THE PROBLEM-FREE
HORSE

THE PROBLEM-FREE
HORSE

The Owner's Guide to Safe,
Sensible Horse Management

CLAIRE LILLEY

J. A. ALLEN

LONDON

© Claire Lilley 2007
First published in Great Britain 2007

ISBN 978 0 85131 919 3

J.A. Allen
Clerkenwell House
Clerkenwell Green
London EC1R 0HT

J.A. Allen is an imprint of Robert Hale Ltd

The right of Claire Lilley to be identified as author of this work has been asserted
by her in accordance with the Copyright, Designs and Patents Act 1988

British Library Cataloguing in Publication Data
A catalogue record for this book is available from the British Library

Design by Judy Linard
Edited by Jane Lake
Printed by New Era Printing Co. Limited, Hong Kong

Dedication

To Dougald, Amadeus, Trevor…and Sammy

ACKNOWLEDGEMENTS

I WOULD LIKE to thank Cassandra Campbell of J. A. Allen for her encouragement and the publication of this book. My gratitude goes to Jane Lake, who has diligently edited the text and made sense of my scribbles on the pages, interpreting exactly what I was trying to explain. My husband has been a tower of strength and taken over the household chores, made meals, and still managed to pick up his camera at the drop of a hat to take endless photographs.

I am extremely grateful to all the horses and owners I have ever known who have been the inspiration for this book.

CONTENTS

INTRODUCTION

PROBLEMS WHEN HANDLING your horse can happen to any owner at any time and can be a result of thoughtlessness, fear or simply just not knowing the right thing to do at the right time. A badly behaved horse is a danger to himself, you and anyone else who handles him. This book is a common-sense guide on how to cope with all the little difficulties that can turn the euphoric dream of becoming a horse owner into an uncontrollable nightmare.

If you have acquired a difficult horse, it is very important to *always go back to the beginning* and re-educate him to eradicate the problem. There are no shortcuts, and it is important to take the time to make sure your horse understands what you expect him to do. Lessons must be repeated on a daily basis until the bad habits have disappeared. The recommendations in this book all stem from my own experience and have been tried and tested with many different horses over the years. Horses are all individuals: what works with one horse may not suit another and so it is important to understand your own horse's character and disposition and adapt his education accordingly. Common sense must prevail when handling and training horses; it is much easier to prevent a likely problem than to spend weeks or months on remedial training.

The only way to eradicate problems that your horse has acquired while with a previous owner is to treat everything as a training session, i.e. he has to learn to be tied up, move over in the stable etc. Most problems can be eradicated simply by having the time to re-educate the horse, and yourself in many instances. Horses learn from watching others and so if you are lucky enough to have a well-behaved horse in the yard for yours to copy, this can be a great help. However, bad habits can also be picked up and, if there is no good equine role model for your horse to follow, you will have to take the role of 'herd leader', which is not as daunting as it seems once your horse trusts and respects you. My first book, *Schooling with Ground Poles* (published by J. A. Allen), contains useful exercises for most situations, whether for a horse's initial training or his retraining.

The topics covered in this book include the following.

- Assessing and interpreting your horse's attitude towards you is crucial to understanding his personality.
- Developing good behaviour in your horse and solving inherent problems such as aggression, nervousness, and rebelliousness is essential to handling him safely in the stable and to and from the field, and keeping him under control.
- Teaching your horse to lead in-hand is one of the most fundamental aspects of horsemanship. He will need to be led to the field, into the horsebox, into his stable and so on. You need to be able to do this safely without being trampled on and injured.
- All horses need to learn to stand quietly when tied. This assists safe stable work around the horse, control for the farrier and vet, and safety when venturing out to competitions. If your horse will not stand quietly, day-to-day tasks become problematic.
- Having sound stable management practice can prevent many problems and stable vices. Time and money can be saved by having a practical routine that suits both your pocket and your daily life.
- Grooming helps you to develop a close relationship with your horse and is just as important as riding or training him; it also gives you the opportunity to assess his condition and his demeanour. However, grooming can be a problem if your horse behaves badly.
- Determining your horse's feeding requirements is essential in order to keep him healthy and manageable. The wrong diet can result in him becoming difficult to control or even dangerous. The correct feeding regimes are of vital importance for overweight horses, horses of a nervous or temperamental disposition, elderly horses and youngsters, and are all based on common sense.
- Good foot care is a major part of good horsemanship but if you have

difficulty in picking out a horse's feet, you will be unable to care for them properly or to check his feet for potential problems. Preparing your horse for the experience of shoeing can solve many problems such as mistrust of the farrier and anxiety about being shod, and inevitably makes the farrier's job so much easier.

- Training your horse to accept wearing a rug is often overlooked. Avoiding common mistakes can prevent your horse from being frightened of having rugs put on and taken off and developing problems such as always trying to get a rug off or damaging them.

- Correct procedures for tacking up and untacking are often brushed aside as it is assumed that all horse owners know how to do it. A horse can be spoiled for life by a saddle and bridle being put on roughly when he is young. Time must be taken to retrain the horse methodically and to resolve the problems.

- Assessing when your horse is off-colour is so important to his well-being. Recognizing behaviour that is not normal for your particular horse is the first indication that something is wrong and that he may need medical attention. You need to know your horse well enough to pick up small indications that something is amiss and when to call for the vet's assistance.

- Clipping can frighten a horse if it is introduced incorrectly; it is very important to know how to clip safely, especially around areas that are awkward to clip and/or particularly sensitive.

- Preparing your horse for the experience of travelling by using obstacles and unfamiliar surfaces on the ground to step on helps to give your horse confidence when meeting unfamiliar situations. Gaining his trust is an essential part of safe loading into a horsebox or trailer. Overcoming problems caused by previous bad experiences can take time and much patience, and unloading your horse correctly is equally as important as getting him in safely.

- Following a safe, sensible procedure for turning your horse out in the field, either on his own or with other horses, or bringing him in from the field can prevent many problems such as your horse breaking away from you or, conversely, pushing and barging you, not only makes life a lot easier but, importantly, also saves you from injury.

- Lungeing is an art, involving knowledge of how your horse moves and what equipment to use, and for what purpose. If done well, lungeing can bring about a huge improvement in your horse's way of going; if done badly, it can stop many good horses reaching their full potential. These skills are worth learning, as there is no shortcut to teaching your horse to be more athletic, and to stretch and use his back correctly.

- Long-reining, and double lungeing are both useful ways of training your horse from the ground. The use of pole work helps to keep his concentration during work. A horse that is happy in his work is usually easier to handle in the stable.

- Loose schooling your horse using poles on the ground and small jumps can build a horse's self-confidence, but it is important to stand in the correct place in relation to your horse so that he understands what you want him to do.

1 ASSESSMENT AND HANDLING

ASSESSING YOUR HORSE'S training, or lack of it, acquired before he came to you is vital to knowing how to proceed. If you are fortunate enough to have a well-trained horse you need to know how to manage him to prevent problems occurring in the future. It is most important that you have the time to train your horse, especially youngsters that need daily repetition of new things until they have understood what is required from them.

FIRST STEPS

Finding the right horse

The easiest way to have a problem-free horse is to choose the right one in the first place! This is easier said than done, and it is easy to be fooled by sob stories from a less than honest vendor. It is so important to find a horse that suits your own capabilities and to view the horse with someone more knowledgeable than yourself; even if you have a lot of experience it is always wise to get a second opinion.

The description in the wording of advertisements may need interpretation. 'Bold, forward-going' might mean a horse has braking problems. 'Quiet to handle and shoe' is good but is the horse quiet to clip? Vendors are not going to mention their horses' problems in an advertisement and it is up to you to ask pertinent questions when you enquire about a horse.

If a horse seems fine when you try him out but turns into a demon when you get him home, it would be wise to speak to the person from whom you bought the horse. You need to find out if he has behaved like this before, or whether this is something new. It is to be hoped they will

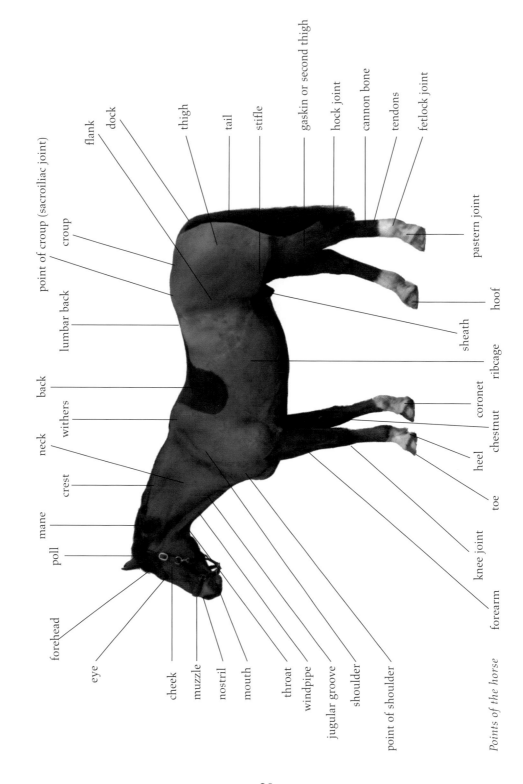

poll
mane
crest
neck
withers
back
lumbar back
point of croup (sacroiliac joint)
croup
flank
dock
thigh
tail
stifle
gaskin or second thigh
hock joint
cannon bone
tendons
fetlock joint
pastern joint
hoof
sheath
ribcage
coronet
chestnut
heel
toe
knee joint
forearm
point of shoulder
shoulder
jugular groove
windpipe
throat
mouth
nostril
muzzle
cheek
eye
forehead

Points of the horse

20

be truthful about this, but they may well say he was fine when they sold him to you!

Always have a horse vetted before buying him: the type of vetting will be dictated by the intended use of the horse. If, for example, you are intending to event competitively and want to be as sure as you can that he can cope with the work, you will need a full vetting which covers lung function at speed, flexion tests on the legs, and heart and eye tests, etc. If you are just intending to hack and do local riding club shows, a partial vetting may suffice. It is important that you are honest with the vet and tell him exactly what you will be doing with the horse so that he can vet him accordingly. A blood test is advisable for detecting foreign substances present, i.e. drugs, as well as giving an indication of the health of the horse. If a horse is very quiet when you buy him but becomes unmanageable shortly after you get him home, he may have been given something to quieten him down. Unless you have had a blood test done, however, it is very unlikely you will get your money back.

The vet can also verify the horse's age, which is important. I knew someone who was told that the mare they had bought was twelve years old, only to find that after a few months work she became stiff or lame, struggling to do what was asked of her. On asking the vets to verify the age, it turned out that the horse was actually twenty-two!

New environments

Some horses can be traumatized by moving to a new environment with a new owner, particularly if they have been at their previous homes for a long time, and could well behave erratically unless they have absolute faith in you right from the start. It is so important not to take on a horse of your own unless you have the experience and confidence to do so. Any sign of anxiety and lack of confidence from you can cause even the most experienced 'schoolmaster' to be upset and anxious, especially if he previously had confident handling (Figure 1.1). If someone with less knowledge, or who is nervous, purchases such a horse, the animal will, over time, become confused and problems are likely to arise. Ironically, novice horse owners are often advised to buy schoolmasters but a 'push-button' horse is only so if you push the right buttons. It takes skill to handle a schoolmaster, as well as to

Figure 1.1 Amadeus takes moving to a new yard in his stride because he has confidence in his owner.

ride one, and this is achieved by having the correct instruction to help you on your way.

Gaining experience

The best way to learn how to handle horses is by gaining practical experience by helping at a yard, sharing a horse with a willing friend, or taking a training course on horse management, combined with reading books on the subject, before going it alone. If you get into difficulty, always ask for professional advice.

If your horse has a history of bad behaviour, anxiety or stress, remedial training is essential to developing trust and understanding. Learning about your horse's character is the only path to successful training and a problem-free horse. Horses are not generally inherently nasty and 'out to get you', but they can become defensive if they have had a tough life and rough handling. They can be naughty and not listen to you, but this is usually because they do not understand what you mean rather than blatant disobedience, though there is always the exception to the rule.

Handling your horse safely with appropriate equipment and keeping necessary items to hand at all times is the only way to avoid accidents. If you do not know your horse well, or are attempting something new with your horse, such as leading him to a new field, always wear a protective hat, sensible footwear and a decent pair of gloves. The unexpected can always happen. I cannot emphasize enough that good old-fashioned common sense is vital to having a successful partnership with your horse.

ASSESSMENT

Interpreting your horse's behaviour towards you is crucial to understanding his personality.

A sensitive horse needs to be treated with care and more gently than a tougher-natured horse. Always give a horse the chance to be sensitive. If you try to dominate him roughly because he looks 'a bit of a brute', you will make him aggressive, born out of self-defence, and handling him will not be a pleasure but a sequence of domination tactics and battles, most of which the horse will win purely by strength. People often resort to breaking a horse's spirit to solve the problem, resulting in a depressed animal with no will to please his owner, but that obeys under sufferance.

Vital signs
EYES

It is often said that a horse has a 'good eye': a horse with a friendly expression, kind, alert eyes, and taking an interest in his surroundings should be far easier to train and handle than one that is putting his ears flat back and gnashing his teeth at you. The latter type should be avoided at all costs unless you are prepared to retrain him. This confrontational behaviour could be a sign of pain or discomfort and needs to be investigated by the vet.

TAIL

Swishing the tail a lot can indicate bad temper but if it is high summer it is natural that a horse will want to swish flies away; being able to recognize the difference is important. An excited horse will carry his tail high in the air and a relaxed horse's tail will swing freely as he moves along; both signs which will help you assess your horse's mood.

EARS

The ears tell you a great deal. If they are both pricked sharply forwards he is alert and listening for danger. Spooky horses usually do this before jumping, possibly on your foot, so beware. A calm relaxed horse will carry his ears slightly apart and at 'half mast'. If they are laid flat back it is a warning; get out of the way as it is likely you will get bitten or kicked. (Figures 1.2a–d.)

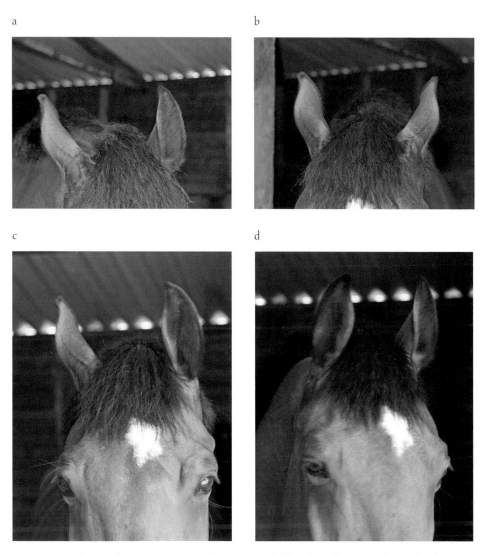

Figures 1.2a–d Your horse's ears can tell you an awful lot about him. a) What is he doing next door? b) I am not really interested. c) I think I can hear someone in the feed room. d) Great, it's definitely lunch time!

VOCAL COMMUNICATION, INDIVIDUAL MANNERISMS, BODY LANGUAGE AND UNDER-STANDING

Friendly horses neigh at each other or you, if you have a carrot in your hand, and neigh even louder at meal times. They often squeal at each other when feeling playful and mares frequently squeal a lot when they are in season. Getting to know your horse's individual expressions and mannerisms is vital to avoiding problems. Looking for the early warning signals can prevent many mishaps and injuries by enabling you to react more quickly than your horse in potentially dangerous situations.

Horses are attuned to the smallest shifts in our body language. If, for example, you are fearful or defensive you will probably be making yourself smaller, crouching in a timid fashion, which sends alarm signals to a horse causing him to worry. Stand tall, with your chest lifted and shoulders relaxed, breathing calmly, and you will send reassuring signals to a horse.

To own and train a horse you have to develop a good relationship, rather like being in a happy marriage; there has to be give and take and each must be willing to try to understand the other. A large horse may well be more sensitive that a small pony, so size is immaterial. Some breeds of horse are more sensitive than others. Hot bloods such as the Iberian breeds, Arabs, and Thoroughbreds are generally quick-thinking, sometimes too quick for their owners, and responsive; cold bloods such as draught horses are very friendly and kind, but take longer to think things through; Warmbloods come somewhere in between. This is a bit of a generalization, but it is important to take your horse's hereditary attributes into account. It would be unfair, for example, to stable a native pony twenty-four hours a day when he would be far happier living out at grass, or to leave a Warmblood used to a European training regime, with a set routine and regular meal times, to his own devices in a field. My horse, Trevor, is an example of the latter. He had been imported from Holland where he had been trained as a show jumper in a professional yard. In England, his owner had so many problems riding him that she was frightened to get on him. Consequently he was turned out in a field for several months, occasionally fed and watered by the girl's family. Left on his own with only the rabbits for company, he became extremely stressed and deteriorated even further. When I went to see him, he appeared

Figure 1.3 It can take time to adjust to new surroundings; Trevor dreaming about his next meal in his new home.

to be kind but misunderstood. He was very polite to lead in-hand and never pulled or barged me. I put him in a yard with a good routine, regular meal times and a calm atmosphere, and within a few days he was back to being a happy horse, keen to work and have something to do, which was a sound basis with which to start for the many months of training ahead (Figure 1.3).

BACK FROM THE BRINK

You have to be a very experienced horseman to take on a horse with problems instilled by someone else. It may seem very noble to rescue horses from the abattoir but bear in mind that these horses have usually gone too far down the line for the average owner. It takes years of experience to be able to bring a horse back from the brink, buying him for meat money and spending a couple of years retraining him. It is extremely satisfying if it does work out, but horses remember bad experiences all too well and may have flashbacks of behaviour throughout their lives if you inadvertently do the wrong thing at the wrong moment.

There is a huge difference between being cruel and rough and using intelligent discipline. You owe it to your horse to train him properly, for your own sake, your horse's and that of a future owner. Spending a life sentence in a field just because he has not been suitably trained should not be the fate of any horse. With time, patience and correct handling you can establish a good training regime that will make sense to your horse, and give you both an easier, less stressful life.

HANDLING

A horse's daily routine is as important as his training regime. Horses love routine and are far less likely to become stressed and unmanageable if they know what the system is: when he is to go to, and come in from, the field; schooling time; feed times, etc. Again, each horse is an individual and over time, as you get to know him, you will work out his particular requirements; for example, is he easier to train if he has been out in the field beforehand, or does he concentrate better if you work him first and then turn him out afterwards to relax?

A horse that is easy to handle is a pleasure to look after. You can tie him up to muck him out, you can put his rugs and tack on and take them off without getting pushed about and you can lead him to and from the field safely. Willing friends are more likely to say 'yes' when asked to look after him if you are ill or on holiday if they are not risking life and limb to do so.

Developing good behaviour in your horse requires you to set the pecking order (see Chapter 13) You have to be superior to him, but he must **trust** you and you must both have **respect** for each other (Figure 1.4).

An aggressive horse thinks he is of a higher rank than you and may be rebellious as he tries to prove it. He requires a calm, strong-minded and determined owner who is not afraid to set the rules but must be rewarded with soft, quiet handling as soon as he is more submissive in his attitude. When firm handling is

Figure 1.4 Trust and respect are vital in developing a good relationship with your horse. Amadeus asking, 'Which foot did you want me to pick up?'

27

required, this does not mean beating him into submission, but outwitting him, so that he realizes you are cleverer than he is. You will need quick reactions and the ability to reprimand him both with your voice and physically but you will never win a horse's trust by shouting and being rough. The tone of your voice is very useful. I find a stony silence works well in conveying my displeasure to my horses. They both hate being ignored and so if one of them has been misbehaving, and it's usually Amadeus, I walk off and say nothing. After letting him reflect on things for a while, I go back and make friends again.

A nervous horse will be way down in the pecking order and will, therefore, need a lot of reassurance from you to boost his confidence. He requires calm quiet handling but do not be too gentle because if he feels you are not in control of the situation he can become even more nervous. He must feel that he can trust you and that you will do him no harm. He needs to have more self-confidence, which you can develop throughout his training, making sure he understands exactly what is required of him at all times. Dithering about will not help a horse like this at all and will make him more nervous.

Control

Having control over your horse is a result of handling him correctly and, again, is about trust and mutual respect and these are the important underlying factors with all the issues covered in this book. Horses boss each other around to sort out the pecking order but they also need affection and friends, one of which must be you.

Without control, enjoying a long-term relationship with your horse becomes impossible. You will be afraid of him, and he will have no confidence in you. This factor alone makes training a horse a daunting task. Some horses resort to extreme, often dangerous, behaviour to avoid co-operating but this usually stems from rough handling at a young age. An immature horse can be spoiled for life with ignorant careless 'training'. Other horses will take advantage if they are not handled firmly enough to keep them under control, taking advantage of well-intentioned owners. There have been numerous occasions when I have heard, 'He won't like me if I tell him off'; an attitude resulting in a dangerous horse that takes every opportunity to intimidate his owner, who then retreats to the safety of the tack room for a therapeutic cup of tea and says, 'He's not in the mood, I will try tomorrow'. The other common solution is to take a trip to the tack shop for solace in equine retail therapy.

If you cannot control your horse, he was maybe the wrong choice for you but if you wish to sell him, you need to train him. Sending him away for professional training is an option but you need to be present to learn how to do it yourself. It is pointless sending a horse away for a couple of weeks and expecting him to return a paragon of virtue because, if you do not change the way you have been dealing with him, he will revert to his previous behaviour extremely quickly; you will have wasted your money, and the trainer's time and expertise will all have been in vain.

LAYING DOWN THE GROUND RULES

Horses control each other with the flick of an ear or a certain look, or, at the other end of the scale, booting each other in the belly, chest or anywhere else in reach, biting and squealing at each other. You need to develop your own 'language' with your horse that he understands.

A basic ground rule is to do to him what he has done to you. If he whickers at you welcomingly, talk back quietly. If you are handling a young horse that is neighing at the top of his voice for back-up from another horse, shout back in response while handling him firmly but fairly; he has to notice you, otherwise you risk being trampled, or pulled over. He will then realize that you are the 'other horse' answering his distress call. Within a day or so he will stop calling for help because he will begin to trust you and regard you as his friend. He will then behave gently with you, and you can reciprocate.

In order to control your horse and ensure that he understands you, you have to think how another horse would react to him. If he bites, another horse would bite him back; similarly a horse being kicked by another horse will respond with a kick. Your personal 'biting and kicking' response is something you have to work out between you and your horse. What works with one horse may not work with another, but you must always use discretion and never retaliate in anger. Always react to the horse's actions and do not be the instigator of a fracas, otherwise you will undoubtedly come off worse.

On the other hand, it is just as important to acknowledge signs of affection from a horse. In a field horses will groom each other, nibble each other's necks, stand companionably swishing flies off each other with their tails and often graze close together. This is why grooming your horse is so important, it gives you the opportunity to mimic the behaviour of a friendly horse. Amadeus shares his hay with me by stuffing it down my shirt at the back of my neck while continuing to munch! All my horses are happy for me to sit in the corner of their stables or in the field near them while they eat.

You can often witness control problems at horse shows when several young horses are being shown in-hand. They spin around and charge about dragging their timid handlers with them neighing loudly at the others because they do not have the faith in their owners to take charge of the situation. While judging such classes, I have often had to resort to barricading myself in a corner of the ring between jump wings out of harm's way! All the competitors say, 'Oh, it's his first show. He's not normally like this'. Well he wouldn't be. He has probably just experienced being in a trailer for the first time, leaving his familiar field, and is expected to react calmly when being led around an arena surrounded by burger vans, pushchairs, dogs, unfamiliar horses leaping around, plus the noise from the gymkhana ring and a booming voice coming from the public-address system. All this is a lot for a novice horse to cope with and can be daunting for any owner. For your own safety, it is so important to know that you can control your horse in any situation. This calls for good powers of observation, anticipation and an ability to stay calm and confident at all times. Avoid putting yourself and your horse in situations you cannot handle. Over time, as you and your horse come to know each other, you will learn to cope with more unusual circumstances together as long as your horse trusts you.

The speed of your response to your horse's actions is vital to his understanding that he has overstepped the line and that you are number one in the pecking order. As stated, your horse should not be allowed to bully you; you have to be the 'herd leader' if you are to stand any chance of training him. I know people who, when bitten, claim to bite their horse back when necessary, but I find that a good pinch on the neck is a good substitute for a bite. If he refuses to move over with a verbal instruction, for example, you may have to give him a shove. The most effective place to do this is just behind his elbow, where your leg aid would be when riding him, as this area is very sensitive. Use your fist to give him a move-over aid with your knuckles. This should be quite sufficient to gain a response from most horses but if yours is particularly stubborn, prodding him with your thumb nail can be effective.

Problems in the stable

Some of these problems can occur either in the stable or outside, or both, but, in many cases, retraining is best tackled in a safe enclosed area.

A DISLIKE OF BEING TOUCHED

Some horses are more sensitive to touch than others and, again, it is important to assess your horse as an individual and respect his personality. If your horse previously had a nervous owner who 'fiddled about' with him he may have

learned to intimidate this owner, and other nervous people who do this, by pulling aggressive faces, or even biting. Grooming is essential to accustoming him to be being touched all over, but be workmanlike about it and not fussy. If you are too gentle you may tickle him, which can annoy him just as flies do when they land on him. Touch him confidently, gently and carefully. Hitting him with strong pats may make him tense and so stroking is preferable.

If a horse has been mistreated, especially around the head, he will become anxious if you raise your hand to his face. To rectify this, hold a brush in your hand and touch

Figure 1.5 Touching your horse's head with a brush is sometimes easier than touching him with your hand at first if he is head-shy.

him on the shoulder, the neck and then on the side of his face and brush him gently. Most horses associate brushes with grooming and will accept a brush on the face as a first step (Figure 1.5).

A brush is inanimate and will not transmit any tension to a horse as a hand would. The same applies to grooming the rest of him; see Chapter 5 for more details.

Touch him when and how you need to but do not make a nuisance of yourself. He will tolerate a certain amount of contact but if he becomes tense, freeze where you are until he relaxes, then continue a moment longer, so that you finish on a good note before leaving him alone again. He will gradually work out that you mean him no harm, and thus learn to relax and allow you to handle him easily. This could take many months – even a couple of years – and if he has been ill-treated, his intolerance to touch might be triggered at any time; always respect this.

When handling the hind legs, grasp the tail below the dock, and hold it against the leg you are touching; this can help because horses do not generally kick against their own tails. Do not fiddle around with the hind legs; do what you have to do, then leave them alone. Never kneel down near his back legs but just crouch so that you can move out of the way quickly should the need arise. (See Chapter 5.)

PUTTING ON EQUIPMENT

Assessing your horse's reaction to items of tack is a prerequisite to having a safe, controllable horse (see Chapter 9). If you cannot handle him all over, particularly around the head and ears you will find it difficult to get a head collar on him, let alone a bridle. If, however, he is accustomed to being groomed and is handled correctly you should not have a problem but wear a hat if you have any doubts about his reactions.

Always be positive when putting tack and other equipment on your horse. He is not going to stand still for hours on end while you fuss with things; you will probably make him tetchy and might get bitten or kicked, or at least head-butted out of the way! On the contrary, it is important that you are never rough and clumsy. The consequences are much the same in both cases, and if your horse is of a nervous disposition anyway, you will make him afraid of you.

If he resents you stroking his back, it is a safe bet that you will have a problem with him accepting a saddle. When you approach with his tack he may demonstrate his fear by shying away from you, or he may show signs of distress such as biting or kicking. If he is sensitive around the girth area, you will have difficulty with rollers, girths and anything else that fastens around his middle.

Spend time grooming him with a brush or a cloth if he resents your hand. This is particularly important if you are nervous. Again, the inanimate objects between your hand and the horse will block the transmission of your nerves, which will help you to gain confidence. Once you are confident, your touch will be as well and your horse will be far more relaxed when you are with him.

Being able to handle your horse's legs is not just important for being able to groom him and pick out his feet but you will also need to put on leg bandages and boots at some point for either work or travelling. It is all too easy to be hurt when handling your horse's legs. I was putting bandages on Amadeus a few minutes before doing a demonstration. I was in a hurry, he became fidgety and raised his leg at what he thought was a fly, but was actually my head. I had to do the show with concussion and a large sticking plaster (courtesy of the on-duty vet) on my forehead. (Yes, I should have been wearing a hat!)

FIGHTING WITH NEXT-DOOR NEIGHBOURS

When stabling your horse next to new neighbours, keep an eye on them for a while. Initially, there is bound to be a little squealing and so on, but if it all turns violent and the horses do not settle down within a couple of days, they may have to be moved. Sensibly designed stables permit horses to see each other without being able to touch. Others have 'talk grilles' between them, which enable horses to touch but not cause harm to each other, it can still cause stress if they do not get on at all, however. When my second horse, Trevor, came along, Amadeus and he would have fights over the stable doors, resulting in them looking as though they has been in a street brawl; moving them apart so that they could chat but not actually touch was the logical answer in their case.

DEALING WITH AN ESCAPE ARTIST

A horse usually tries to escape from a stable owing to boredom, hunger or thirst; good stable management is, therefore, essential to ensure that he is happy in his box and has enough water, hay and clean bedding. Turning all the horses in the yard except yours out in the fields can cause him a lot of stress because he will want to be with the herd, namely his field mates. In this situation he is not misbehaving if he tries to get out but simply does not understand why he has been left behind. If your horse has to stay in his stable on box rest because of an injury or illness, then it would be sensible to leave another horse in the yard, where he can see him. Bringing one horse in for the morning shift and another for the afternoon would be wise.

Some horses have a mischievous streak and need a lot of mental stimulation, which you must provide or they will find their own amusement such as trying to undo the door. This usually happens accidentally the first time: playing with the bolt causes it to slide across and, hey presto, freedom! Once your horse has learnt to do this, he will usually try it again.

Amadeus is a real Houdini and has been since he was a youngster. We have been through every type of stable bolt on the market (there is only one he cannot undo) and so it is most important that his stable has a bottom bolt. Even now, at thirteen years of age (he should have grown out of it by now), he will still test his skill if he can. He rarely leaves the stable as he quite likes his home and will stand happily with the door wide open, but he still enjoys the satisfaction of being able to undo the door.

FEAR OF BEING CONFINED

A horse that hates being stabled may have had a bad experience in a confined space, such as a fall in a trailer, a bad travelling experience in a horsebox, or being shut in a stable – possibly a small dark box – for a long period of time without proper care such as adequate water, food and bedding.

If a horse has been living out for years quite happily, a sudden change to being stabled can be a huge shock to his system. Changes like this have to be made gradually to avoid problems. To help a horse overcome his fear, bring him in from the field for pleasurable things, such as food (which always works) or for grooming.

If a horse received poor initial training while he was backed and was stabled during the process, he may associate the stable with rough handling or bad riding.

All the above examples prove that it is most important to try to find out his past history if you can to help you analyse the cause of his fear.

The cure is the same in any situation. He must learn a new pleasurable association with being stabled. If other horses are in the yard and stabled next to him within sight he should settle fairly quickly. As with the equine escape artists, make sure he is not the only horse left in the yard when the others have been turned out. If you are in a DIY yard and cannot get to the yard to turn your horse out or bring him in, ask a friend to turn your horse out with hers and to bring them in again at the same time. This will establish a routine of field/stable/field which should help your horse tremendously. At first he may cope with the stable for only half an hour or so but over time he should be able to stay in all day or night. A deep bed, plenty of hay, fresh water, i.e. four-star accommodation, will encourage him to relax in a stable.

REFUSAL TO MOVE OVER

If you have tried to get your horse to move over in the stable and failed, you may need to tap him on the thigh to get him to move. Have a schooling whip, a short length of hosepipe or a lead rope nearby with which to flick him, should you need it quickly. It is no good reprimanding a horse after you have been across the yard to find a suitable implement; he will not understand any punishment after the event and will begin to mistrust you. Never, however, go into a stable with a whip if your horse is of a nervous dis-position or if he has been beaten with one in a stable in the past, otherwise you will just frighten him.

A broom with stiff bristles comes in handy as a tool to persuade him to move away from you and I have found this method far more effective than using a whip. Use the broom as an extension of your arm, and hold it parallel to your horse's body. If he swings his backside towards it, then bump him quickly on the side of his rump and say, 'over'. He should step away imme-diately but if he does not, and moves towards it more, do it again. Make sure that you do not allow him to lean on the broom and push it because he can undoubtedly push harder that you. You have to give a quick 'aid' by poking him with the bristles to surprise him so that he moves away himself. As soon as he has stepped away, reward him by telling him he was a good boy and stroking him on the neck, making sure you leave your broom by the door out of the way. You should only have to do this once or twice. The next time, just extend your arm out parallel to him and say, 'over', as you did before. He should now move away from your arm. Praise him.

The next stage is to just give the verbal aid of 'over'. You might need to move your hand towards him so that he sees the same movement you made before. Within a week, you should have a horse that moves over for you on command.

If you feel that you may be cornered or kicked when teaching your horse this lesson in the stable, take him into the school or a field and conduct the lesson there first (Figure 1.6).

Once he has learnt to move away from you, introduce the command 'stand' as soon as he has moved to the right place; this will let him know he has done the right thing. When he stands, approach his shoulder and stroke

Figure 1.6 Teaching your horse to move over in the school or field helps him to learn the lesson without you getting cornered or kicked in the stable.

him. In this way he learns to stand still so that you can tie him up, groom him, put a rug on, etc. Teaching him to 'stand' can be useful in many circumstances. For example, I once inadvertently let go of Trevor when I was lungeing. I yelled 'STAND' at the top of my voice and amazingly he stood rooted to the spot until I retrieved him, thus avoiding a nasty tangle with the lunge line.

If you do need to reprimand your horse at any time, a quick response from you will mean the aid you need to administer will be barely a touch. It must be

36

enough to be effective, but that is all. If your hands are full with a rug, for example, and your horse sidles towards you, wave your leg at him as though doing a karate kick. He should move away as he sees your leg coming towards him, if you do it fast enough, as he would if another horse were trying to kick him. Aim under the belly where the strong abdominal muscles are, or between the front legs where the pectoral muscles are just in case your toe does make contact. *Never* aim at the horse's ribs which bruise easily.

BARGING

Some horses try to walk all over you in the stable and will try to barge you out of the way to get out of the door. This bossy, dominant behaviour must be eliminated quickly or a horse will learn that he does not have to stand still for anything, and may spin around before you can tie him up. Try putting a rug on a rotating horse; you will probably end up wearing it yourself!

With a horse like this, carry a secret weapon: a hoof pick. This technique is an extension of asking your horse to move over as covered in the previous section.

Go into the stable and stand quietly, with authority. Have a quiet, commanding attitude and think of the stable as your territory; you are allowing him to stay in your space and he must accept your presence there. If he approaches you as though you were an inconvenience that spoils his view over the stable door, hold your fist closed around the hoof pick in your hand with the rounded handle just protruding under your thumb As he shoves into you, hold your fist in front of your body with your elbow close to your side, stand your ground and be ready to 'body block' him. Let him push into your fist so that he makes contact with the hoof pick handle *but on no account attempt to stab him with it*. He should jump back in surprise. Remain quiet, and approach him. If he stands quietly, stroke him and tell him what a good boy he has been. If he has another go, then repeat the same procedure but *never* get angry.

After a couple of days, he should stand still and actually notice that you are in his stable, so you will not need your 'secret weapon' any more. This has taught him the valuable lesson of respect, which is essential to you being in control of the situation and he should respond the next time to a light touch from your hand. Aids in the stable should coincide with aids given when riding, i.e. they should be firm enough to work instantly; if they are too soft, you will receive no reaction, too firm and you create tension and resistance. Always reward the horse as soon as he has understood what you are asking of him.

As a child, I had weekly lessons at the local riding school where I rode a small strawberry-roan pony called Cobweb that used to deposit me in the same patch of nettles every week. When trying to untack Cobweb after a particularly unsuccessful attempt to ride without stirrups, she decided that she had had enough of my ineptitude and cornered me in her stable. I had been given a small hunting crop for Christmas with a pointed horn handle, the use for which escaped me until I prodded Cobweb in the ribs with it and she moved away from me in surprise. The next time I rode her, I held the crop upside down, with my hand through the leather loop, so that I could poke her if she tried to dump me again but, unfortunately, the instructor noticed before the lesson began and made me hold it properly!

STRIKING OUT WITH A FRONT LEG

This behaviour is particularly dangerous when it occurs in the stable but it can occur anywhere and is often seen in a field when a horse is trying to assert his authority over another horse he has just met. A newly acquired horse may try this with you to see if he can intimidate you. It must be tackled immediately and your response should be to do it back to him. Some horses respond better to the retraining when it takes place in the stable but there will always be those with whom it may be necessary to retrain in a secure but larger area so that you can get out of harm's way easily.

If you have managed to get a head collar and lead rope on him and he strikes out at you, give a short, sharp tug on the rope with one hand, then 'strike out' with your other arm aiming at the middle of his chest. Accompany this with a large growl and repeat it as many times as he does. He should stop doing it after a few strikes. This method also works in the arena if he tries this when on the lunge. Once he has accepted that you are in charge, continue with whatever it was you were doing before he struck out as though nothing has happened. If he does this to keep you out of his stable, and you cannot get near him, use the broom /lead rope/piece of hose pipe to 'strike' towards him. Once he stops, be very quiet and put your implement outside the door before approaching him slowly. Reward him, and then leave him alone to think about it. After a few minutes, calmly approach him in the box, without staring him in the eye, and touch him on the shoulder. When he lets you touch him, you should be able to put his head collar on. If he does not let you touch him, stand still and do nothing. Once he relaxes, try again and you should be successful. You may have to repeat this a few times with a very obstreperous horse. If he neighs and shouts for help from other horses, shout back at him. He has to learn that you will answer him and he does not have to find another horse for moral support. Once he actually seems to acknowledge you, he should calm down and be more compliant.

VANDALIZING STABLES

This can manifest itself as chewing wood or kicking at the walls or door. It can be a symptom of boredom, frustration, stress or attention-seeking, e.g. banging the door at meal times.

Make sure your horse has plenty of hay to eat. Ideally he should spend some time out in the field grazing, which in itself is a relaxing pastime. A horse needs to chew to be relaxed and so giving hay ad lib in the stable is vital to his well-being. To prevent a greedy horse wolfing his hay down, feed him little and often. Giving too much at once can result in hay being trampled into the bed and wasted, especially if your horse is restless in his box. A lack of roughage will make him chew wood. Stables constructed of cheap wood will suffer more than those built from more expensive, harder wood varieties. For equine vandals, brick stables with good quality doors are a better option. There are many horse toys available now, one of which may distract your horse from his destructive behaviour.

If your horse bangs the door for attention, or because it is dinner time, one solution is to have a chain across the open doorway so that he has no door to kick; another is to deaden the noise with rubber matting fixed to the inside of the door because some horses like the noise the banging makes and will stop doing it if the banging does not have the desired effect. Shutting the top stable door as soon as the door-banging starts is another effective solution; the horse has to move away from the door as he cannot stick his head out. Once he has been quiet for a few minutes, open it again. If he recommences the banging, shut the top door again. He should get the message that banging does not get results. Once he stands quietly with the top door open, praise him, or give him his dinner. In busy yards, if the banging is feed induced, it is a big mistake to feed the door banger first just to keep him quiet because it simply reinforces the behaviour and causes a long-term problem.

Kicking at walls may jar a horse's legs if the walls are built from brick or concrete blocks, and so installing wood or rubber panelling up to kick height (about 120 cm [4 ft] from the ground) can be advisable. Kicking at walls can be the result of a horse taking a dislike to his neighbour, or finding a stable too small (claustrophobia). If your horse is extremely irritated by flies in the summer, he may kick out; try to find a way of dealing with the flies, hanging fly paper in the box, for example, and make sure you skip out regularly to discourage them.

Make sure your horse receives sufficient work to keep him interested, and that he is slightly tired after his training. He will be mentally relaxed if he understands what is being asked of him but if your training methods do not suit him, he may well become stressed in the stable, restless and destructive. Look for early warning signs such as disturbed bedding. Some horse are naturally more restless than others, however, and so it important to understand your horse's own individual personality.

HANDLING A CHARGING HORSE

Some horses can be very territorial and defend their stables from intruders. This may be because a horse has been badly handled, in which case you will not be allowed in for fear that you cause him harm or it may be because he thinks he is the herd leader and in his eyes you do not stand a chance of being the boss. It is crucial to establish that you are in charge otherwise you will never be able to train such a horse. This calls for clever tactics to outwit him.

A friend of mine who bred show ponies used to wrap a single mattress around his middle and secure it with baler twine when approaching youngsters that had not been handled. He would quietly stand in the stable, unharmed by flying hooves until the pony in question settled down, and allowed himself to be caught. My friend was, however, an experienced horseman and this should **not** be attempted by novices.

I once had a young Anglo-Arab mare to break in. Indira was rather bossy and indignant at being sent to a new yard, and took an instant dislike to me. I was not too keen on her either as a result! She was going to be with me for four months and it was important that we reached an agreement in the first week. Her first tactic was to canter at me from the back of the stable with teeth bared and ears flat as soon as I opened the door. There was no doubt in my mind – or hers – that she wanted to be boss horse; I therefore had to remedy the situation immediately otherwise I would not be able to train her at all.

The nice approach was clearly not going to work and so I armed myself with the newest yard broom with the best bristles. Using the philosophy, 'if your horse does it to you, do it back', I hid behind the door, opened it quickly, and assumed a rugby player's stance, broom out in front, so that if she ran at me she would run into the broom and get a pricked chest before she was close enough to reach me with her teeth. She started to launch herself at me but changed her mind, eyeing me and my trusty broom with a bemused look on her face before pulling faces at me from where she stood. I left the stable, shut the door, composed myself, and did the same thing again. By the third attempt she had categorized me as a bit potty, but realized that I was 'boss horse' in this yard. By the third day I could lead her in and out of her stable without her dashing off and by the end of the first week we were on pleasant enough terms to get by. Interestingly, by the end of four months we were the best of friends, she was easy to ride and I was sad to see her go back home.

Horses can charge at you in the field or school as well. The problem is sometimes best dealt with in the confines of a safe school, as shown in Figures 1.7a–e, rather than in the stable.

BITING AND KICKING

Biting and kicking often accompany charging at you or trying to corner you in the stable. The best way to handle your horse without getting hurt is to

a

b

c

d

e

Figures 1.7 a–e This Icelandic pony stallion was intimidating his nervous rider by rearing up, tipping her off and then running at her; I took over on the spur of the moment to set out a few ground rules. (Don't follow the example I am setting in the photographs, always wear a protective hat and gloves when doing this.) The four poles laid in a square on the ground marked out my space and enabled me to prevent this pony charging at me. Note the difference in his attitude in the last photo. It took about fifteen minutes for him to work out that he could trust me and did not need to be aggressive. He behaved well for the rest of the weekend both for me and his rider, once she stopped being afraid of him.

put a head collar on him to at least give you control over the front end. You stand very little chance of avoiding both ends without having hold of him! Initially, it may help to leave the head collar on your horse – once you get it on him – to make it easier to catch him in the stable, but on no account make a quick grab at it, otherwise you will cause him to shy away from you, which gives him a chance to kick at you, if he is inclined to do so. Should your horse turns his backside on you as soon as you open the door and threaten to kick, you need to out-manoeuvre him. Horses that threaten in this way usually stand at the back of the stable. Enter the stable quietly with some feed in a feed scoop and a lead rope held clip-at-the-ready in your hand. Talk quietly to him, and wait for him to approach you before attempting to clip on the lead rope; clip it on without startling him while he is sampling the feed you have offered him. Horses usually bite or kick as a form of self-defence, which often comes about from rough handling, or pain associated with being handled; the best way to tackle this problem, therefore, is to be calm and confident. If there is a physical cause, you will not find this out until you can catch and tie up the horse – how is the vet to examine him otherwise?

Again, it is a good idea to use a door chain with a horse like this because it allows you to get out of the way quickly. Have the trusty broom handy. If your horse does launch both barrels at you, give him a swift prod on the backside immediately. He will then think you have kicked him back. If he kicks again, you use the broom again but on no account start shouting and panicking or you will just wind him up. Once he stands still, praise him. Offer the feed scoop. He may be too mad at you to accept it at first but, if you are patient, he should come to you after a few minutes. He will have then learnt that kicking provokes a 'kick' from you, and approaching you quietly earns him a treat.

Biting accompanies charging at you and so the broom in the chest works well, as described on page 41.

Max, a young Arab, had come to me for training because he had been turning his back on his owner as soon as she approached him in his stable. I used the following approach with him. As I went into his stable, he shot to the back placing his back end towards me in a threatening manner. I stood inside the stable by the door and turned my back on him, mirroring what he had done to me. I just watched the cat playing in the yard with a half-dead mouse, thinking of nothing in particular. It is important to empty your head of all thoughts. If you are willing him to come to you or trying to give him 'good vibes' he will sense that he is under pressure to respond. On the other hand if you have negative thoughts such as, 'I'm not going to get him. What do I do if he kicks me? Do I make a run for the door?' he will be more afraid and probably do what you are thinking. Within a couple of minutes Max come up behind me. He paused and then walked up to me, looking over my shoulder to see what I was watching. I stroked him, put his head collar on, and that was that. I never had another problem with him as he looked upon me as a friend not a foe. Once I had finished with Max, I went to deal with the cat and his petrified toy.

RUNNING TO THE BACK OF THE STABLE

Some horses run to the back of the stable when you open the door, especially if they have had harsh handling in the past. This is not to be confused with a horse moving to the back because he has been trained to. If your horse rushes to the back and appears tense it is the former reason, and if he looks as though he is standing still and to attention, it is the latter, in which case be grateful that you have a well-mannered horse!

If your horse is afraid and shoots away from you, avoid looking him in the eye, which can make him feel intimidated. Stand still until he settles and stays in one place. Look and talk to his shoulder and approach very slowly. Try to think of nothing at all, empty your head of all thoughts, as described above, breathe normally and walk towards him as though it is easy to approach him. If you make it easy, it will be. Most often it is the owner who causes the problems by being tense and unsure. Look at it from this point of view: would you rather shake hands with a calm, smiling, confident person who presents you with a firm handshake or someone who creeps up to you surreptitiously and offers clammy, limp fingers?

Once your horse lets you approach, stand next to his shoulder and stroke him gently. Give him a titbit so that he knows you are friend, then withdraw from the stable and leave him in peace for ten minutes or so before repeating the process. If he is afraid of the door opening, have a chain across the doorway to make it easy to get in and out without the palaver of opening and closing the door each time. It is important to train him to be calm when you go in and out. Go in to the stable to give him his hay, feed, and fill his bucket in a matter of fact way, without approaching him. He will learn very quickly that you are not a threat and relax in the stable with you.

Our latest acquisition, Heinrich, a six-year-old Trakehner gelding, has just become used to his new home. He was bred and handled by a good friend of mine, and I have known him since he was a foal. However, since his birth he had known only the one home and it took him about a month to get used to his new stable companions and me. At first he barged and tested my authority; I, therefore, had to utilize the if-I-open-the-door-you-move-back training with the help of the ubiquitous broom. Once he understood this, we went through the don't-you-come-near-me-or-I-might-kick stage, when he would swing his backside towards me. To deal with this, I had the broom in one hand and sugar lumps in the other. It took him an afternoon to work out which end of him I wanted to come towards me.

Horses do go through phases and progress from one dodge to the next before they accept you and decide to co-operate. You have to be prepared to go through each phase calmly and take time to correct each problem as it arises, which will take as long as it takes.

2 LEADING IN-HAND

TEACHING YOUR HORSE to lead in-hand is one of the most fundamental aspects of horsemanship. He will need to be led to the field, into the horsebox or trailer, into his stable and so on. It should also help you iron out some of the problems commonly confronted when you begin working him on the lunge. You need to be able to lead a horse safely without being trampled on and injured; you must establish that you are in charge of the situation.

It is not unusual to find horses that have been abandoned in a field simply because they were difficult to handle, even to the extent of being chased with a whip from stable to field and back again. With basic training,

Figure 2.1 In-hand work teaches your horse to be obedient and respond to your aids in preparation for ridden work.

done in a controlled manner, even the most nervous horse will respond to being taught to lead. It is most important that you, as owner and trainer of your horse, can remain calm at all times in all circumstances. Most problems can be avoided with a bit of forethought, such as removing potential hazards, that old car axle leaning against the field gate, for example, is a certain trap for wayward limbs should your horse leap in the air and land on it. You need to develop trust and understanding between yourself and your horse in order to work together safely and so taking time and care with what seem pretty mundane aspects of horse training can have beneficial effects on future schooling. (Figure 2.1.)

It is very important that you allow sufficient time for the lessons that establish solid training foundations so that you are not stressed by a tight schedule. Ten minutes before you leave for work is not the best time to start.

IN-HAND EQUIPMENT

Clothing

Wear clothes that you can move easily in. Stout footwear is advisable, preferably with steel toecaps. Horses can move very quickly when frightened, and a spooking horse jumping on your foot often ends in tears: yours. Avoid lace-up shoes that could come undone and trip you up; a problem that is not dissimilar to lungeing while wearing your spurs!

A hard hat is vital, especially with a horse you do not know as his reactions will be much more difficult to judge than a horse you have owned for years.

Gloves are another essential. They need to be a little on the large size so that you can slip your hand out easily should the lunge line get caught around your hand. If your gloves are skin tight, and the line winds around your hand or wrist, you risk a broken wrist, or at least a finger or two.

Schooling whip

You need a whip that is comfortable to hold and long enough to touch the horse on his belly behind you as you lead him positioned next to his shoulder. The whip shaft must be stiff enough to be effective. A whip with too much flexibility tends to waggle and flap against the horse rather than deliver the right amount of flick.

Head collar

If you are leading your horse in and out of the stable, or to the field and back, a stout head collar should suffice. A 'control halter' is a useful item of equipment should you need to have more control but an old-fashioned rope halter works in a similar way: both tighten around the horse's head if pressure is put on the lead rope, then the pressure is released once the rope is relaxed.

Lunge cavesson

A lunge cavesson needs to fit well around a horse's face. Ideally three rings are present on the noseband of the cavesson to allow the lunge rein to be attached either in the centre or on either side. The centre ring is useful as you do not have to alter the position of the lunge line to change direction, but there may be occasions when you need to attach the line on either of the side rings.

Snaffle bridle

Leading in-hand using a bridle is a good way of introducing the bit to a young or spoiled horse. A simple snaffle bridle, with a mild bit such as a double-jointed snaffle, a training bit with a lozenge in the middle, which generally sits nicely in the mouth, or a snaffle made of synthetic material, of which there are many on the market, is perfectly adequate for lungeing your horse. For safety, always remove the reins so that there is no risk of them dangling down and your horse putting his foot through them.

Lunge line

Training a horse to lead in-hand is better done with a lunge line than a lead rope, as it gives you more leeway should your horse jump away. A lead rope can be pulled out of your hand more easily and using the first old frayed lead rope that comes to hand is asking for trouble should you need to give a horse a sharp tug to reprimand him: you will end up with a few strands in your hand and no horse.

If you have never handled a lunge line before, you will have to get used to the length. Obviously it is much longer than a lead rope, about 8 m (26 ft), because its first job is to allow for lungeing on a large circle. Soft cotton webbing is comfortable to hold, and notches along the line give a trainer good grip. A hand loop is necessary so that you can put your hand through the loop ensuring that you have a secure grip on the line should your horse try to pull away and you have to let the line out to its full extent. A swivel clip to attach the line to the lunge cavesson is easier and quicker to fasten and unfasten than a buckle. Ease of getting equipment on and off quickly and quietly is vital to avoid problems. Losing your horse between unclipping your lunge line from one side and getting it on the other side is most embarrassing, as is watching your horse have a mad five minutes around the school while you get your act together again.

Leg protection

It is advisable to put boots or bandages on your horse's legs to protect them from knocks if he gets nervous or escapes from you. Make sure that whichever you use is securely fastened; boots flying off can frighten a horse and trying to get them back on an upset horse again is extremely awkward unless you have a handy assistant around. There is also the risk of being kicked in the head while trying to refasten boots. It is better to return the horse to the stable, retrieve the boots and start again. This may take longer but at least you will live to see another day.

HOW TO LEAD IN-HAND

Make sure that the area you are working in is secure. Any level-surfaced area in the school, field or stable yard should be fine, as long as it is properly fenced and/or enclosed, and should be clear of all unnecessary clutter such as jump stands and wings. **Shut all gates**.

With yourself suitably attired and your horse with bridle (minus noseband), cavesson, and leg protection, attach the lunge line to the nearside cavesson ring in preparation to lead him around the school. Stand by his left shoulder with the line coiled in your left hand, with your hand through the loop for security. Hold the lunge line lightly in your right hand about a foot from the swivel clip attached to the cavesson. Carry a schooling whip in your left hand and hold it behind you so that the horse's belly is in reach should you need to tap him.

Start to walk purposefully forward, looking straight ahead; if you turn to look at the horse uttering terms of endearment, he will look at you as though you are mad and not budge. Pulling at the line will not work because he will just resist the pull. As you walk forward, expect your horse to come with you. If he does not, give him a quick tap with the whip on his belly. As soon as he walks on, continue for a few strides and then stop, remaining by his shoulder. If you get in front of his head, you will end up dragging him along and it will be difficult to stop again. When you stop, remain looking straight ahead, and reward him with a stroke with the back of your hand on his neck, without letting go of the line.

Walk on again, and then stop. Repeat this all around the school/yard until he walks when you walk, and stops when you stop. If he does not stop immediately, remain by his shoulder and walk a couple of steps with him, giving quick tugs on the cavesson with the line using your right hand. As soon as he stops, stroke his neck again. Keep your voice quiet, and limit your vocabulary to 'come', 'stop', and 'good boy'. He will understand these simple words far more quickly than a full-scale lecture on when he should stop and when he should walk on. Once he understands you, he will stop and walk with you, following your chosen route without you needing to tap him or tug at him. Then try the same process leading him from the right side.

If you are starting from scratch with your horse, this first leading session will be enough for him. Work him for fifteen to twenty minutes before returning him to his stable, or turning him out in the field to relax. With a very young horse, ten to fifteen minutes will be sufficient.

LEADING PROBLEMS

Refusing to move

If your horse refuses to walk out of the stable with you, remain by his shoulder, tap him on the belly with the schooling whip and walk out of the stable looking directly ahead. Stay by his shoulder and expect him to come with you. If you are at all anxious, he will pick this up and react either with fear or obstinacy, depending on his demeanour. Remain calm and repeat the same walk-forward-and-tap routine with more determination and a sharper whip aid. Shouting and anger will not work, on the contrary a stony silence works very well while he is resisting you, but be ready to stroke his neck and be pleased with him as soon as he responds correctly. If he takes one step, then stop, stay with him, allowing him to stand where he is, but not allowing him to reverse. A quiet steady contact on the lunge line or lead rope should be enough. If you tighten your grip to the point of pulling, he will almost certainly hit reverse gear and drag you back into the stable. If this happens, quietly repeat the whole process again.

Running off

If your horse attempts to run off when you lead him, try to be quick enough to prevent him getting ahead of you. Stay by his shoulder even if this means running along with him for a few steps. You need to give quite sharp tugs on the cavesson but a system of tug and release works far better than just pulling. If you pull and try to hold your horse with a dead hold, he will lurch against you, unbalance you and probably charge off around the school, at which point you will probably be desperately trying to remember if you followed the shut-the-gate rule! If he is too strong for you to hold, let go, unless you have the willpower to hang on, though you are more likely to get hurt being dragged along the ground. If your horse runs around the school the lunge line usually trails along behind, and will not get caught up in his legs if he is travelling in a straight line, though if you have left jump stands etc. around the school, the line could get caught on these and panic your horse. This is why a clear arena is vital for leading or lungeing in. If you have let go, most horses only run a few yards and then stop, as there is nothing on the end of the line to pull against (namely you). This is when the advantage of a lunge line over a lead rope is made apparent: you can retrieve it more quickly than a lead rope. Once the horse has stopped, walk quietly towards him, picking up the end of the line, and calmly looping it up as you walk towards him. Once you reach him, keep quiet and resume your leading exercise again as though nothing has happened. If you tell him off when you reach him, you are punishing him for stopping, instead you should stroke him briefly to calm him, and resume training.

Barging

When you begin leading your horse around the school, he may be distracted by his surroundings, tending to shy away from the edge of the school, and could barge into you. If he does this, remain by his shoulder, and quickly press your right elbow firmly against his shoulder. You may need to give him two or three sharp prods to make him move away from you. You must maintain a tall and strong posture, with a 'bossy headmistress' attitude to counteract his thuggish behaviour. There is no reason to shout, as mentioned earlier; a stony silence works best in these circumstances. Once he walks nicely beside you, stroke him and praise him. If he starts barging again, repeat the prodding. He should stop barging within a few minutes if your reactions are quick and firm enough.

Turning to face you: the stand-off

If a horse gets too far ahead of you when you are leading him, he may turn to face you head on, challenging your authority. In this situation, stare him directly in the eye, face him with your body, standing tall in that 'head-mistress' stance, and challenge him back, hence the stand-off. With whichever hand is not holding the lead line, make a fist and use it against his chest to push him back away from you. Short sharp punches work better than one continuous push. These punches need to be firm enough to be effective but not too firm: if your horse takes no notice of you, you are being too gentle; if you frighten him, you are being too strong. If you shove yourself against him, he will lean on your arm. As soon as he takes even one step back, stroke him. Repeat the punches two to three times and stare at him until he looks away from you. Do not look away first, and try not to blink! Once he looks away, lower your eyes, come out of 'headmistress' mode and resume the leading-round-the-school exercise normally as soon as you can.

Keeping your horse's attention

If your horse is more interested in what is happening in the next field or watching low-flying aircraft go by, you have to use your imagination. Place poles on the ground and lead him over and between them to focus his attention (Figure 2.2). In addition, you can introduce him to objects such as

Figure 2.2 Poles on the ground can make training interesting for your horse.

black rubbish sacks, paper bags, balloons, etc. at this stage to acclimatize him to objects he might find frightening (see the next two sections).

INTRODUCING STRANGE OBJECTS

Attach various items such as balloons, paper feed sacks, tinsel etc. to the fence at various points around the training area. Do not look at the items yourself and lead your horse past them as though there is nothing there. Focus on where you are going. Your horse sees what you see and so focusing on an open space ahead of you will encourage him to come with you. On the other hand, staring at the object as though you expect him to be frightened of it will put doubt into his mind as to how to deal with it. He may want to look at it, which is fine, but keep walking past it slowly, quietly and firmly, taking control of the situation. As he is only close to the object for a second or two, he has no time to be afraid. If he is the type of horse that becomes scared easily, showing a potentially frightening object to him head on will probably cause him to leap away.

Stay by his shoulder as you lead him past the object; he should walk past it beside you. If he is afraid he might want to tuck in behind you and follow

53

you, which is acceptable to start with but during each successive leading session encourage him forward so that his nose is just in front of you. In this way you will be in the best position to watch his facial expressions and therefore judge his reactions. If your horse is behind you, and he spooks, he may shoot forward and knock you over. Also, if you allow your horse to walk behind you where you cannot see what he is doing, beware of the horse that can slip his head collar, or detach his rope, because you certainly feel rather foolish walking along holding the end of a rope assuming he is following you, when he has actually sneaked off to the neighbour's fence and is stealing apples! Believe me, I speak from experience.

Successfully getting a horse accustomed to strange objects will help make hacking out and going to shows at a later stage so much easier and safer. If he learns to trust your judgement when being led, he will continue to do so when you ride him.

OBSTACLE COURSES

Obstacle courses can be simple or elaborate, depending on how much time you have available and the items you have to hand. Four poles or logs are very useful, as are buckets, plastic blocks and a piece of tarpaulin.

Set two poles randomly so that you can lead your horse over them, and two parallel to each other, like tram lines, so that you can walk between them. Some horses will go over poles more easily than walking between them, and vice versa. Practise walking and halting before and after the single poles and halting between the tram lines; this exercise prepares your horse for being mounted, as he becomes accustomed to standing still for a few moments when and where you ask him to. It can be a good idea to get him used to standing alongside the fence or wall should you ever need to mount from a mounting block in the future.

Walking over a tarpaulin can be a good way of introducing your horse to the sensation and sound of different terrain beneath his feet (Figure 2.3). Secure the tarpaulin by weighting it down with two poles so that it does not blow in the wind and frighten your horse. Walk next to your horse's shoulder and focus ahead into the distance. Lead him towards the tarpaulin. If he stops a long way before it and looks at it with suspicion, lead him around it in a small circle so that he initially just gets used to being near it.

Figure 2.3 Leading your horse over different surfaces, such as a tarpaulin can be useful preparation for trailer training.

Gradually take him closer and closer to the tarpaulin for brief periods at first using the walk-halt-walk technique described above. Once he has relaxed, walk purposefully towards it, and step on it yourself. The sound it makes may horrify him but just halt for a few moments. If he backs away from it, stay with him and as soon as he stops, walk forward again.

Repeat this circling method a few times and he should walk with you over the tarpaulin after a few minutes. If he does not, resume the circling around. Do not labour the exercise if he is really not happy with it. Get him as close to the tarpaulin as you can and finish on a positive note, which may be a circle around it, or standing with one foot on it. Reward him if you are sure he has done his best, and try again the next day and the next until he is relaxed and will walk quietly over the tarpaulin. He may rush over it the first couple of times, but keep up with him, stay calm and he should relax fairly quickly. If it still does not work, make sure your handling technique is sound and that you are not unwittingly transmitting your own anxiety feelings to him. (See also Chapter 12.)

3 TRAINING YOUR HORSE TO TIE UP

ONCE YOUR HORSE stands still in his stable politely and calmly, he must learn to stand quietly tied up. Trying to tie him up before he has learned to respect your presence in the stable could end up with him fighting any restraint and, if he breaks away, you will have a major problem with tying him up again.

Being able to tie up your horse is essential to safe horse management. If your horse is not so disciplined, he is potentially dangerous and impossible to restrain; he cannot be allowed to just wander wherever he likes around the yard. He might not go very far (next door, perhaps, to eat the fuchsias) but he could gallop off onto the road, or get into a field of unfamiliar horses, where fights could break out. A loose horse will take fright if he meets unusual or unfamiliar objects or incidents, such as a noisy tractor. He will probably panic and run wild, causing other horses in the vicinity to panic as well.

From a practical point of view, your farrier will not be impressed if he cannot tie your horse up to shoe him if you are late for his appointment, no-one will be able to look after your horse safely for you in your absence and when attending a horse show you will have to hold your horse all day.

If a horse is not used to being tied up how do you start? Just do it. The more fuss you make about doing it, the more problems you might give yourself. Tie him up for a few minutes at a time for specific things such as feeding and grooming so that tying up is connected to a good experience each time but never leave him unattended (Figure 3.1). Tie him where he can see another horse tied up so that he learns by example. Gradually extend the

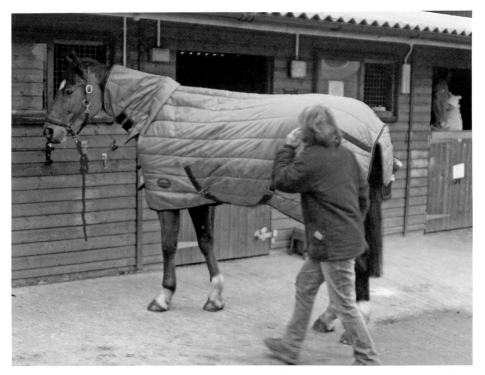

Figure 3.1 If your horse is tied up in the yard, do not leave him unattended just in case he takes fright.

period of time so that he can be tied long enough for the farrier to shoe him, or for you to give him a thorough groom and tack him up; about an hour should suffice. Sometimes long waits are involved at shows. If you have to tie him up to the horsebox or trailer for longer than an hour and a half, it might be better to put him back inside for a while in case he becomes bored and gets up to mischief.

If, however, tying-up problems do present themselves, you have to know how to combat them.

THE QUICK-RELEASE KNOT

How to tie a quick-release knot should be one of the first things you learn. If you were a member of the Pony Club, or able to help at a stables in exchange for lessons, you will have had this drummed into you on the first day. Tying a horse with any knot that does not release quickly is asking for trouble. If you cannot undo the knot, particularly when the rope is pulled taut, you will end up with a broken head collar, a chunk out of your stable (if the ring was fixed to wood) or an injured horse.

Tying the quick-release knot

Tie your horse leaving him no more than 0.6 m (2 ft) of slack rope. If the rope is too long he can move around too much and might get a leg over the rope and panic.

1. Put the end of the rope through the tie ring and pull it through.
2. Holding the rope the stated 0.6 m (2 ft) from the end attached to the head collar in your left hand, make a loop by crossing the other end over it and holding it in place.
3. Fold the remaining rope into another loop and push it through the original loop; pull it taut to make a knot (Figure 3.2a).
4. Leave the end of the rope just long enough so that it can be pulled to release the knot.
5. If your horse has learnt to pull the end and 'quick release' himself, you may need to pass the end of the rope through the loop to prevent him undoing it (Figure 3.2b).

Figures 3.2a and b a) A quick-release knot; b) Put the end of the rope through the loop to prevent your horse pulling it to untie the knot but it is quicker to undo in an emergency if you leave the end free.

EQUIPMENT FOR TYING UP

The head collar or halter

Wearing a head collar or halter is the first stage in introducing head gear to your horse; once he is happy with this, the bridle is the next stage.

It is best to use a head collar as it will not tighten if the horse pulls back. There are many types of 'control halter' available which do tighten if the horse pulls back. These are more suitable for leading work but can be useful for retraining a horse that pulls back when he is tied up, providing that you pass the rope through the tie ring and hold it in your hand rather than tying him with a knot just in case he panics. It is not advisable, however, to use a halter on horses that are sensitive around the poll area, or that have been injured behind the ears, because, should such a horse pull back, too much pressure will be put on the poll and he may panic. If your horse is frightened of being tied up with a head collar, try using a neck strap instead (see page 60).

TRAINING YOUR HORSE TO ACCEPT A HEAD COLLAR

The best way to handle your horse easily and safely without getting hurt is to put a head collar on him to give you control over the front end at least, but if your horse has never been trained to wear a head collar, getting him to accept this is the first hurdle to overcome. Enter the stable quietly with a head collar strategically placed over one arm just in case you have a good opportunity to catch him. Stand just inside the door, and pull it to, but have your hand on it so you can make a quick and quiet exit if necessary, or use a door chain if you feel you need greater freedom to get in and out of the stable.

If your horse does not approach you willingly to have his head collar put on, turn your back on him and look out into the yard admiring the scenery. Stay very still and relaxed. After a couple of minutes, quietly exit the stable and close the door, ignoring your horse. Go out of sight and watch what he does next. If you have aroused his curiosity, he should come to the door and look for you. If he does, approach him calmly and let him sniff your hand; do not be tempted to pat him on the head otherwise he may shy away again.

If he is relaxed and pleased to have contact with you, quietly open the door enough to slip inside and stand beside him. Avoid eye contact as this can be taken as aggression if your horse is in a defensive frame of mind. Gently stroke his neck and talk to him and then leave the stable again. It is a bit like playing hard to get!

Go through the same routine again, but this time, when you have stroked your horse's neck, place the head-collar rope gently over it and leave it there a minute or two. Slide it off again, and stroke him. Repeat the process again, and this time you may be able to ease the head collar over his nose. If you discover that he is afraid of the rope coming towards his neck, it might be easier just to slip the head collar over his nose directly while he is looking out of the door. If he flinches, stay where you are holding the head collar in the same position, neither forcing it on, nor removing it. If you get any adverse reaction from your horse, stay quite still until he relaxes, then try again. Once your horse is calm, reach under his throat and gently flip the head strap over behind his ears, slip it through the buckle held in your left hand and buckle up the head collar. Move him into position to be tied up, pushing against his shoulder or belly to manoeuvre him if necessary. Again, if your horse becomes tense at any stage, start again but if you feel you have got as far as you can for the day, leave it and try again the next day. It should not take more than a day or two to solve this problem.

Using a neck strap

If your horse will not accept a head collar, try a neck strap instead. A sound stirrup leather with sufficient holes punched in it is ideal. You can clip an old lead rope clip onto the buckle for attaching a lead rope, which is easier than clipping the lead rope directly onto the buckle each time.

To accustom a horse to a head collar, tie him up to the neck strap and just let him wear the head collar. He can then be tied up with a short rope on the neck strap and a longer one on the head collar. If he does pull back, he will feel pressure on the neck strap rather than the head collar and should not, therefore, panic. Move behind him to send him forwards to relieve the pressure on the neck strap. Gradually make the ropes the same length and then remove the neck strap, tying him up solely to his head collar. This stage could take days or weeks depending on the severity of the problem, but daily training is essential.

If you have taken the right amount of time, and made sure he feels confident during each training session, he should now tie up easily without panicking. There is always the unexpected low-flying jet, motorbike, etc. which may alarm your horse but if your horse does become tense and pulls back slightly, your first reaction should always be to send him forwards from a movement of your arm towards his haunches, swinging a spare lead rope at his back end, or tapping him with a schooling whip if he is being very difficult. Once he is happy being tied up with the head collar on his head, he should happily stand tethered with it around his neck (like the neck strap) in order to have his head groomed, and his bridle put on.

Day by day your horse should accept his head collar more easily. Another good ploy is to put it on and take it off every time you pass the stable whether you are going to do something with him or not. Putting it on at feed times also works well. In a short time he should be completely accustomed to the head collar being put on and taken off, especially if he sees you putting head collars on his neighbours; it helps if he is close enough to smell and touch the head collar, which is easy to do in a field if he and a companion are turned out with their head collars on. But remember to keep an eye on them to make sure that there is no risk of them getting the head collars hooked up on anything.

Ropes and chains

You need a **stout rope** with which to tie your horse or a **chain** fixed to a **tie ring** in the wall that will not break. The wall must be sound; if the horse pulls back, there is no point in the rope and head collar staying intact if a great chunk of the stable comes away. I have seen a horse break away when tied to a tap, the result being a torrent of water and a large bill for plumbing! Two rings in the wall either side of a passageway between stables are useful for tying up with two ropes or chains. With ropes, the quick-release knot described on page 57 is recommended and with chains it may be advisable to use **quick release fastenings** attached to the tie ring. It is much easier to unclip the chain at the wall ring than having it attached to the head collar because, if he sticks his head up in the air out of reach, you will be left fiddling around under his chin trying to release him. In addition, the chain that unclips at the wall ring gives you something with which to keep hold of the horse because the chain will be still attached to the head collar. These fastenings are often called 'panic hooks': the hook is hinged and the end is secured by a metal collar; by grabbing the collar and pulling on it, you can release it very quickly (Figures 3.3a and b).

Many people believe tying a horse to a short loop of string attached to a tie ring is safer because if he pulls back the string will break, thus preventing damage to the rope, head collar or horse. But this system does have its disadvantages, except for some horses that are very quick to turn it to their advantage: if they pull back hard enough, they can break the string and enjoy their freedom. This can result in the perpetuation of the pulling-back problem and unwittingly encouraging a horse not to remain tied up. If this is what you are dealing with, you need to use another method of tying up.

One of the best methods is one I remember from my childhood. Ponies and horses at the riding school I attended were tied in stalls during the day and secured by passing the rope through the tie ring and fastening it to a small log, threading the rope through a hole in the middle, and securing it with a quick-release knot. This enables the pony or horse to move back a certain amount without finding his head collar and rope tightening up thus reducing the risk of him panicking. The rope should not be so long that it

a   b

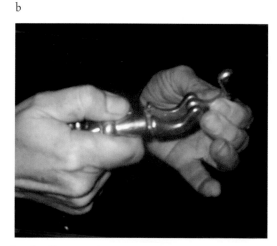

Figures 3.3a and b a) The 'panic hook' attached to the head-collar ring; b) Pressure applied to the 'panic hook' collar releases the hinged hook.

will get caught around a front leg but he should be able to reach the ground to eat.

Trevor is a first-class escapologist and will always test any attachments for breakability. Strangely enough he does not do it if tied up short with a rope directly to a ring, or to a ring at eye level, as he is unable to get any leverage. He has tested chains of various types and found that if he pulls back sharply enough he can break away. (I use him for market research because, if anything will break, Trevor will demonstrate this willingly every time.) The most interesting test we carried out was on a rubber rope. The first time I tied him up with one, he pulled back to test the stretch limit and pulled it to four times its length before stepping forwards again. He tried the 'quick snatch' the next day and the rope broke, pinging away about six metres in one direction, with Trevor 'pinging' in the other. He looked around to see if anyone was watching (I was hiding out of sight in the hay barn) and casually proceeded to graze. I think he felt a bit of a fool. I do believe, however, that if a young horse less balanced than Trevor had done this, he could easily have fallen over when the rubber gave way.

A rubber rope can be useful if your horse is prone to panicking when tied, but never leave your horse on his own until he is totally relaxed, otherwise you are just tempting fate and he is bound to pull back and break it. Rubber ropes are acceptable as long as your horse has already learned to tie up using a conventional rope, but a horse that pulls back will revel in the challenge of finding the breaking strain of rubber (Figure 3.4).
I do, however, find rubber ropes useful when travelling because, again, they do prevent most horses panicking when in a trailer or horsebox and there is little risk of them catapulting themselves about, as they are in a confined space.

WHERE TO TIE UP

Where you tie up your horse is all important and it must be done somewhere safe. If he has any problems with being tied up, tie him in the safety of a large, airy stable and treat being tied up as part of the daily training. If you are tying him up in the yard or stable passageway, make sure

Figure 3.4 A rubber rope can be an optional method for tying some horses, as long as they have already learned not to pull back.

that the gate/door is closed in case he should break free. It is also a good idea to tie him up to your horsebox or trailer as practice for when you later take him to a show. A day will seem very long if you have to hold your horse the whole time.

In the stable

When tying him in the stable, tie him to a ring on the same wall as the door or window, so that he can see out. If he is not used to being in a stable, it is likely he will be a bit restless and could swing his quarters around, so make sure that you have a clear exit to the door. Having a door chain across the entrance not only makes getting in and out easy but I have also found that some horses panic less with the 'open' doorway than if you tie them up and then shut them in by closing the door. Eventually, you should be able to tie your horse facing any direction with the door closed.

Make sure his water bucket is moved out of the way; the last thing you want is for him to knock it over and frighten himself. Initially it may help to give him a hay net so that he can nibble while tied up, but it is important to get him to stand quietly without it eventually, otherwise the result will be a fat horse that will not stand still unless he has food and you will be poor from the expense of feeding him all the time!

Horses that respond only to food can become very bossy and pushy. There is nothing wrong with a bit of bribery to encourage a horse at first, but neither you nor your horse must become totally dependent on the use of treats. If your horse has achieved something new or difficult he deserves a treat but rewarding him for very little simply teaches him to be greedy and might lead to the development of stable vices (see pages 78–83).

Outside

Once a horse has learnt to stand quietly when tied in the stable, progress to tying him up outside. Start by tying him just outside his stable which should be familiar territory to him now. The presence of his stable companions will reassure him but do not tie him up within biting range of a neighbour because he could throw his head up and panic and undo all your hard work. For the same reason, avoid over-hanging roofs, gutters, etc., to ensure that your horse does not bang his head should he raise it suddenly.

If you tie him to the trailer or lorry, make sure it is parked in an enclosed space, such as the corner of a field or yard and away from anything hazardous such as a chain harrow or other such farm implements. Do not park other vehicles too closely; they and, more importantly, the horse could be damaged if he is restless at first. A horse that will stand tied to a trailer or horsebox, quietly eating his hay, contributes so much to having a nice day out at a show. Chasing a loose horse around a showground gives you a bad name, and the embarrassment might contribute to your decision to never go to a show again. Amadeus got loose at a dressage event (while I was seeking the nearest Portaloo) and went around admiring all the other horseboxes (they were smarter than his) until someone got fed up with him and tied him up again – to the right trailer. I wonder how they knew he was mine…

TYING UP

Tying up with two ropes

If a horse has a tendency to swing his neck or hindquarters towards you, tying him up with two ropes may prevent this, as long as they are short enough. Clip one rope on either side of his head collar and attach them to separate rings set at about 1–1.5 m (3–5 ft) apart on the wall either side of his head and at chest height, which should be the right distance and positioning to keep him standing straight. Put the rings on a side wall to ensure you have space to move all around his back end and a clear run to the door if you need to exit rapidly. Tying your horse to rings on the back wall does not allow him to see what you are doing as you enter the stable and he could intimidate you with his hind legs because they will be aimed at the stable entrance.

When you move from one side of him to the other, always duck under his neck in preference to walking around his hind legs unless you know him really well and are sure he will not kick you. Be calm and confident at all times; jumping around like a rabbit and being afraid of what he might do to you is not the way to carry on. You will just annoy him which increases the possibility of him kicking.

If a horse has had a bad experience while being tied with two ropes he may be happier being tied up with a single rope instead of two but you will only find out by trial and error. Just take care and watch your horse closely for signs of stress, such as putting his ears flat back, swishing his tail, restlessness and so on.

Introducing tying up by leading in-hand

One way of introducing tying up is to teach your horse to lead in-hand (see also Chapter 2). This method works with horses of all ages and is a good remedial method for older horses with a tying-up problem. Wear gloves, a hat and sturdy boots and use a strong lead rope or lunge line in case the horse gets too exuberant. He must walk when you do, and stop when you do.

Start by leading him from the left side, although it is sensible to practise this on the right side as well to get him used to being led from both sides. Position yourself by his shoulder and purposefully walk straight ahead; do not turn round and stare at him. He will go with you if you remain by his shoulder, with a relaxed but closed hand on the lead line and keep moving forward. Have a schooling whip in your other hand so that you can reach behind you and give him a quick tap with the whip on his side if he does not immediately walk forward with you. When he does walks with you, keep the line loose. Then, stop walking; he should stop immediately you do if his attention is focused on you. If he does not stop, give a quick **tug** on the lead line and release it again. If you **pull** continuously on the lead line, he might spin around towards you and so it is important to keep your right elbow pressed against his neck to ensure that he cannot spin round. When he stops nicely for you, stroke him with the back of your right hand. Do not pat him too heavily as this will make him tense.

Once he has learnt to stop correctly, concentrate on getting him to stand still next to you for a few moments without wandering off. If he does start to creep away, give a sharp tug on the rope, and say 'stand'. As soon as he stands again, relax the lead line. Repeat the lead, stop and stand, until it can be done with a relaxed contact and he stands for a little longer each time without pulling.

When this technique is mastered, take him into his stable or yard, wherever you both feel most comfortable, and tie him up while you take off his bridle. Because horses like the attention, groom him lightly, even though he may not be dirty, and then leave him for a few minutes, observing him from a distance. Remember to always tie him up with a quick release knot so that the rope can be undone in an instant if he does panic. You should not need to tie him to a loop of string if you are paying attention and can get to him quickly (see page 62).

Dealing with a horse that pulls back

As stated, when teaching a horse to tie up you should never leave him on his own, even in a stable. If, however, you know, or discover, that your horse pulls back, this rule is even more pertinent. Pulling back is an important issue to deal with and quick reactions from you are essential because it is potentially very dangerous. You cannot even just take a few seconds to go and do this or that assuming he will be all right for a moment. If you have to leave him, untie him, and then return to continue the training session.

If a horse does pull back, the best way to deal with it initially is to have a broom or spare lead rope to hand to send him forwards to release the pressure on the rope he is tied with. (Use a schooling whip only if you know he is not whip-shy or of a nervous disposition.) You should only need to use an 'implement' to touch him with a few times. Once he understands that he has to move forwards when he sees something coming towards his back end from the side, he should react to you touching him on his belly (where a leg aid would be applied). Watch him closely and at the first sign of tension, which usually manifests itself in a raised head and stiffened neck, move your arm towards his haunches to prevent him from stepping back. You have to move quickly to drive him forward again and make sure you praise him when he stands quietly with the rope slackened. If you are a little slow and he steps back, tightening the rope, prod him in the belly with your knuckles and say 'forwards' or 'no' or some other word of your choice that you must use consistently every time he steps back. The instant he steps forwards, praise him and stroke him. In a few days he will learn to stand quietly and not to pull back.

If you have a horse with a strong tendency to pull back, work with him in a stable so that he cannot run too far backwards, break the rope and get away. Use a lunge line or very long rope. Pass it through the tie ring, and fasten the clip to the head collar. Hold the end of the line in the hand nearest your horse's head, keep it slack and wear gloves in case he shoots back and pulls the line through your hand. Groom your horse, keeping the line in your hand and if he pulls back, let the line slide through your hand allowing him to move backwards a little but let him feel gentle pressure on the line; do not tighten it too much otherwise he will pull against it even more. Keep calm and say, 'stand'. Once he is standing still, move behind him as before and send him forward closer to the ring. Continue with the grooming. If you need both hands, to pick out his feet for example, place the line on the floor under the ring close to the wall to ensure that your horse cannot stand on it. If he pulls back, grab the line with one hand, but do not pull him, just maintain a gentle pressure as before. When this method helps him to stop panicking and running backwards, move on to using a normal lead rope through the ring to make your horse think he is tied, but do not secure the rope. Again, if he pulls back, send him forwards with your arm. Once he responds with confidence and stops panicking, you should be able to tie him up conventionally.

If the pulling-back problems recur at a later date, start the whole process again. A rubber rope (see page 63) may work in this circumstance, but do make sure it is not likely to break causing him to panic him even more. I have found tying horses to string loops encourages them to not only break free (see page 62) but also induces further panic; they pull back, feel the string break, and frighten themselves. This then becomes a habit and a vicious circle: 'I'm tied up, I'm frightened, I have to break away, now I'm even more frightened'. It is much better to send a horse forwards to slacken off the lead rope.

Tying up foals

Teaching a foal to tie up should be done in a matter-of-fact way next to his mother. Tie up the mare and groom her, the foal should stand beside her contentedly, learning from her example. Brushing the mare, and then brushing the foal teaches him that standing still results in nice things. Before the foal gets bored, return them to the field, leading the mare with the foal following on.

The next stage is to tie up the mare, groom both mare and foal and, at a point when the foal is really relaxed, quietly put a foal slip on him. Let him get used to wearing it for a while each day, especially when you need to handle him. It makes life so much easier if he readily accepts a halter being put on and taken off rather than the process becoming a big drama.

Following on from the grooming and foal-slip-wearing stages, have an assistant lead the mare to the field, and you lead the foal. If he stops and refuses to budge, ask another assistant to give him a gentle push from behind to help him on his way. When you turn him out or bring him in from the field, clip the lead rope back on his foal slip and let him follow his mother, keeping the lead rope loose so that, although you are holding the end of it, you are not yet influencing him, and walk beside him. On no account resort to pulling him along as this will just make him tense, and could damage his young neck. He should soon, over a few days, be happy to be led to and from the field following his mother.

As soon as he is confident **following** his mother, lead him **beside** her, and then take him **in front.** Over the next few days, start to drop back with the mare, increasing the distance gradually until the foal eventually accepts being led on his own. If you time this training right, he should be able to be led on his own at weaning time.

4 STABLE MANAGEMENT

GOOD STABLE MANAGEMENT is essential to keeping your horse healthy and a healthy comfortable horse is likely to be a better-behaved horse; a horse's surroundings can dictate whether or not problems develop.

Walls festooned with cobwebs leads to an accumulation of dirt in the environment. Non-circular feed bowls and water buckets harbour germs and dirt in corners and old and spilt feed encourages rats and mice. A clean, tidy yard discourages vermin and makes it easier to locate equipment if you are in a hurry (Figure 4.1). For example, rummaging through a pile of rugs thrown on the floor, searching for your horse's New Zealand rug because of

Figure 4.1 A clean, tidy yard runs much more efficiently than one in which you cannot find anything when you need it.

a sudden downpour is frustrating and time-consuming, particularly when you are already late for work. Inefficiency can lead to a frayed temper which, in turn, could be directed at your horse causing him to retaliate with bad behaviour.

MUCKING OUT

A poorly mucked-out bed can cause problems for your horse such as thrush from standing in wet bedding, and breathing problems from dust or mould. Throwing out too much clean bedding with the soiled material is wasteful and can increase your bedding bills. If you muck out properly, your horse will be cleaner because he is not lying down in his droppings, his feet remain clean and hard and his stable rugs will not need cleaning so often. If you have a busy life, you do not want to spend hours mucking out, and utilizing a system that fits into your day means that the job can be done as quickly and efficiently as possible, leaving you free to get on with other things, such as riding!

Having recently acquired my own yard, becoming used to mucking out my horses after several years with them on livery has been an enlightening experience. As I am usually short of time in the morning, I tend to skip out in the morning and muck out in the evening when I am under less pressure. My back complained during the first week, even though I have only three horses to do as opposed to the ten or so in my charge when I was in my twenties. Age probably had something to do with the back pain, but I now have got back into the swing of it and have worked out the best technique for me. Mucking out can be very therapeutic (especially after an afternoon arguing with someone on the phone about my internet connection) and is one of the most underrated jobs in the stable yard.

Whether you use straw or shavings, or one of the other types of bedding available, it takes a bit of know-how to do a good job and something that always makes the job easier is knowing your horse. If you have recently acquired a horse you will not be immediately familiar with his toilet habits. These vary considerably from horse to horse. Amadeus is very tidy in his box, and defecates around the edge, leaving himself a clear area to lie down in the middle. He always urinates in the same place as well and so it is easy to find the dirty patch straight away. On the other hand, Trevor tends to trample everything together in a mess, which makes selecting the dirtiest bits a bit of a challenge, and he likes to dunk his hay in the water bucket, thus making the front of his bed rather soggy. Familiarizing yourself as to where the wettest bedding will be saves you a lot of time searching for it.

The most inexperienced stable employee or helper is always given the mucking out as an initiation. At first, tools seem to have a mind of their own, wheelbarrows have a tendency to fall over and the muck heap is difficult to clamber up. Progress is slow, as the initiate tries to choose between clean, slightly soiled and dirty bedding, and deciding what to throw out and what to keep. Mucking out a stable can take ages at first, much to the dismay of the yard manager, but novices have to be allowed time to get up to speed. An experienced groom should be able to muck out a stable in 10–15 minutes, including putting in fresh bedding and refilling the water buckets (automatic waterers are fantastic time-savers, see page 78).

Having had to rediscover the art of forking, shovelling, wheel-barrowing and sweeping, it has been easy to write it all down.

Mucking-out tools

Have all the tools you need to hand.

Wheelbarrow A strongly made plastic wheelbarrow is lighter than a metal one when full of muck. Choose one with a broad rim so that you can get more in it, which saves you making so many trips to the muck heap. When filling the wheelbarrow, throw a forkful of dirty bedding into each corner, fill in the middle and then flatten the load. Add another layer, keeping it as flat as possible to make sure it does not all fall out on your way to the muck heap.

Fork Four-pronged forks are better than those with five for scooping up a good forkful as the tines go through the bedding more easily. A two- or three-pronged pitchfork is useful for throwing the clean straw about to lay the bed again.

Shovel A shovel is required for removing the sweepings from the floor

Broom Use a stiff-bristled broom for wet material and a soft-bristled one for sweeping up dry bedding.

Preparation for mucking out

Remove the horse from the stable; it is easier to get into all the corners without your horse standing in the way or trying to push past you. If you are in a rush, however, it can save you time if your horse is trained to move to the back or the side of the stable on command and to stand there while you skip out. It takes no longer to do this than taking your horse out of the box providing he is well-behaved. If your horse is in the stable, place your wheelbarrow across the door; this prevents him escaping and makes it easy to fill the barrow. Anything that drops off the sides of the wheelbarrow falls in the doorway from where it is easy to pick up. If you put the barrow a long way from the doorway, it is further to fling the muck, and will make the work more tiring. A chain across the door makes mucking out easier because you can go in and out without worrying that your horse will sneak out when you are not looking. Alternatively tie him up, but you will have to take care around him when mucking out the corner in which he is tied.

Skipping out

Removing the droppings throughout the day helps to keep the stable clean, prevents your horse trampling them around his bed and gives you less work when you next come to muck out. In the summer, droppings are a magnet to flies and so removing them can help to reduce the number of insects bothering your horse.

Mucking-out methods for different bedding
STRAW

Remove the piles of droppings on the surface of the bed first. Slide your fork underneath each pile, picking up the layer of straw beneath them as you do so. This keeps the piles intact while you transport them to the wheelbarrow. Tip the droppings off the straw into the barrow, and fling the straw (which should be clean as it was on the top of the bed) to one side. Putting the droppings in the barrow first means they do not roll out on the way to the muck heap. Once you have removed all the droppings start flicking the clean straw to the sides of the box. You will find the bed is layered and underneath the clean straw you may discover hidden droppings, which should be removed. A horse will usually defecate about eight times in twenty-four

73

hours and some piles are bound to get covered up with the cleaner straw.

Clean straw is easy to see, as is the wet solid stuff near the floor but deciding which of the remainder is clean and which is dirty can be confusing. As a guide, all straw that is brown is dirty, and all that is any shade of yellow is clean. If you stick your fork in and find the straw easy to fluff up, it is clean enough to stay in the box. If you hit a solid lump, it is wet and should be put in the wheelbarrow. The wettest bit is usually in the centre of the box and so you should end up with the central area of wet bed to remove and all the clean stuff around the walls. Once you have removed the final wet patch, sweep the floor clean to remove all remaining soiled straw/bits of dropping. On average, a clean horse will need one barrow load taken out, a dirty horse two. Bed 'mashers', like Trevor, sometimes supply three or four loads!

If you are unfortunate to have a horse that tramples everything in together, take out a couple of barrow loads of the worst bedding, and leave the rest as a base. Put sufficient clean straw on top so that he will not be standing or lying on dirty straw overnight. If the bed is a real mess, then you have no other option than to take everything out and start again. A good way of keeping the bed under control in this situation is to remove the wettest patch morning and night before the horse has a chance to trample the clean bedding into it.

Use the fork to fluff up the remaining bank of clean straw and spread it over the floor in an even layer. Some people like to leave a bank around the edge which they feel prevents the horse from getting cast by encouraging him to lie down in the middle but I have found this to be a myth and like a level bed. Banks encourage some people to just muck out the middle of the bed and not the edges as it is hard work digging out muck from the banked sides.

If, when fluffing up the clean straw, you find wet patches you missed on the first fork-through, remove them. Top up the bed with sufficient clean straw to make sure the horse will not be lying on bare floor. A good bed-depth guide is to stab your fork into the bed: if you hit concrete, it is not thick enough; if you find it difficult to muck out the next morning because of mountains of clean straw, you have put in too much.

Finally, sweep the doorway and leave an area clear for water buckets. Spilled water does not then soak the bed. If you have a horse that plays football with his buckets, place them in an old car tyre to stabilize them.

SHAVINGS/HEMP

With bedding materials like these, the easiest method of mucking out is to arm yourself with a pair of rubber gloves and a skip. Remove the droppings by picking them up, and then proceed to remove the wet bedding as described above. You may find a shavings fork easier to use as the prongs are closer together or, alternatively, use a shovel. This type of bedding is more absorbent than straw and lends itself well to deep-litter beds.

DEEP LITTER

Deep-litter beds can save a lot of time but bear in mind that you will have to set aside a morning periodically to dig it out completely and start again. Suitable deep-litter materials are straw, shavings, or hemp. The principle is to remove droppings, level the bed by banging it down with a fork to make a firm base and then to put the fresh bedding on top. The important thing is to leave deep litter alone and not to poke it about to see what it looks like underneath. If you do this, the bed will become mashed up, damp and smelly. If you leave it alone until it is at least 30 cm (1 ft) thick, the heat generated underneath will ensure that the top few centimetres will be dry. The damp is absorbed by the underneath layer of the bedding. By allowing the bed to settle and become dry, your horse's feet will remain in good condition. With a mushy bed there is the risk that the horse will develop thrush.

A deep-litter bed is warm and comfortable for a horse and easier on his legs than a thin bed on concrete. Some people clear the bed out every week, others every month, and some leave it even longer. The time to clear it out and start again is when it gets about 60 cm (2 ft) high, otherwise it is a hard task to dig out (you need a back that can cope with heavy digging). On the plus side, the manure is well rotted and very good for compost!

RUBBER MATTING

Rubber matting is popular at the moment; it provides a horse with a comfortable surface on which to lie down and stand, and it is said to mimic bare earth. The mats do, however, have to be sealed to make a waterproof floor otherwise they have to be lifted periodically to hose the stable floor underneath, which can be an unpleasant job, and they tend to be heavy, so you will need help and a strong back.

Sealed mats just require a toilet area of absorbent bedding such as shavings to keep the floor dry, or you could lay a half-sized bed for your horse. Some horses make a mess all over the place and not in the toilet area, which means that they sometimes lie in the dirt and wet more often than with conventional beds, and can get filthier, particularly greys, as I know to my cost! Once your horse is used to having a smaller bed, he should work out and separate his toilet area from the lying-down area, unless you have a horse like Trevor that likes to spread his bedding and muck all over the floor in a thin layer and play with it all night.

Muck out the box as normal, but this can be done quickly and easily because the bed is smaller than a full bed. You may need to hose down the mats occasionally to keep them clean.

Rubber matting combined with a half-bed of absorbent material is ideal if you have a horse with breathing problems or dust allergies.

The muck heap

This can be a work of art or an eyesore depending on how it is looked after. When I was a lowly working pupil, we all had to climb on the muck heap after doing the stables to trample it and flatten it down. Much fun was had in muck slinging competitions to see how much we could get down each other's boots and shirts – but it did look neat and tidy when we had finished. We also had a muck-heap ritual for birthdays: the unlucky recipient was first dunked in the water trough and then buried in the muck heap.

The serious reason for trampling the muck heap is to pack it down in order to aid the rotting process and keep it compact, which means that it takes up less room and grows more slowly instead of erupting into a messy mound. A smaller volume will cost you less to remove and save you money over the year.

Situating your muck heap miles from the stable in a sea of mud is totally impractical. If you are in a position to be able to plan the situation of your muck heap, make sure you can get to it easily and quickly. A plank placed against the heap enables you to run the wheelbarrow to the top of the heap and save time (and backache) throwing muck up from ground level. The muck heap should be removed at regular intervals before it turns into Mount Everest. Shaping it into a neat rectangle in layers helps it rot down and prevents muck falling back down the sides. My own muck heap is sloping with a 'runway' up the middle, for ease of tipping out the barrow (Figure 4.2).

Figure 4.2 One style of muck heap: the sloping runway up the middle makes it easy to wheel the barrow to the top and empty it.

WATER

All horses need constant access to clean, fresh water. If you use buckets, make sure they are kept clean and place them where your horse is least likely to knock them over, while bearing in mind they need to be easy to reach for filling up. Standing them in old car tyres works well to keep them upright and to discourage rough games where buckets are hurled across the box and kicked about (one of Trevor's favourite games, which has been put a stop to by using a large rubber container in the biggest old tyre I could find). Filling buckets up with the hose from the doorway saves carting buckets back and forth to the tap during the day and can help to accustom your horse to the hose pipe. Have the hose on a gentle stream at first so that initially you do not alarm him and gradually increase the pressure to get him used to the noise of the spray (see page 94 in Chapter 5).

Automatic waterers

Automatically filling drinking bowls are a great labour-saving invention. There are no buckets to heave around and your horse has constant access to water. They come in various shapes and sizes. If your horse is a dainty drinker, a smaller one will suffice but there are larger ones if he prefers to submerge his nose and take a large draught. The bowls should be wiped clean daily with a sponge. Place an empty bucket underneath the bowl, raise the flap at the back and hold the small ball cock up to cut off the water supply while you wipe out any dirt into the bucket. Once the bowl is clean, release the ball cock and replace the cover and let it refill. One school of thought is that an automatic waterer makes it difficult to tell how much water your horse is drinking each day but I would rather know a horse has continuous access to water. It is no different from your horse drinking from a trough in a field; you would not know how many times he drank unless you sat in the field with him all day.

If your horse likes to dunk his hay in the stable, it may be wise to give him a 'dunk bucket' to use rather than stuffing the waterer with it and if your horse prefers drinking from a bucket, give him one and use the waterer as a back-up supply.

Make sure the plumbing is tucked out of reach in a corner to discourage vandalism. In Germany I used to look after Wenko, a show jumper that would frequently chew through the copper pipes and be standing under his own en-suite shower in the morning. I became a dab hand at turning off the stopcock when half asleep at six in the morning. Make sure you lag the pipework and know how to turn the water off if you get a leak.

STABLE VICES – SIGNS OF BOREDOM AND STRESS

Stable vices can occur when a horse is bored or stressed and are, therefore, indicative of poor management. Horses can copy vices from other horses but, in my experience, they usually have an inherent tendency to weave, crib etc., before they pick it up. Titbits are also a cause of stable vices and should not be given in the stable just for the sake of it; it is far better to use titbits in the school or in the yard as a training reward. A horse will co-operate much better if he understands that if he does what you ask, he gets a treat. Horses that get titbits from passers-by soon start to nip and bite in the absence of the goodies.

I know many yards where several horses each have their own idiosyncrasies, but this does not necessarily mean that every horse on the yard will follow suit. Some people treat a horse with a vice as though it has some infectious disease and shut it away in the furthest corner of the yard in isolation, which is the worst thing you could do because the horse will become more stressed and his behaviour deteriorate rapidly. Normality is the best treatment for such problems.

If you have bought a horse with a stable vice, all is not lost; understanding the cause of the vice requires observation and assessing when and why your horse does what he does. Once you have an idea why he does it, you can adjust his feed/work/care routine to hopefully eradicate or at least manage the problem. Some horses display their vices when someone is around, hoping they will be given food. The way to tell if this is the case is to walk away from the stables, and hide somewhere where you can see your horse but he cannot see you. If he stops what he is doing when you go away, you can assume the vice is titbit related. If he continues to do it, then it is most likely stress related. Other people in the yard can exacerbate the problem. If a horse weaves as a way of asking for attention or a treat, people standing outside your horse's box saying, 'Oh look, this one is weaving', would just make matters worse as he would continue to weave in case anything was forthcoming. Ask them politely to move away to another part of the yard to continue their conversation and leave your horse in peace. Most horses stop weaving when left alone.

It is important that horses with stable vices spend as much time as possible out at grass but ensure they also have sufficient work to keep them relaxed, healthy and happy. A tense stressed horse will crib on a fence in the field as well as in the stable if you do not take heed of his feed and work requirements. I have known horses with various degrees of stable vice, but this has not affected their work and they have been otherwise well-behaved and friendly horses.

I think that the description 'stable vice' implies that a horse is deeply traumatized or even dangerous. I would rather describe these behaviours as 'stable habits' as they are on a par with finger-nail chewing in humans. If your horse has any of these 'habits' they should be mentioned when he is sold as they could affect his value slightly, though it does depend on the severity of the problem. This can, however, often be outweighed by other attributes a horse has such as a good competition record, or perfect manners.

Weaving

A weaving horse sways incessantly from one front foot to the other in a rocking motion swinging his neck from side to side over the door. The usual, most effective, deterrent is to put a weaving grille, which has a V shape in it, on the top of the door allowing the horse to put his head out but discouraging him from swaying from side to side. Confirmed weavers will stand back from the door and weave in the stable, or even in the field. In the worst cases, the horse can suffer joint problems and lose weight. Some horses may swing their necks (without rocking the body) a few times when feeling stressed, or if they think a titbit is in the offing, but they will stop if you ignore them.

The first sign of a true tendency to weave is a slight rocking of the shoulders from side to side but if you nip this in the bud, it is possible to eradicate it. If you see your horse swaying a little, he must be told not to do it; if you do nothing, it is probable he will continue. Flick his chest with the end of a lead rope (this is easiest to do if you have the stable door open with a chain across it) and say, 'No'. Your horse should step back from the doorway. You must then give him some hay as a distraction, leaving some in the doorway so that he associates looking out of the door with a relaxing nibble rather than winding himself up. This works best with young horses; older ones may be more difficult to completely retrain, but you should be able to minimize the occurrence.

Weaving can also be a sign of claustrophobia; I knew a young horse that was very reluctant to go into a stable at a new yard, planting himself firmly in front of the door, refusing to budge. Once he was persuaded to go in, he began to weave when the door was closed. I spent an afternoon leading him in and out of different stables in the yard, until he did it easily, tapping him with a schooling whip to encourage him in, and rewarding him with a treat every time he stood quietly in each stable. When he was left in his own stable, he no longer weaved. I made sure he was worked properly and had sufficient turn-out, and he relaxed very quickly as he settled into his new regime.

Cribbing (crib-biting)

A horse that cribs will grab hold of the edge of the door, draw in air and belch it out again. This, again, is very often caused by too many titbits. In the worst cases, cribbing results in severely worn-down teeth and the development of tight muscles around the throat area (where the head joins the neck), which can make a horse reluctant to flex at the poll when ridden. Mild cribbing usually appears at meal times, and only lasts a few minutes. You can purchase cribbing collars which fit around the throat to prevent the horse from belching. Although this works, I have found that the horse becomes more stressed when not allowed to crib and does it even more frantically once the collar is removed. As with weaving, say 'No' each time you see your horse doing it and make sure that he has hay to keep him occupied, that he is left in peace in his stable and that he is not being made nervous or excited by people standing next to his stable, who may give him titbits.

Wind-sucking

Wind-sucking often develops from cribbing when the horse learns to arch his neck, suck in air and belch without having to grab onto anything. I have never seen a confirmed wind-sucker, cribbing being more common. If the problem of cribbing is managed well, and the horse has adequate work and the correct amount of feed and turn-out, wind-sucking can be avoided.

Managing stable vices

Using good quality straw as bedding, usually barley or oat straw, can act as 'bed and breakfast'; the horse can 'graze' on the straw in his stable, which helps to prevent stable vices. You will not then have to feed him so much hay, and as straw is cheaper you can save some money. Stables damaged by chewing can be costly to repair and so it is preferable for your horse to eat his bed than chew the walls and stable fittings. If your horse is stabled on shavings or another type of inedible bedding, you must ensure he has hay ad lib to keep him occupied while he is in his box and make sure he is turned out each day. Horses with vices benefit from spending time in the field first thing in the morning while you muck out and last thing at night while you skip out. He will be less stressed in the morning because he will look forward to a pleasant graze, and also go to bed with a full belly and in a relaxed frame of mind.

Anxiety may cause cribbing and weaving to appear frequently at feed times, particularly when horses see you enter the feed room, in which case it best not to take too long over feeding the horses. The less time a cribber or weaver has to wait, the less chance he has to become anxious.

Some horses crib or weave if they have become tense during schooling. Always make sure you finish a training session on a good note, and allow your horse to relax on a long rein, or go for a short hack to calm him before putting him back in his stable. An alternative is to put him in the field for a while after he has worked. Grazing is extremely therapeutic for a tense horse and is the best way to distract the horse from stable vices. A horse with a stable vice should spend as much time

Figure 4.3 Toys can encourage 'grazing' to help your horse relax and to occupy his time so that stable vices do not develop in the first place.

as possible out at grass, as this usually cures the problem, but some horses that have a long-term cribbing or weaving habit will do it even in the field.

A good solution to weaving and cribbing is to leave the door open as much as possible and use a door chain across the doorway. By 'removing' the door, many horses feel more relaxed, and cease to be stressed. Wind-sucking and cribbing require a surface to grab hold of with the teeth, or to press against with the lower jaw; if, therefore, the means to perform these vices are removed, including feed mangers, the horse stops.

Toys in the stable can help. Hollow balls that can be filled with food are useful; as the horse rolls the ball around, the food falls out of a small opening, thus encouraging 'grazing' (Figure 4.3). Make sure he always has hay to nibble once the ball is empty to stop him reverting to cribbing or wind-sucking.

Box-walking

Box-walking is not so much a vice as a sign of stress. A horse will trample around his box and be reluctant to settle, a common occurrence when changing to a new yard. It may be a bit of a shock to find your newly purchased horse cantering around his stable sweating up. The normal response would be to put him in the field to 'work it off' but usually the poor horse runs around, still in a panic, neighing loudly, risking injury, or even jumping out of the field. It is better to leave him in his stable, preferably with a neighbour next door for company. Try not to hang over his door in trepidation. Just make sure he has hay and water and leave him in peace to become accustomed to his new surroundings. He should calm down over a couple of days and then he could be lunged to tire him a little before he is turned out thus making him less likely to run around in an anxious state. This behaviour will be seen in the field as well as in the stable and so it is advisable to leave him out for only a short time, and bring him in before the anxiety manifests itself. Once he is settled in his stable, he should be relaxed outside as well. Make sure he has sufficient work and the right amount of food to keep him occupied and content but not enough to cause him to get fat.

5 GROOMING

GROOMING A HORSE thoroughly is important to his well-being both physically and mentally. Making sure your horse is properly groomed reduces the risk of minor injuries such as sore spots or girth galls caused by not cleaning the girth and saddle area, or sore patches on the face where dirt or sweat has not been removed before putting on the bridle, and picking out a horse's feet thoroughly is important to keeping the hooves in first-class condition.

As well as promoting health, grooming gives you the opportunity to assess the condition of your horse by observing his muscular development, the way he stands naturally, i.e. his posture, and his demeanour. If he resents you touching his back, he could have sore muscles caused by a poorly fitting saddle or bad riding (this reaction is not to be confused with the horse's natural reflex to dip his back away from pressure on the muscles either side of his spine); or it could be that you groom him too roughly and he is simply reacting to pressure from you rather than actually being in pain. Brushing his belly firmly can cause him to reflexively hump his back and this is often used by vets to test that reflex action of the back muscles when assessing a horse for purchase.

Care should be taken when grooming between a horse's back legs, and when handling the legs in general. Keep an eye on your horse's face so that you can detect any signs of resentment. Tail swishing and stamping the feet often precede a kick, watch out for early warning signs, therefore, and make sure you are not in the firing line. If you are not familiar with the horse or if you know he may be inclined to kick, wear a safety helmet.

Horses enjoy being groomed, they do it to each other to establish and cement relationships, and grooming can help you to establish a good rapport with your horse, ensuring that you are a herd member. (Figure 5.1.) All horses have ticklish places and areas they like you brushing firmly but these will vary from horse to horse.

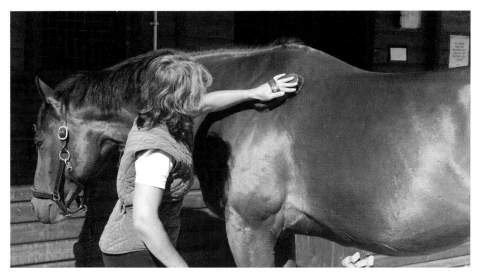

Figure 5.1 Horses enjoy being groomed and it is worthwhile investing in a decent body brush with real bristles to get your horse really clean.

My horses have different attitudes to grooming. Amadeus has always enjoyed being groomed and pampered and, in particular, loves having his withers scrubbed with a rubber curry comb, a sensation that makes him wobble his lips in delight! I take advantage of his sensuousness when I ride: scratching his withers with my fingers rewards him for good work and shows him he has done well.

Grooming Trevor daily helped him learn to trust me. When I first had him he would run to the back of the stable, with his head up in the air, expecting something awful to happen, which could have been caused by careless handling around the head, but after a while he would stand with his head lowered, relaxing and enjoying being brushed gently. He was very ticklish at first and so I would stroke him gently with a grooming glove until he accepted my touch. Gradually I progressed to a body brush and rubber curry comb but even now he does not like being groomed too firmly straight away; he still likes the stroking first!

The act of grooming is an ideal opportunity to have a close contact, and to reinforce your relationship, with your horse, which is just as important as riding or training him. It can be a way of spending time enjoying each other's company during inclement weather; far preferable for both parties that trudging down the road in the pouring rain.

GROOMING KIT

A few key items are all you need to keep your horse clean and healthy.
- Hoof pick
- Dandy brush
- Rubber curry comb
- Plastic curry comb (optional)
- Metal curry comb (optional)
- Body brush
- Water brush
- Stable rubber (tea towel)
- Grooming glove (optional)
- Mane comb
- Two sponges (for hygiene reasons, one sponge should be kept for the nose and eyes and one for the back end)
- Mild shampoo
- Sweat scraper or piece of baler twine

Care of your grooming kit

Wash the brushes and curry combs from time to time using either shampoo or washing up liquid to remove all grease. Leave them to dry thoroughly before repacking them in your kit, as the brush bristles can rot and metal curry combs will rust if they are put away wet.

Put the stable rubber and grooming glove in the washing machine occasionally. If they are stiff with dirt, they are not going to be effective.

Replace sponges before they fall apart.

WHEN AND HOW TO GROOM

When I was a working pupil, we were taught to **brush-off** the horses before exercise, and give them a thorough groom, known as **strapping**, later in the day.

It is easy these days, when life seems hectic all the time, to get into the habit of just brushing-off, i.e. picking out the feet and removing the worst of the dirt from, mainly, the saddle and bridle areas. If you never actually get round to giving the horse a thorough groom, dirt and grease builds up in the coat, your once glossy horse will feel distinctly grubby and you risk causing skin conditions, the tell-tale signs of which are a build-up of grease under the mane along the crest and in the coat. I have seen a distinct line on some horses where the person grooming has brushed up as far as the mane but not lifted the mane to groom underneath. Grease under the saddle can cause saddle sores which start off as pimples; if you do not notice them at this stage, the subsequent sores will stop your horse being ridden for some days.

Check your riding boots after you have ridden. If the insides of the heels are covered with thick white grease, then your horse is filthy and in serious need of a good clean. Run your hand against the coat over the top of the rump – another area often missed – if it is full of dust then you have been neglectful. There is no point in just brushing the horse up to eye level, if your horse is too tall for you to reach his back from the ground, stand on a box and get to work properly.

Horses and ponies that live out all year round do not need such a thorough grooming. Obviously they should be clean but rigorous removal of all their natural grease leaves them without nature's protection against the elements.

The best time to strap your horse is when he is slightly warm after exercise, but not sweaty. The grease is much easier to remove and he is more likely to stand still and relax if he is a bit tired. It is rather like you going to the gym for a rigorous work-out and then having a nice shower and massage afterwards. There are all sorts of grooming and massage machines available these days but I do not think you can beat spending time grooming manually. A thorough groom should take you about half an hour, whereas brushing-off can be done in five minutes.

Tie your horse up either in his stable or outside if it is a nice day. If the stable is poorly lit, tie him up near the door for better visibility. It is possible to groom properly by feel but it does help to see what you are doing! If it is chilly and your horse is clipped, undo his rug but leave it on his back so that he does not get cold and fold it accordingly to expose the area on which you want to work.

Picking out the feet

Pick out your horse's feet first thing in the morning to remove droppings and soiled bedding and pick them out each time he leaves his stable, comes in from the field and when he has been shod. This may seem excessive but you soon get into the routine. Obviously, picking out a horse's feet should also be part of the grooming routine when it is best done first so that you do not forget to do it. If you are short of time, this must take priority. The condition of the feet can deteriorate very quickly; thrush, for example, can appear after just a couple of days of neglect (see Chapter 10 for treatment).

The **hoof pick** should be used from the heel of the foot towards the toe, scraping out dirt from the grooves (clefts) either side of the frog and around the inside of the shoe but without gouging into the sole. Digging too deep causes small fissures in which dirt can hide, resulting in thrush. As you pick out the foot, use a small brush to clear away loosened dirt so that you can inspect the foot for anything unusual such as a smelly frog, discolouration of the sole (a bruise) and to check the general condition of his feet and shoes (See Chapter 7). Leave a hoof pick hanging by the stable so that it is always to hand.

Some yards insist on the feet being picked out into a rubber skip but this can be awkward if you have a fidgety horse that may put his foot into it and frighten himself. It can, therefore, be safer just to pick them out onto the ground, provided you sweep up the dirt as soon as you have finished grooming and put the horse away.

Brushing-off (removing surface dirt)

A **dandy brush** with stiff bristles is one of the best items of equipment for removing dried-on mud, stable stains and loose hair (it is also handy for brushing loose hair off your saddle cloth). It can be used on the body and the legs in a scrubbing motion but should not be used on the horse's face. An old dandy brush with less stiff bristles can be used on the mane and tail if your horse has thick bushy hair; many ponies have this type of mane and tail hair. It should not be used on horses with fine manes and tails as you will break the hairs. Separating the hairs from the lumps of mud is best done by hand in this instance. The same applies to feathers on the legs, use the dandy brush to get the worst of the mud off and then use your fingers.

The **rubber curry comb**, used in a circular motion, is great for removing mud, stable stains and loose hair.

A **plastic curry comb** is useful for removing mud from thick manes and tails and from the legs but tends to twist in the hand more than a rubber one when used on the body, making it harder to keep an even pressure on the horse's coat.

Strapping (thorough grooming)

For this you will need the **rubber curry comb** and the **body brush**. Apart from removing surface dirt, a rubber curry comb is ideal for bringing the grease in the coat to the surface. Begin on the nearside (left side) of the horse at the top of his neck. Hold the body brush in the hand nearest the horse's head, i.e. the left hand, and the rubber curry comb in the right hand. Use the curry comb in a circular motion against the coat, lifting the hairs to release the underlying grease, and then remove the grease by using the body brush in the same direction as the coat. Repeat the same rubber curry comb/body brush routine until no more dirt comes out and then continue cleaning the whole horse in this way. Any build-up of grease and hair in the rubber curry comb can be knocked out on a firm surface and it can be used to clean the body brush after every couple of strokes by drawing the body brush firmly across the rubber teeth. Some people prefer to use a **metal curry comb** for this but it is all too easy to grate the inside of your wrist in the process if you do not take care. Clean bristles are more effective at cleaning your horse than those clogged with grease and hair. Real bristles will remove far more dirt from your horse than synthetic ones and the real-bristle brush lasts longer. Be gentle over the joints and bony areas as they are not protected by muscle and remember to lift the mane to clean underneath it.

Once the horse is clean, you could 'wisp' him to tone his muscles (Figure 5.2) Wrap the **stable rubber** round the rubber curry comb and bang it gently over muscled areas such as the neck and rump. In the good old days we used to make a wisp, or pad, out of plaited hay and use this in the same way. Wisping helps to tone the muscles by making them twitch in response to gentle thumps (this is the same principle as a machine toning your stomach muscles with electrical impulses).

Figure 5.2 Wisping helps to tone muscles, both yours and the horse's!

To give a nice sheen to your horse's coat, shake out the stable rubber and use it to smooth the coat down in the direction of the hair.

The head

When you have finished grooming your horse's body, he should be used to your touch and relaxed enough for you to groom his head. Undo his head collar and fasten it around his neck to prevent him wandering off. Have the body brush or, if your horse is very sensitive, a **grooming glove** or folded stable rubber in the hand furthest away from his head. Reach under his chin with the other hand and slide it around his nose to place it on his nose bone between his eyes and his nostrils. Placing it too near his nostrils and squashing them may cause him to throw his head up as will making a grab towards his eyes. If he puts his head up before you get your hand around his nose, just keep your finger tips touching his cheek so that he learns that you are not going to remove your hand just because he is putting his head up in the air. If your horse has a tendency to do this, stand on a sturdy grooming box to make sure you can still reach him.

Carefully place the body brush on his cheek, and quietly brush him. Some horses accept the touch of the brush rather than that of your hand. Trevor was extremely head shy when I tried to put my hand on his face but I managed to overcome this by stroking his neck with a stable rubber at first, and gradually creeping up over his nose. He then let me touch his head with the body brush, and eventually my hand. Brush the coat in the direction in which it lies, making sure you clean underneath the forelock – another area that frequently is forgotten. You could also brush the forelock at this point so that you do not forget it when doing the mane.

THE EARS

If your horse hates his ears being touched, the most important thing is to not make a big issue out of it. The more worried you are, the more stressed he becomes. It is a mistake in these circumstances to keep trying to handle his ears all the time as this will just make things worse. At first, just use the body brush near the base of his ears, where they can get sweaty, to judge his reactions. His ears should not be dirty unless he has been out in the field and given himself a facial in the mud, in which case your fingers are the best grooming tool. You can fool him into letting you clean his ears by pretending to stroke them first, before giving them a light rub. Do this for a very short period the first few times until he realizes it was not as uncomfortable or frightening as he first thought.

THE EYES AND NOSTRILS

Finish cleaning his face by wiping the dust from his eyes and nostrils with the **face sponge**. Take care when cleaning around his eyes and, again, use your fingers to gently rub away the dirt if he objects to a brush.

When you have finished grooming the head, replace the head collar.

The stomach

Some horses are ticklish around the stomach, and may resent this area being groomed too firmly. Be very gentle to start with and watch his facial expressions; if you are being too rough they will reflect his displeasure although he will not be able to turn around and nip you if you have tied him up. Revert to the grooming glove or stable rubber if it makes things easier. Swishing the tail is another sign of his displeasure and can be an early warning signal of a kick coming your way. It is important, therefore, to keep your ears open as well as your eyes! Talk to your horse to calm him, many a bad incident can be avoided in this way, which is preferable to, and less aggressive than, hitting him. Only reprimand him in this way if he goes to kick or bite you out of malice (See Chapter 1).

The legs

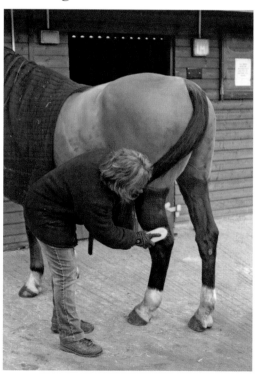

Figure 5.3 Holding your horse's tail against a hind leg will discourage him from kicking because he will not kick out against his own tail.

Use the rubber curry comb to rub off any stray lumps of mud and to lift the grease out of the leg hair for removal with the body brush. Brush the hair in the direction of growth. A build-up of grease on the cannon bones can lead to sore skin, which if left unattended can become infected by bacteria in the mud in the field and result in mud fever. Grooming the front legs is usually straightforward, but take care when grooming the hind legs. Holding the tail against the leg can discourage the horse from kicking out (see Chapter 1) (Figure 5.3). Brushing the inside of the opposite leg while keeping a hand on the hock nearest to you is a safe way to clean the inside of the legs. It is also easier to see what you are doing rather than trying to peer round the back of the leg you are working on and putting your head in a dangerous position.

The mane and tail

If you did not brush the forelock when you groomed your horse's head, do it now. Then, part the mane into sections and brush the mane out with the body brush. Once most of the tangles are out, finish with the **mane comb.** Using the mane comb before you have used the brush can pull and break the hairs and cause your horse discomfort. Once the mane is smooth, wet the **water brush** and use it to 'lay' the mane so that the hairs do not stick up. The other option is to use a detangle spray, especially if the mane is long and fine.

With the tail, take the whole thing in one hand and brush out a small section of hair at a time until all the tangles are out. It is important not to forget the end of the tail because, when this gets missed the hairs become matted, forcing you to trim off the ends with scissors, and if this has to be done too often, your horse will have no tail left.

The kindest way to groom the tail and avoid breaking the hairs is to use your fingers (Figure 5.4). Divide the hair into sections as before and run your fingers through it, like a human comb. Once you think it is tangle-free, comb it gently with the mane comb to check for any missed tangles. If you find any, use your fingers to deal with

Figure 5.4 Groom the tail with your fingers to prevent the hairs breaking.

93

them. Again, a detangle spray works wonders and should keep your horse's tail tangle-free for a few days.

Finally use the **back-end sponge** to clean under the horse's tail. On no account use this sponge on his face!

WASHING

A good groom should remove all stable stains, muddy patches, etc., but if you have a grey or pale-coloured horse, there may often be the odd stain that brushing does not remove and that requires washing. It is best to groom the horse first; otherwise you will end up washing everything and not grooming your horse properly. The horse's coat and skin condition will improve far better with thorough grooming rather than constant washing. Grooming encourages the skin to release oils which coat the hair and protect them, putting a sheen on the coat, but washing too often strips the oil from the coat leaving it dull and dry.

Horses do enjoy a bath on a hot day, and it can be useful for special occasions to make the horse pristine, but it is a good idea to bath him a day or two beforehand to allow the oil to build up in his coat to recover the shine. There are many products available these days to use on your horse's coat but, as with your own hair, if you over-use these you will not be doing his skin a lot of good in the long term and it may become dry and flaky.

Bathing your horse with a bucket and sponge and a water brush should not produce any particular problems whether you are just removing a stain or washing the whole horse. Using a hose saves a lot of time but some horses will have to be conditioned to accept this (Figure 5.5).

It is best introduced on a warm, sunny day after exercise when he is a little tired. Either tie the horse up if you are giving him a full bath, or you could hold him by the rope if you are just giving him a quick spray on the legs and feet. Set the nozzle on a gentle spray; giving him an icy blast is the best way to frighten him. As with all new experiences, keep the first few hosing sessions brief, after which you should be able to wash him all over but avoid spraying near his head, particularly if he has a tendency to be head shy.

Figure 5.5 Getting your horse used to a hose saves a lot of time when washing him. Amadeus appreciating a cool shower on a hot summer's day.

Amadeus loves a bath and will drink out of the hose very happily. Trevor, on the other hand, hates being titivated, and will fidget if I take too long about it and so I have to be quick and quiet and not make a fuss.

The easiest way to wash a horse quickly is to dab small amounts of mild shampoo (baby shampoo is fine) on the coat and using your spare hand to rub the dirty marks away while washing the shampoo off with the hose. Make sure you rinse all the shampoo out of the coat because any residue will build up in his coat. Remove the excess water with either a **sweat scraper,** drawing the blade across the coat in the direction of the hair, or stretch a piece of baler twine taut between your hands and use it in the same way.

Make sure you work the shampoo into the base of the mane and the dock of the tail to remove the thick grease that can build up in these areas, and rinse very thoroughly.

If your horse is really frightened of the hose pipe and will not let you anywhere near him with it, try to let him see you washing another horse – or the dog – if possible. Failing that, don your Wellington boots and wash them with the hose so that he can learn that it is not dangerous. Have a calm assistant hold him near where you are doing the washing so they can reassure him if he becomes anxious. If he is calm, tie him up to let him watch. Once you have washed the horse, dog or boots, keep the spray on a gentle jet and spray his front feet. If he fidgets, keep the hose on his feet. Most people's instinct is to stop spraying if the horse is afraid, but this teaches him that if he fidgets, the spray stops; consequently, every time you use the hose, he will fidget more and more until it is turned off. The correct way to handle the situation is to keep spraying until he accepts it, continue for a few more moments, while telling him he is a good boy, and then turn it off and praise him again. That way he will learn that the spray will be turned off if he stands still and accepts the wash calmly. It is important to praise him while he is being good and not afterwards so that he understands exactly what it is he has done well.

Do not use the hose pipe tentatively, expecting it to make your horse nervous, treat it as part of your everyday equipment so that he gets used to seeing and hearing the long, yellow snake trailing across the yard, filling buckets, damping hay and spraying the stables or yard. Often it is the noise of the jet that alarms a horse, so vary the nozzle setting from low to full jet as you go about your business over a few days. If the hose is part of everyday life, your horse will soon take it in his stride, and forget his previous worries. If he misbehaves and stamps about when you wash him, give a sharp tug on the lead rope and say 'Stand' with authority. You may need to repeat this if he persists. Make sure you relax your grip between tugs and keep some slack in the rope but be ready to tug again if necessary. Holding the rope tightly and pulling against the head collar will just make your horse more cross and he will want to fight you. Once he stands still, praise him. Keep the hose on as before until he accepts it calmly, and then turn it off.

Once he lets you hose his front feet, try the hind feet. He may well wriggle around a bit, but follow the above procedure again. Keep spraying until he stands quietly while you wash him, praise him, and then turn it off. The same applies when you progress to the saddle patch, and between his hind legs, though by this time he should be happy enough to stand still with you either holding his rope or tying him up. You need a week of warm weather to teach your horse to have a bath, building up each day to a full wash by the end of the week.

Removing mud

Washing mud off is best done with a hose. Let the water wash down the leg taking the wet mud with it. Using a water brush when you wash the legs can drive the mud further into the coat where it comes in contact with the skin, which can lead to skin problems such as cracked heels and mud fever (see Chapter 10). This often happens with horses that have hairy legs or feathers, where wet mud takes ages to dry and can chap the underlying skin. It is not the mud that causes mud fever so much as incorrect grooming. If you wash mud off, dry your horse's legs with a towel and make sure you allow him to dry off completely by standing him in a clean stable. Horses that are clipped are easier to wash and dry than those left unclipped.

6 FEEDING

ASSESSING YOUR HORSE'S feeding requirements in order to keep him healthy and manageable is an essential part of horse management. An unsuitable diet can affect the performance of your horse during training, his mental attitude, and can cause physical problems. Feeding a horse more food than he needs causes him to become overweight and can make him highly strung. If this in turn makes him difficult to handle, his bad behaviour can frighten and intimidate you. Small ponies on very rich grass can prove to be too much for children, and most adults, to deal with, and ponies are particularly suscepti-ble to weight-induced problems such as laminitis.

On the contrary, not feeding a horse enough can lead to a loss of weight and condition, he will not be able to do his best when worked, and his physical strength will be affected. A hungry horse is a miserable one, and he could become snappy and aggressive. Feeding this horse even less because he is grumpy will compound the problem. It is important to get to know your horse's character (see Chapter 1) in order to be able to feed him properly.

Some horses are picky eaters, though I have not known very many; they have their likes and dislikes but horses that do not eat up their feed are often not receiving the correct type of food or are simply getting too much. Horses' appetites will also be affected by the seasons: when the pasture is lush in the spring, horses often go off their hard feed and their hay simply because they are getting sufficient nourishment from the grass (Figure 6.1); once the grass is less nutritious in the winter, they will tuck into everything you give them with gusto. Horses will not generally eat mouldy hay or musty feed unless they are deprived of a balanced diet and really hungry.

Figure 6.1 Good grazing has great feed value as shown by the good condition of this mare and foal.

Horses like routine and this is certainly true when it comes to food: they need to know when their next meal is going to appear. Before we bought Trevor, he was fed once a day, if he was lucky, and he never knew for sure if anything was forthcoming. Once we had him in new surroundings, he was very possessive about his food, pulling the most awful faces to fend off anyone who came near his stable. He would neigh madly in anticipation every time anyone went near the feed room to make sure he was not forgotten. Three years on, he has mellowed and knows he gets fed with everyone else, though he still neighs hopefully at feed times. He certainly knows if dinner is late!

RULES OF FEEDING

There are certain basic rules to feeding horses than should be adhered to if you want to keep your horse healthy and happy.

- Do not exercise him when his stomach is full; this applies whether he has a belly full of grass or hard feed. Always allow about an hour before exercising him to ensure he has digested his food. Think how uncomfortable you would be jogging around the block after eating steak and chips!

Use this time to give him a good groom and attend to odd jobs around the yard.

- Make sure that he has access to fresh water at all times so that he can drink what he needs when he wants to. If he is given a bucket of water at the same time as his feed, it is likely that he will eat first and then drink a lot after his meal, which can wash undigested food out of his stomach. Most horses will drink after they have been exercised but not excessively unless they have been left without water for any length of time. Endurance riders train their horses to drink whenever it is offered, sometimes adding apples to encourage 'apple bobbing' so that the horse takes in fluid.

- The equine digestive system is designed to deal with frequent small quantities, i.e. the horse should eat little and often. Consequently he also needs to drink little and often in order to aid his digestion. In the wild a horse always has to be ready to run away from danger, and this would not be easy on a full stomach. Damping feed or adding soaked sugar beet to feed also keeps the fluid intake up. Dehydration in a horse can cause all manner of digestive problems such as food becoming impacted in the gut.

- Always feed the best-quality food and hay that you can. This is more economical because good-quality feed and hay is more nutritional than poor quality foodstuff and you will, therefore, need less of it.

- Changes to diet must be made gradually over a couple of weeks to allow the bacteria in the gut to adjust to digesting the new food. Sudden changes to totally different types of food can upset a horse's system causing loose droppings or, more seriously, colic. If the new feed is similar to the old feed, i.e. changing from a pasture mix to a riding mix of the same brand, then the change is not so extreme and a week should be adequate for the changeover.

- Feed at about the same time each day. It does not have to be exactly to the minute: I know of horses that wait happily for their owners to get home from work if they have been delayed an hour or so. It is more important to make sure all the horses in the yard are fed at the same time. Feeding some horses and not others leads to problems such as door banging, weaving and crib-biting.

- Feed according to work. If you give your horse a day off or go away for a couple of days, cut the hard feed by half so that on your return he is not too 'full of beans'. (This expression originated in the days when hunters were fed peas and beans as high protein food to give them energy.) The consequence of not cutting down the protein on your horse's day off is a hyperactive and hard-to-manage horse. If you forget to cut his rations, lunge him before riding to work off some excess energy. If, on the other hand, he is lacking in energy when you work him, he may need his feed increased.

- Keep feed bowls and water buckets clean to prevent contamination of fresh food and water.

- In a well-organized feed room (Figure 6.2), the feed bins are cleaned out once they are empty and certainly before refilling. Tipping new feed on top of old results in a layer of musty feed at the bottom of the bin which will taint the new stuff. Store your hay and straw somewhere dry. Damp hay quickly becomes mouldy and inedible. If a horse does eat it, he may develop a cough or an allergic reaction to mould particles, in which case you will have to wet his hay, or substitute haylage for the hay.

Figure 6.2 A well-organized feed room.

DIFFERENT FEEDING REQUIREMENTS

Overweight horses

If your horse puts on weight easily, replace some of his hay with oat or barley straw as it is lower in feed value (calories). Make sure he is being worked enough to get him fit. The more muscled a horse is, the better he is able to burn calories, and so a fit horse will utilize his food far better than a fat, unfit one. Lazy horses need more motivation, you will have to maintain a really upbeat attitude when you lunge or ride a lazy horse in order to generate a bit of excitement in his demeanour and it may take a few weeks to change his attitude to work. Horses that do not receive the right kind of, and sufficient, work to challenge them mentally as well as physically will have one interest in life: eating. You will, therefore, have to work out a realistic work and feeding routine that fits in with your daily schedule and will help your horse become fitter and healthier. Feeding high-protein food will just make him fatter but a mix designed for the average riding horse should suit him. Good old-fashioned oats fed with chaff and carrots can be a suitable diet for this type of horse. The overweight horse often bolts his food; dividing it up into smaller more frequent meals, and making sure he has sufficient hay or straw to pick at between meals, can help. Make sure his schooling is interesting, work him sufficiently to burn off what he eats and spend time grooming him and paying him attention to give him a more varied day.

Nervous and temperamental horses

A common reaction when dealing with a horse with a nervous or tempera-mental disposition is to cut down his food. Starving him will not calm him down but, because he is hungry, probably cause him more anxiety, which may well manifest itself as aggression. There are many types of food on the market designed for all types of horse and if you have a nervous horse, a riding-horse mix should be suitable. Feed containing a low level of protein will not provide sufficient nutrition and the horse will lose condition because nervousness burns off more calories than calmness. It would be far better to work him sensibly to ensure that he finishes his training sessions in a relaxed state. Correct training results in a generally calmer horse which means that both his nervous and physical condition improve over time with a normal diet.

Feed containing oats can make some horses 'hot', i.e. too excitable, but less-heating barley can be a useful feedstuff. Sugar beet can help to keep weight on a horse, but make sure it is properly soaked first. Unsoaked sugar beet will, at least, cause colic or, at worst, death because it swells in the stomach when it absorbs fluid from the gut. It is, therefore, most important that dry sugar beet is kept in a secure bin and clearly labelled so that it is not fed accidentally as dry feed. This type of horse must have access to good grazing to help him relax and gain nutrition at the same time. If he tends to be picky with his food and not eat it all, divide his feed ration into smaller feeds and feed him more frequently so as not to over-face him at meal times.

Youngsters

A young horse coming into training for the first time (or a horse returning to work after having been laid-off) should start with a large proportion of the food ration as hay (roughage) with small meals of chaff, carrots and a handful of hard feed once the training regime is underway. He will cope with short work sessions on the lunge for a week on hardly any hard feed; when he starts to get tired and obviously needs more energy to cope with your demands, you will know it is time to up the ration. Feeding large feeds in the hope of working it off is not a good strategy because if you are not able to stick to the training schedule, because of bad weather for example, you will have to deal with a young horse brimming over with excess energy, which may be channelled into bad behaviour.

Older horses

Some older horses develop problems with chewing. Their teeth naturally slope more with age and may wear down to the point where the horse has difficulty biting off the grass when grazing, in which case you must ensure they have access to soft hay or haylage which is easier to eat. They require hard feed to keep them in good condition and feed mixes made specifically for older horses, which give them sufficient nutrition without sending them into orbit, are recommended. Feed may need to be soaked to make it easier to eat, which makes sugar beet a valuable foodstuff for the older horse. Damping the feed makes it easier to eat and reduces the risk of choking. Even if your old horse is not in work, he will still require hard feed to maintain his weight, especially in colder weather.

Fit and unfit horses

A fit horse will require a different diet from that of an unfit horse. I know many unfit clipped horses and athletic hairy ones and so it is important to follow the rule of feeding according to work not the amount of coat your horse has. Clipped horses do not need more food just because they are clipped; conversely, woolly horses at grass should not be rationed just because they are hairy. Clipping your horse unnecessarily and taking off too much coat can cause him to lose condition, in which case you will need to increase his hard feed temporarily to rectify this. Once his weight has returned to normal, keep him warm with an extra rug and reduce his feed to his regular amount. (See Chapter 11.)

Horses that spend a lot of time at grass need less hard feed if the grazing is good quality and they have sufficient energy to work happily (Figure 6.3).

Figure 6.3 A well-established meadow of mixed grasses and wild herbs provides a nutritious diet for this Icelandic pony

If the grass is poor and they lose weight through work, they will require more hard feed to compensate.

A thick woolly coat can disguise a thin body and so your horse's condition must always be checked by feeling him with your hand: you should just be able to feel the surface of the ribs, which should be covered by a layer of flesh, not be able to see them. If there is no flesh over the bones, your horse is too thin. If, however, you cannot feel the ribs at all and there is a thick layer of blubber, your horse is overweight and unfit. If you can feel and see well-defined muscles, your horse is fit.

Sick horses

If your horse is sick, or has been off work due to injury, you need to adjust his diet accordingly. If he is on box rest, his diet should consist wholly of roughage, i.e. hay or straw. So that he does not feel left out when his stable-mates are fed, he could have a token feed of a handful of chaff and a little soaked sugar beet, which is high in fibre, or carrots. Feeding hard feed to confined horses can cause them to become stressed and naughty due to too much protein in the diet. He must have fresh water at all times. Toys can help to keep him occupied during his confinement as can grooming and attention-giving visits from you. If medication has to be given, you may have to administer it in a handful of something tasty. If he has lost condition, there are many types of feed on the market to help him regain it. Haylage is higher in protein than hay and so is a good feedstuff to improve condition while making sure he has a lot of roughage.

SUPPLEMENTS

If you have good grazing, high-quality hay and feed which suit your horse's work load, you should not need extra supplements. Feed mixes are designed to contain a balanced diet and so if you add a bit of this and that to the feed without reading the contents label properly, you will alter the balance of minerals, salt, etc. in your horse's feed.

If you feed 'straights' such as oats and barley, you can make small adjustments to your horse's diet easily without having to buy a whole new feed. If your horse sweats a lot during work, you should add a small amount of salt to replace that lost in the sweat. Sugar beet can replace sugars lost in the same way. Electrolytes can be bought as a supplement for horses that sweat profusely such as endurance horses, racehorses, and top-level eventers but these should not be necessary if your horse just gets a bit damp around the ears on a hack!

There are many vitamin and mineral supplements and herbal remedies on the market but, again, a good compound feed mix should contain all your horse's requirements and so supplements of this type should only be necessary if your horse needs a short-term boost of vitamins, after illness for example.

If you suspect hormone problems, allergies etc., the first port of call should be your vet for a proper diagnosis.

Products that claim to calm your horse can work in many circumstances but I do believe there is a psychological element to it. Knowing that you have given your horse a calming supplement can make *you* more relaxed, which in turn keeps your horse calm. If the rider takes a calming potion, this often has a more dramatic effect than giving it to the horse. I sometimes take Rescue Remedy before a dressage test if I am feeling jittery. I used to give it to Amadeus on a sugar lump as well to be on the safe side. It appeared to work, and we were both very laid-back. He then realized I was doctoring the sugar lumps and refused to eat them. Needless to say, it made no difference; as long as I am relaxed, he is!

FEEDING PROGRAMME

Drawing up a simple feeding programme to suit your horse and your own daily routine is straightforward to do and ensures that ratios of hard feed to roughage are adhered to.

The first thing you need to do is to work out your horse's weight. One of the easiest ways is to buy a tape measure which gives a weight measurement based on your horse's girth size.

A simple way of working out the total amount of food (hay and hard feed) required per day in pounds is to double the horse's height, e.g. a 16 hh horse will need *about* 28 lb (12.5 kg) of food (2.2 lb = 1 kg)

There is a useful formula in the book *Horse and Stable Management* by

Jeremy Houghton Brown and Vincent Powell Smith and I have used it many times myself. The following is my own simplified version of the formula.

An averagely built 16 hh horse will weigh about 500 kg (1,100 lb).

To work out how much feed he should have per day, use the following formula (which is actually less than the double-the-height guesstimate):

500 divided by 100 X 2.5 = 12.5 kg (28 lb) of hay and hard feed per day.

The following table will give you an idea of how to adjust the amount of hay/hard feed to give your horse according to the amount of work he does.

Amount of work	None	Light (schooling/ lungeing for half an hour)	Medium (intensive schooling for an hour/ long hacks/ lunge work)	Hard (competition fit)
Feed	None	20 per cent	40 per cent	50 per cent
Hay	100 per cent	80 per cent	60 per cent	50 per cent

7 THE FEET AND SHOEING

CARING FOR A HORSE'S feet is essential to good horsemanship. 'No foot, no horse' is an old saying, which is still valuable advice today. Potential problems can usually be avoided with common sense and sound, practical basic care. Trying to save a few pounds by spreading out the farrier's visits, for example, is false economy. Leaving the feet unattended or waiting until your horse loses a shoe before calling the farrier, makes it difficult for him to maintain the correct shape and balance of your horse's feet.

If you want your farrier to come on a regular basis to shoe your horse he will only come if he is not risking life and limb to do so. You owe it to the farrier, and indeed anyone who might have to handle and care for your horse, to train him to stand quietly tied up while he has his feet attended to (see Chapter 1). The vet, for example, cannot be expected to examine your horse's feet and legs properly if the animal is misbehaving and putting both you and the vet in danger of being kicked, trampled on or pulled over. Most lameness problems begin with the feet, and this will be the first area your vet will check before progressing further up the leg.

Picking your horse's feet out to clean them should be part of your daily grooming routine (see Chapter 5) and this familiarizes the horse with the routine of picking his feet up when asked and allowing you to care for them. Keeping your horse's feet in good condition means checking them for potential problems as well as assessing the wear and tear of his shoes. It takes far less time to make a quick check of the feet than to spend days or weeks treating damaged hooves or rotten frogs.

Good stable management is most important. Clean bedding is essential and no horse should have to stand for long periods of time in wet and muddy conditions as this can affect the health of the feet and result in minor ailments (see Chapter 10).

FEET IN GOOD CONDITION

The same rules apply to the condition of the feet whether the horse is shod or unshod. Feet that are in good condition are well shaped and should be the correct size and shape for the horse. For example, you would expect big broad feet on a Shire horse but not on a Thoroughbred. The angle of the hoof wall to the ground at

Figure 7.1 A well-shod foot should show correct pastern/hoof alignment

the front should match that of the horse's pastern (Figure 7.1). There should be no cracks or splits, and the shoe must fit the foot. The sole should be level and the frog large and healthy with no smell emitting from it.

FEET IN POOR CONDITION

Hooves in poor condition can cause all sorts of problems. If the farrier does not attend to the feet regularly, the hooves might split, shoes could be loosened or lost completely and, if the hoof has not been trimmed, the frog can lose contact with the ground (frog pressure), which affects its ability to pump blood around the tissues of the foot and up the leg as part of the circulatory system. A shrivelled frog cannot function properly; if the feet are not kept clean, the frog can become soft and spongy (it should be hard and firm) and thrush can develop. Brittle feet can be a sign of poor condition in a horse that has not been fed correctly (see Chapter 6). If the pastern/hoof angle is not correct, the joints, ligaments and tendons of the legs can be put under stress resulting in poor movement, signs of strain (swelling) or lameness.

TRAINING YOUR HORSE TO PICK UP HIS FEET

To pick up the feet, start with the near fore (horses are most used to being handled from the nearside [left], so make life easy for yourself and take the easy option). Stand next to the leg, facing the back of the horse, run your left hand down the back of the cannon bone and grasp the fetlock in your hand. Give an upwards tug, using both hands if necessary (Figure 7.2), and give an appropriate voice command such as, 'Foot' or 'Up'. Once your horse understands your voice command, he should lift his feet for you without you having to tug; a tap on the cannon bone with your hand as you say 'Foot' should be sufficient. As soon as the horse has raised his foot, slide your left hand under his hoof to support it but do not allow the horse to lean on you, make sure that he holds his own leg up (Figure 7.3). When working from the offside (right), use the right hand to pick the hoof up.

Picking the feet up in the same order can help to teach your horse to lift each foot on command. If you work from both sides of the horse you can do them in the following sequence: near fore, near hind, off fore, off hind, or

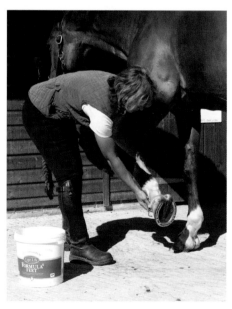

Figure 7.2 Use both hands if necessary to raise the foot.

Figure 7.3 Support the foot but ensure that your horse holds his own leg up and does not lean on you.

110

you can do all four feet from the nearside: near fore, off fore, near hind, off hind.

When picking up a hind foot, make sure that you cup the hoof in your hand as lightly as you can, and allow the horse to hold it up at a comfortable height for him. If you pull it up to high, you risk getting kicked. Make sure that your arm is *in front* of the cannon bone. If your arm passes behind the cannon bone and your horse does kick back, he would probably break your arm (Figure 7.4).

Never kneel down; a horse could suddenly put his foot down on your leg and you would not be able to get out of the way. It is best to crouch down with your knees bent so that you can move away quickly and quietly without the risk of getting your head in the firing line should he also kick.

Refusing to pick up a foot

If your horse refuses to pick up his foot, lean against him with your shoulder and push his weight onto the opposite leg, making it easier to lift the offending leg. Do this with a rocking motion instead of just leaning on him continuously which will just give you backache! Rather

Figure 7.4 When picking up a hind foot, keep your hand under the hoof and your arm to the front of the cannon bone so that your horse cannot break your arm if he kicks out behind.

than physically heaving his leg off the ground, grab hold of the hair under his pastern with the hand nearest to him and give a few short, sharp tugs until he lifts his foot. If on the nearside, lift the foot with the left hand, and place the right hand under the foot to support it but if you wish to pick the foot out, for example, you will have to change hands so that the left hand is supporting the foot, thus freeing the right hand to use the hoof pick. Pick his foot out quickly and then lower his leg gently. Try not to let it bang down onto the ground, as he will remember this discomfort and be even more reluctant to pick it up the next time. Pick the same foot up and put it down three or four times until he does it more willingly. Praise him and move to the next foot. You cannot rush things when dealing with problems like this, allow yourself plenty of time.

If the horse becomes rigid and absolutely refuses to lift a leg, either make him step backwards or tug on the lead rope to make him take a step forward so that he 'unlocks' his legs (make sure he is not tied up too short to do this). Then quickly proceed as above. Repeat the whole process as many times as necessary until he lets you pick up his foot. You may have to be satisfied with one foot at the first attempt, another on the next and so on. Then you should be able to do both front feet at one session, followed by both hind feet at another. After a few days you should be able to pick up all four feet in the same session. If necessary, have two or three attempts in one day, spreading them out as they fit into your day's routine.

A horse may have difficulty picking up his feet for you if he has a weak back or an old injury, or he may simply be getting on in years and becoming rather doddery. I had an elderly mare, Lizzie, who, in her last few months, would roll each foot forwards onto the toe so that I could pick out her feet without them leaving the ground, as she was worried about balancing on three legs.

It is important to introduce foals to having their feet handled early on and to keep this training up. To stop doing this because you think a foal has learned the lesson thoroughly is asking for trouble; if you try handling his feet again a few months later when he needs his feet trimmed, you will find that you are dealing with a bigger, stronger individual that has probably developed a 'Why should I?' attitude. You will have to start all over again and retrain him but you may require extra persistence now to ensure that he picks his feet up correctly every time you ask him.

KICKING

If your horse kicks as you approach a hind leg, grasp his tail at the dock, and run your hand down it until you have a good grip on his tail. Bring his tail around the outside of the offending leg and hold it against the leg with the hand nearest the horse. Horses do not like kicking against their own tails. Run your other hand down the cannon bone to the fetlock a few times and then pick his foot up just a little way off the ground and put it down again; keep doing this until he allows you to do so without resenting it. Once you have achieved this, you should be able to pick his leg up with the hand nearest the horse (without holding the tail) and clean or examine his foot normally.

If this does not work, you have to be stricter. As your horse kicks out, aim a swift punch at his belly, i.e. do to him what he does to you; you should only need to do this once. (**_You must do this in a calm and controlled manner, never in temper, and you must be aware of exactly what you are doing._**) The next time, a quick tap on the leg with your hand should be enough to stop him. Remember to praise him when he complies. This should be enough to stop the kicking but if he kicks again, the lesson must be repeated because you were not fast enough to discipline him in the first place. (See also Chapter 1.)

If your horse lifts his leg and then waves it around, calmly keep your hand under his hoof, say nothing, and wait for him to find a comfortable position in which to hold it. Once he is still, do what you need to do to the foot and lower it to the ground. He may pull his foot out of your hand before you are ready and so you must keep repeating the process, praising him when he allows you to hold his foot up for the required time.

If your horse becomes really cross about having his feet picked up and resorts to cornering you in the stable, treading on you or kicking you, take him into the school or field and teach him to pick up each of his feet in turn in the open. Lead him with either a bridle or cavesson and a lunge line in case he gets really cross and tries to make a run for it. You then have the option of lunging him for a few minutes until he is calm enough to begin his lesson. Once he stands still, tap each leg in turn on the cannon bone with a long schooling whip and say 'foot' until he picks each foot up and puts it down again without kicking out (Figure 7.5). If he does kick, give him a quick, sharp smack on the same leg. This shows him that you can 'kick' as well, and you should only have to do it once if you timed it right. Touch him again on the cannon bone, gently this time, and he should pick his foot up and put it down again calmly and without kicking. Praise him when he does this.

Figure 7.5 Teach your horse to lift each leg in turn by touching him with a schooling whip.

Follow this by returning to the stable, tying him up and asking him to pick up each foot in turn by just touching each cannon bone with your fingers. He should pick his feet up on his own for you. Hold each hoof in your hand by the toe so that he cannot lean on you. Proceed to pick out or check his feet, rewarding him after each one. (A pocketful of sugar lumps helps!) This procedure should be repeated on a daily basis until your horse has learned to pick his feet up for you politely, don't forget to use your chosen voice cue. It is very important to distinguish between touching a horse's legs to ask him to pick up his feet and running a hand down them as you would to feel for injuries or to groom him with a brush. If you are too vague about what you want, your horse will become confused, frustrated and may kick as a consequence. It is to be hoped that, in time, you will only have to use the verbal cue, and he will respond instantly.

If your horse continues to lift his foot for you but then kicks out if you try to hold it still, another solution is to slide a lead rope around his cannon bone, and lower it until it is just under the fetlock. Say 'foot' or 'up' and at the same time, ease the leg off the ground with pressure on the rope. Once your horse lifts his leg, hold it steady with the rope until he relaxes; if he does kick, at least your head will be well out of the way! When he lets you lift the leg without him waving it around, let the rope fall to the floor out of the way and place your fingers under the toe of his foot to support it. Pick out or examine the foot quickly and calmly before returning the foot to the floor gently.

CARE OF THE FEET

In addition to the hooves being picked out to keep them clean, the horn needs attention. It requires a certain amount of moisture to remain hard. Excessively wet and muddy conditions and wet bedding is detrimental to the state of the feet, but careful washing and drying preserves their moisture content. Washing them every couple of days or so, especially in dry weather, allows the hooves to absorb necessary moisture before letting them dry naturally. Coating them after washing with a thin layer of Vaseline has the same effect as you putting hand cream on after washing your hands: it keeps moisture *in*. Using hoof grease or hoof oil on dry hooves *actually prevents the hoof from absorbing necessary moisture from the air* and so the feet will dry out and become brittle.

TRIMMING AND SHOEING

Foot balance, i.e. ensuring that the ground surface of the hoof is evenly loaded, is most important to prevent wear and tear of the joints and improve the musculature of the whole horse. Trimming the feet incorrectly can lead to joint and back problems. If you wear shoes that do not fit and give no support to your feet, you will have aching legs and probably backache as well. This also applies to a horse. Long heels can lead to tendon problems and long toes can cause stumbling because the foot cannot 'break over' properly as the horse takes a step forwards. If your horse starts to trip when you ride him, providing it is not caused by sloppy riding, his toes may be too long, making him stumble.

Different breeds have differently shaped feet, and should be shod according to the type of breed they are and the work they are doing.

Booking the farrier's visits too far apart can result in the shoes working loose owing to the foot growing longer and forcing the shoe out of position. When the clenches (ends of the nails) lift away from the hoof wall the shoe will come loose, come off or the horse can stand on one branch of the shoe causing it to twist. In the latter case the shoe must be removed as soon as possible to prevent injury to the horse.

A horse's front feet are usually a different shape from his hind feet, and feet are often not a perfect pair, in the same way that we usually have one foot slightly bigger than the other. It is a mistake to make them the same size because the foot will revert to its natural shape and pull at the nails making the shoe come away from the foot. The different sizing is not a problem unless the underlying bones and tissues of the foot are unhealthy. You will only know this for sure if the vet takes an X-ray. Feet that are naturally set at different angles should, again, not be forced to match because this can cause problems with the leg joints. A horse with crooked feet but clean legs may move with a 'dishing' action with his front feet, i.e. he throws the lower part of his front legs out in a semi-circular motion, but may well be perfectly sound.

There is no such thing as a perfect horse and so all aspects of foot shape and joint movement should be sensibly weighed up. A skilled farrier will assess the shape and type of your horse's feet, his breed, the type of work he will do and be able to make minor adjustments to the balance of his feet to help him to move as well as he can. If your horse has a serious problem with his feet, you will need to seek the advice of a remedial farrier who specializes in such work and who will collaborate with your vet.

Is shoeing necessary?

Weighing up the pros and cons of shoeing or whether to keep your horse barefooted, depends on the condition of his feet and the type of work you will be doing with him. Some horses, such as the Iberian breeds and the Arab, have tough, small, bell-shaped feet that are well adapted to rough terrain as the sole is clear of the ground and horses of this type can even compete in endurance rides unshod. Thoroughbreds tend to have flatter, broader feet with the sole closer to the ground and therefore prone to bruising, and they are less likely to be comfortable unshod.

If you want to try working your shod horse without shoes, make the change gradually allowing time for his feet to adjust and the horn to harden and become more resilient. Make sure that you check your horse's feet daily and watch for signs of splitting or other damage; good foot care is essential to keep them in good condition and regular trimming by the farrier will prevent splitting. Just because your horse does not wear shoes does not mean that you do not need the farrier. It is most important that your horses are professionally cared for in order to maintain the correct foot balance to ensure your horse is comfortable and moving well.

If your horse has the type of feet that can cope with being left unshod, this is the safest way to avoid slipping on the roads as the horn of the foot has more grip on tarmac than metal shoes. Road studs in metal shoes can create jarring of the limbs because they do not allow any slippage at all and a horse could lose balance and fall as a result of not being able to slide a leg outwards to save himself if necessary.

If you do not want to use metal shoes, or if your horse has a strong aversion to having metal shoes nailed on, there are very good stick-on plastic shoes on the market these days but you should discuss them with your farrier to decide if they are suitable for your horse.

Quite often, front shoes are sufficient for average work. The front feet tend to be flatter than the hind feet and also wear at the toes more. Sand arenas, for example, can wear away the toes; to protect the toes and prevent them splitting, therefore, shoeing may be necessary but you may only need front shoes in this case. Take the advice of your farrier as he will be aware of the toughness of the horn in your horse's feet and how they cope with abrasion. If you are working your horse daily and on different surfaces, then a full set of shoes will protect his feet.

The shoeing stages

All farriers have to get on with the job, but most are willing to take things in easy stages to accustom your horse to being shod. Initially a youngster will just have his feet trimmed until he is in ridden work and the feet show signs of wear at the toes. Front shoes should suffice at this stage; it is a better idea just to have the hind feet trimmed as before which makes the visit brief and gives the horse a shorter time to have to stand still and behave himself. When being hot shod for the first time, some horses are surprised by the smoke and its smell as the shoe is placed on the foot but they soon get used to it. Hind shoes can be introduced as necessary and, if feasible, it is a good idea if the farrier makes a separate visit to do them so that all four feet are not done at once. When a full set is really necessary, your horse should be well-enough established in his training to behave for an hour to have his feet trimmed and the shoes put on.

Preparing for the farrier

Mistrust of the farrier and anxiety usually stem from the horse being handled by a nervous owner or could be the result of a previous bad experience, which may not actually be caused by being shod but by a related incident that the horse associates with the farrier's visit.

I once had a phone call from a very worried owner. She was concerned that her horse was so difficult to deal with when the farrier visited, that sedation was necessary even to trim his feet. His previous owner did admit to him being 'a bit fidgety' when being shod, and had sent him away to a burley chap to have him 'sorted out'. He was duly returned, and apparently cured of the problem, but was immediately sold on to Debby.

The shoeing problem was so bad that Debby's farrier attempted to trim Harry's feet in the field, in the company of his field mates. Unfortunately, while this was happening, one of Harry's elderly field companions dropped dead a few yards away. This caused a commotion in the yard with upset people, horses reacting to the atmosphere, and poor Harry being put off farriers for life. It might seem far-fetched but there is every possibility that Harry now dreads having his feet trimmed in case he drops dead himself.

Patience and confidence are paramount. Nervous owners create nervous horses; if you cannot stay relaxed when your horse is being shod, let a friend or more knowledgeable person deal with it. Your farrier will not take kindly to being kicked, bitten or knocked over by your horse and if you want to remain his customer, you owe it to him to do all you can to make his job easier (Figure 7.6).

There are a few things you can do to prepare your horse for the experience of shoeing. Most importantly, he must be taught to stand still while tied up for the duration of the farrier's visit (see Chapter 3). Picking his feet out daily as a matter of routine is essential and tapping the foot wall and sole with a hoof pick or a small hammer accustoms him to the noise and feel of having his feet shod.

Your horse must also stand still while allowing you to stretch his fore and hind legs forwards. The farrier will need to do this in order to place them on his stand for trimming. In the early sessions, he may place a foot on his thigh to trim, but he is not going to do this if a horse is thrashing about and has no manners. When you can pick up each of your horse's feet easily, hold the toe of the foot with your fingertips underneath the edge, so that if he does pull his leg back sharply, it is easy to let go and keep out of harm's way. Ease the leg into a full forward stretch and hold it there for a few seconds before gently lowering it to the ground. Praise your horse after he has allowed each leg to be stretched. Amadeus has taken this one stage further and has learnt to ask for titbits by raising each of his front legs and pawing the ground three times (Figure 7.7). Stretch the legs in this way daily until it just becomes a matter of course.

If your horse tries to rear up when you stretch the legs forward, untie him and hold the rope or chain in your hand. (This is a prime example of why you should use a quick-release knot with a rope, or a panic hook with a chain.) Give a sharp tug on the rope/chain and either growl at him or say, 'No!' sharply, in a commanding fashion. You must not deal with this dangerous response gently; it must be stopped, otherwise he will rear whenever he does not like something. If your horse is touchy about his poll and panics if he feels pressure behind his ears, the 'karate kick' (as described in Chapter 1) is a useful alternative way to deal with

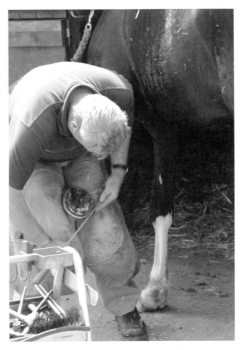

Figure 7.6 Your farrier's work is made far easier if your horse is well behaved and knows what to expect.

Figure 7.7 Amadeus 'asking' for his reward; his interpretation of lifting his legs on command.

this problem. Aiming towards his back end either with your leg or an extended arm should send him forwards.

When horses are used to being handled only by women, the arrival of a strange man, namely the farrier, turning up with a box of spooky-looking tools, is viewed with suspicion. If the farrier comes to the yard for other horses, ask him to spend a few minutes with your horse to get him used to being 'man-handled'. A horse should not be allowed to become 'sexist'; there are many situations when it is likely a horse will have to be looked after by a man. If, for example, you had to sell your horse in the future, limiting yourself to female purchasers could make selling very difficult, and there is no guarantee that female vets or farriers will be available. This problem must be dealt with once and for all.

Try to 'borrow' a calm confident man to help you around the yard. (Do make sure he is fully briefed, and never ask someone to help you if you have not done all the preparatory work.) It also helps if said male can be present at feed times to feed your horse; after all, anyone who delivers the feed bucket must pass the acceptance test. He can also pretend to be the farrier and go through the motions of picking up each foot, and stretching and holding each one in turn. If all this fails and your horse has a real phobia about men, it might be worth looking at your own reaction first. Many women assume that men are going to be rough with their horses and if you are anxious about your horse being handled by a male, be it farrier, vet or equine dentist, your horse will pick up on, and mirror, your anxiety. It is most important to empty your head of any negative thoughts and remain relaxed.

If you do get over-anxious in this situation, provided you have trained your horse to stand still and lift his feet, your farrier will probably get on far better without you in close proximity; go and have a cup of coffee or do odd jobs around the yard to occupy yourself.

Remember that horses learn from other horses. If there is another horse in your yard being shod, ask if you can tie your horse up nearby (but not close enough to be a nuisance) so that he can see what is going on. Stay with your horse and groom him and pick out his feet to keep him occupied. A full hay net can also keep him occupied and help him remain calm, as long as you are also calm. When the time comes for him to be shod, he should accept things more easily.

8 RUGS, BANDAGES, BOOTS AND OTHER CLOTHING

TRAINING A HORSE to wear clothing is an often-forgotten aspect of stable management. Youngsters have to have this equipment put on for the first time and it is all too easy to assume that an older horse is familiar with having rugs, bandages or boots put on and taken off. However, under former ownership and/or a different stable-management routine he may have either never worn these items or had a bad experience with their application.

Throwing a rustling, stiff New Zealand rug, for example, onto the back of any horse for the first time is bound to frighten him and he will undoubtedly react by shying away from this large, noisy monster. You would be lucky to get another rug on this horse without months of retraining and he might always harbour a fear of anything looming at him. With a bit of forethought this situation can easily be avoided.

Try to get into a routine of putting all clothing on and taking it off in the same way so that your horse becomes familiar with the procedure, and when he stays calm and relaxed you can become more dexterous in its execution. You do not have to treat him like a china doll, but be calm, confident and business-like about the whole thing. Tentatively holding a rug out in front of you and moving uncertainly towards your horse will not fill him with confidence and he will probably not let you near him at all. Always believe that what you do around your horse will be successful. If you approach him thinking he might do something untoward, he probably will because he senses your anxiety.

RUGS

Putting rugs on

When you present your horse with a rug for the first time it is vital to get the lesson right and, as with all new experiences, it must be done in stages so as not to frighten him.

Tie your horse up in the stable where he feels secure and comfortable. Groom him as normal to settle him and to make sure that he is in the right frame of mind for something new. If he is at all unsettled, leave the rug introduction for another day.

The following exercises should be done on the nearside of the horse at first to get a system going and reassure the horse by always following the same procedure. At a later stage, you can do the same from the offside if you want to be ambidextrous and accustom your horse to having rugs put on from either side.

In your grooming kit you should have a stable rubber, or cloth, to hand to polish your horse's coat. Do this for a few moments. Standing on the nearside of your horse open the cloth out and lay it on your horse's back (Figure 8.1). Gently slide it backwards and off over his tail. Repeat this a few times.

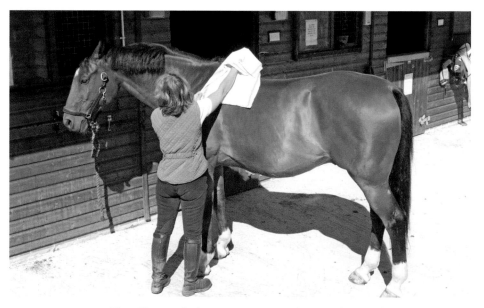

Figure 8.1 Use a stable rubber or cloth to accustom your horse to having things put over his back.

If he tenses his back or is ticklish when you slide the cloth along his back, stop what you are doing immediately – freeze on the spot – do not suddenly whisk the cloth away, just keep it still and talk to your horse until he relaxes again, and then continue to slide it steadily over his back and off over his tail. Repeat this exercise over the next couple of days. Always finish on a good note when he is happy with what you are doing.

The next stage is to have two old coats: a soft fleece that makes no noise and an old waterproof coat that rustles. Repeat the above procedure with the fleece coat for a further couple of days and then repeat it again with the rustling coat (Figure 8.2).

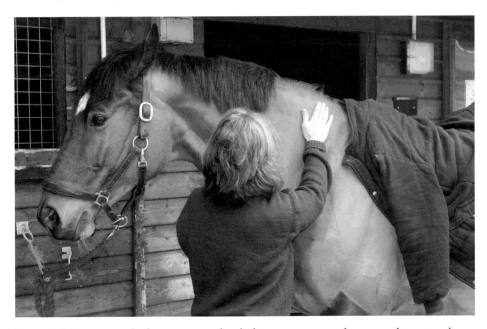

Figure 8.2 As soon as the horse accepts the cloth, progress to a soft non-rustly coat and, when he is happy with this, try a noisier waterproof coat.

The coats give your horse the feel of the material used in his rugs and, as the coats are rather bigger than a stable rubber, he gets used to seeing a larger piece of material being brought towards him. Always present your horse with the coat at his shoulder, gradually moving along beside his body as far as his haunches but do not go behind him, keeping an eye on his facial expression. If the exercise is making him anxious, his face will show this and, again, you must keep still until he relaxes, then continue. If he does feel the need to kick out with his back legs, by not going behind him you are out of harm's way.

When he graduates to his first rug, a lightweight, silent fleece cooler is the ideal choice. Fold it in half widthways so that the back edge and front (neck) edge are together, back to back. Holding it with one hand on each side of the neck edge gently place the rug in one smooth movement over his withers (the front [breast] fastening should be pointing forwards, otherwise your rug will be back to front) (Figure 8.3). Smooth it out, and then gently slide it back over his tail and quietly down to your side.

Figure 8.3 Fold the rug in half and place it over your horse's withers fastening the breast buckle.

It would be a grave mistake to shake the rug out or throw it over the door at any time, as this sudden movement will alarm him. Keep hold of it and go through the above exercise a few times until he is happy with the sensation of the rug being thrown quietly over his back. It is not necessary to swing it up in the air but just a few centimetres higher than his withers so that it does not get caught up against his shoulder. Fiddling with the rug will make him restless and he will get annoyed with you; if you have a problem, therefore, practise your rug-throwing technique over a spare stable door or the fence. Each time you put the folded up rug over your horse, do it with more fluency and speed, as though the horse were an old hand with rugs.

As soon as you can throw the fleece quickly and quietly into place over the withers, a little further forward than its final position, with your horse remaining calm and unflustered, fasten the breast straps then unfold the back half over his back (Figure 8.4). Take hold of the back edge of the rug and slide it back into position so that the breast straps are loosely touching his chest. If you pull the rug back too far, the feeling of the straps drawing tight against his chest might frighten him. If you left the rug like this all day, the straps would be too tight and may rub his chest. It is now time to stand directly behind your horse to straighten the rug from behind and to make sure the centre line of the rug lines up with his tail. He should be used to you working all around him by now and should not, therefore, kick but if he fidgets at any time stand to the side of his haunches and remain quiet until he settles again. Walk around the front of him to the offside and check that the belly straps are not twisted. Come back to the nearside and quietly do them up. You have now successfully rugged up your horse. Untie him and let him wander around his stable. Leave him on his own in the stable to get used to his new outfit, eat some hay and relax, and after about half an hour

Figure 8.4 Straighten the rug, making sure the straps are not tight against his chest, and unfold the rug.

remove the rug again. If you follow this procedure with a stable rug and then a New Zealand rug, within a week your horse should be perfectly happy wearing each type.

It is important that he has his own set of rugs. Once he has dirtied them a little and they smell familiar to him, you should have no problems putting them on.

Taking rugs off

Taking a rug off should be a relatively straightforward thing to do. Make sure your horse is tied up safely, especially until he is totally happy with the procedure.

For safety's sake it is sensible to undo the breast straps first, then the leg straps and then the belly straps (many rugs, including New Zealands, have leg straps to stop them slipping). Leaving the belly straps till last ensures that the rug stay in place until you remove it (Figure 8.5). If you start at the front and undo the breast straps followed by the belly straps, should your horse shy, the rug will end up on the floor tangled around his back legs and frighten him. This can also happen if you inadvertently forget to undo the

Figure 8.5 Undo the belly straps last to keep the rug in place in case your horse spooks. Watch his facial expressions because they act as an early-warning system of anything untoward happening.

leg straps on a dark winter's evening in your hurry to get home. If you undo the leg straps first, however, then the belly straps, leaving the breast straps till last, a quick movement from your horse could sweep the rug off to one side leaving it hanging around his neck and he could easily trample all over it, frightening himself and probably tearing the rug in the process. The correct sequence if you wish to start with the leg straps so that you do not forget them is: undo the back leg straps, then the breast straps, then the belly straps.

Take hold of the front of the rug above the withers, and fold it in half backwards, so that the dirty side of the rug is touching itself. This prevents you covering yourself in mud or droppings. Calmly sweep the rug off over the horse's quarters, holding the rug at the back and front edges to keep it flat (Figure 8.6) Keep hold of the rug as shown in Figure 8.6 and fold it in half again into quarters (Figure 8.7) so that it is easy to carry. Hang it over the door out of the way and then untie your horse.

If you are leaving a rug over your horse when he is tacked up, tie the belly straps out of the way so that he does not stand on them. If the rug has a fillet string, pass it under his tail to stop the back of the rug blowing about,

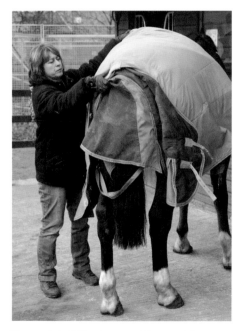

Figure 8.6 Slide the rug off smoothly over the tail.

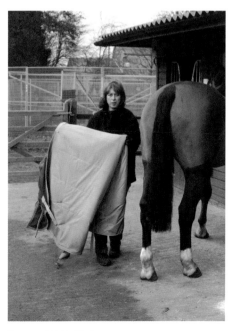

Figure 8.7 Fold the rug into quarters so that it is easy to carry.

especially if you are outside, and do up the breast straps to keep the front secure. If it will not do up over a saddle, leave the fillet string and the breast straps unsecured so that, if it does slide off, it will fall freely to the ground.

Retraining horses that remove their own rugs

Young horses often like to test the rip-factor of rug material and how easily rug straps come undone. Some horses are less curious than others, so hopefully your horse is one of these and not an inherent rug vandal.

If you are turning a young horse out in the field for the first time with a New Zealand rug on, do not put the brand new one on that you have just bought. Find an old hand-me-down from another horse, just in case the rug comes off worse for wear. It can help if your horse goes out in the field with a companion that is also wearing a rug so that he learns by example. If his friend wears a rug without taking any notice of it, he should follow suit. Similarly, if you have a horse that can escape from his rug, the youngster could well learn this handy trick too! I used to own a Lusitano called Leo; he was my then two-year-old Lipizzaner's 'nanny'. This Lipizzaner was Amadeus and until he came along I had no problem with four-year-old Leo and rugs. However, Leo's young field mate could get a New Zealand rug off without undoing any of the straps; an admiring Leo had a go but was not as adept at it. In order to try to foil Amadeus I found him a smaller rug with shorter straps but this rug lasted one morning and I found it neatly ripped into four quarters and mashed into the mud as though he was burying the evidence. He obviously thought that if I could not find it I would not notice that he had lost it!

For your horse's first rug-wearing venture, turn him out for just a short period of time – about an hour – and bring him and his companion back in. As he becomes accustomed to his rug, gradually extend the time in the field but make sure that he is not too hot as he might try to get rid of his rug simply because he is too warm. This also applies in the stable. Amadeus tried his remove-a-rug-and-bury-it trick in the stable and so I left him unrugged until he found the nights rather chilly, after which he appreciated a light rug.

Your horse will remove, or try to remove, rugs that are uncomfortable. His shoulders may become rubbed by a poorly fitting rug or a rug that is too small. A rug that is too big will slip back causing the front edge to dig into his withers. Most problems can be solved by using common sense when selecting a suitable rug for the time of year and of the correct fit.

Some stabled horses will tear their rugs out of boredom. Make sure that your stable routine gives your horse sufficient work so that he is mentally and physically relaxed when in his stable. Horses with too much feed and too little work are usually the ones that develop problems. Frustration with an owner born out of not understanding what is required from them or stress caused by mishandling or cruelty can result in a horse destroying his rugs. A sensible routine and learning to understand your horse's character and needs will solve any such problems but be prepared to be very patient and to take the time to retrain him from the very beginning, just like a young horse. This should fill in the missing piece of his rug training, especially if you do not know your horse's history and how he was treated before you had him.

Types of rug

Using the right type of rug for your horse in a particular environment ensures that he is comfortable both in the field and the stable, thus ensuring he is a happier horse that will not become bad-tempered because of discomfort. Turning him out in the rain in a stable rug that is not weather resistant will result in him wearing a sodden rug all day and not being able to dry off. A thick, heavy outdoor rug worn in the stable may make him hot and bothered and he may damage the rug if he tries to get it off. Allowing a horse to dry or cool off slowly in a rug designed for the purpose prevents him from getting a chill. Experiencing discomfort in the wrong rug could make a horse a confirmed rug hater.

There are many different types of rug on the market these days. When I was a young working pupil, there were two types of rug: a canvas New Zealand rug for wear in the field, and a jute stable rug. On chilly nights, a stable blanket was used under the jute rug, neatly folded around the withers to prevent rubs, and fastened by a padded surcingle to keep everything in place. If a horse was wet, you rubbed him down with handfuls of straw to stimulate his circulation and make sure he was warm; the jute rug was then put on inside out to keep the lining dry for later, with a thick layer of straw 'thatching' under the rug to help the horse dry off. Once he was warm and dry, he was brushed off, and rugged up for the night. Those were the days!

Mind you, on checking through the many mail-order catalogues selling horse equipment recently, I noticed the return of the jute rug which was described as 'good value for money and robust'. I shall be putting my order in.

TURNOUT RUG/NEW ZEALAND RUG

These rugs protect a horse from the elements when out in the field. They can be made of canvas, often lined with wool, or various breathable, waterproof fabrics, which can be either heavyweight or lightweight, and often come with neck covers. It is most important that it comes far enough down your horse's sides to cover his belly, but should not extend to the knees. This type of rug has back leg straps, crossed surcingles, and breast straps to secure it.

NIGHT RUG

These are commonly made from materials such as polypropylene or nylon and filled with polyester padding. They come in different thicknesses and can be extremely warm. Some horses feel the cold more than others: a horse with a fine coat, or one that is clipped, will need a heavier rug than one with more coat. It is, therefore, important to choose the correct thickness of rug for your horse and not what you would like to curl up in yourself!

DAY RUG

Day rugs are lighter versions of night rugs and so, as with the night rugs, you must buy one of the appropriate thickness/warmth for your horse. A jute rug makes a good day rug, and can be scrubbed clean. Fleece rugs come into this category.

SUMMER SHEET

Summer sheets, usually made from cotton, are designed to keep your horse clean when you have just groomed him, and also give some protection against flies. Cotton is cooler for the summer than a fleece fabric and is useful for protecting a horse's back from draughts when in a trailer.

COOLER (ANTI-SWEAT RUG)

A fleece cooler is designed to allow your horse to cool off after exercise gradually. Allowing a sweaty horse to stand in his stable or outdoors at an event with no rug on causes his muscles to cool down too quickly and can result in stiffness. As the sweat has to evaporate for him to cool down, the rug must be thin and porous enough to allow the sweat to wick away. There are some very good rugs now that do this, leaving your horse warm, comfortable and dry. In the summer, a 'string vest' cooler made of cotton works very well. A cooler should be left on just long enough for your horse to dry off; he should then be brushed off and, depending on the time of day, rugged up in his day or night rug. Fleece coolers can also be used as an under-rug for a night rug.

FLY COAT/SWEET-ITCH RUG

These are made of a fine mesh material designed to protect your horse from insects in the field and usually come with a neck cover. The disadvantage is that they are often made from nylon mesh which, although breathable, could cause your horse to sweat on warm days and so do check that he is comfortable and not itchy, as this could cause skin complaints and he may rub himself sore. Natural fabrics such as cotton are sometimes better at preventing sweating. The best way to avoid insects is to keep your horse in a stable during the heat of the day, or at least give him protection in the field with a purpose-built shelter, or a field with trees. In groups, horses stand head to tail, and use their tails as fly swats to keep the flies off each other and so turning a horse out with companions is the best natural way for horses to protect themselves from insects. As midges are the prime cause of sweet itch, avoiding turning your horse out near streams or marshy ground may help.

BLANKETS AND DUVETS

Blankets are of most use under a fitted rug such as a jute rug, which requires a roller to keep it in place. Rugs with surcingles also need a roller if you use a blanket under them, but all this equipment can be a bit cumbersome for your horse. It is better to put a fleece cooler under a rug with surcingles, although there will still be a lot of straps under your horse's belly. It is better to choose the appropriate rug in the first place. Duvets, frankly, belong on your bed at home. I have yet to see a horse looking comfortable with a huge puffy thing under his rug. Again, a duvet needs securing with a roller over the top of the rug otherwise it will tend to slide out from the back and end up in a soggy mess in your horse's bed, and just try passing it off as domestic bedding at the dry cleaners!

Does your horse need a rug?

Different breeds of horse have varying amounts of coat depending on their natural habitat. You would neither expect a fine-coated Arab to live out all winter with no protection, nor would you wrap a Dartmoor pony up in a duvet. Common sense must prevail when it comes to choosing appropriate rugs for the individual animal and the time of year. A horse will tend to feel the cold if he is wet through; it is, therefore, important that he is dry so that his coat can function to keep him warm. If your horse is warm he should look happy and healthy, his coat will be smooth and his ears will feel warm. If he is cold, he may lie down more than usual to keep warm, his coat will feel slightly rough because the hairs will stand on end, and his ears will feel cold. Keep an eye on the weather forecast. If the night-time temperature drops below 8°C, he may then need a light rug at night. If *you* do not need a coat, then your horse certainly does not. As a rough guide I do not normally use the thick night rugs until I need to wear gloves and a woolly hat to keep warm. In spring, once your horse starts shedding his coat, put on a thinner rug, turning him out without a New Zealand on sunny days so that he can have a good roll to shift the loose hair which must really itch.

How to fit/measure a rug

Rug length is measured horizontally from a point in the centre of your horse's chest to where the rug would end at the back end, i.e. just covering the point of buttock (the furthest point back on the haunches). To measure this you need two people, one to hold the tape in the middle of his chest, and the other to measure the distance to the point of buttock. The depth of the rug is measured vertically from the top of the withers down to the lowest point of the belly so that the rug covers his sides completely. Chest depth is measured from the lower part of his neck where the fastenings would be to the same lowest-point-of-the-belly line. Neck circumference is for rugs that extend up the neck and this measurement is taken around the narrowest part of your horse's neck just behind his ears.

Rug accessories and other clothing
ROLLERS, SURCINGLES AND ROLLER PADS

A roller needs to be padded on either side of the withers to avoid pressure on the spine. Rollers with an elastic girth still exert pressure on the horse's back if you do them up tight enough to hold the rug in place. Elastic surcingles are best used for a short time, holding your cooler in place for an hour, for example.

Roller pads, which are cushioned rectangular pads, should be used to protect the spine from pressure or you could use a square saddle pad folded in half. A towel folded to form a pad is also suitable particularly as towelling does not tend to slip out from underneath the roller.

FLY FRINGES AND HOODS

There are many forms of head protection to keep the insects off your horse's head, the best protection being a full mane and tail. If a horse needs a little more protection, however, a fly fringe (Figure 8.8), consisting of a browband with tassels on it, which attaches to a head collar as a 'forelock substitute' works well, as do fly hoods, which cover the horse's eyes and are made of net

Figure 8.8 A fly fringe

material. They fit over the horse's ears and top half of his head but leave the muzzle exposed. Some horses can get very sore eyes from fly irritation, so it makes sense to use a fly hood if you horse is prone to eye infections. Make sure that the fly net you buy fits snugly around the horse's face. It is easy for them to get caught on branches or other protuberances in the field, and you do not want your horse to sustain an injury that may be far worse than a few fly bites. The edges of the hood must be padded to avoid rubbing. Some horses can become sweaty and sore in a nylon hood and so it is important to look out for patches of raw skin.

NECK COVER

This is a hood made of stretchy material, such as Lycra, which is fastened with a zip under the neck. It is designed to protect the horse's head and neck from dirt and to keep him warm. It has holes for his ears and eyes; make sure you put his ears through the correct ones! A neck cover can be useful if you have bathed, groomed and plaited your horse ready for a show, and it can prevent overnight stable stains, particularly with grey horses. To put it on, gather it up in your hands so that it looks like a driving collar; the zip should be uppermost. Place your horse's nose through the hole and ease the whole thing up and over his ears so that it is around his neck. Twist it round to position the zip under the neck and the ear and eye holes will then be on top of the neck. Ease the cover up spreading it out along the length of his neck and over his ears and eyes, ensuring he can see out. Do this gently and as quickly and efficiently as possible because you do not want your horse to think he has been blindfolded. Fasten the zip and stretch the cover over his shoulder area, and fasten the strap that goes from the cover around the belly and comes back up to fasten to itself with Velcro, which will prevent it riding up and wrinkling during the night.

VEST/SHOULDER GUARD

This is similar to a neck cover but just covers the shoulder area to prevent your horse getting rubbed by his rug. It can either slip on over your horse's neck in the same way as a neck cover, or it may fasten in front of the chest. A vest can be useful if you have a horse with a very fine coat, but if your rug fits well, your horse should not get rubbed in this area.

BANDAGES

The art of good bandaging relies on your ability to roll them up! When you buy a new set of bandages, the Velcro or tape fastening is on the outside to prevent the bandages unrolling all over the shop floor. Before you use them you will have to unravel them, and roll them up ready for use. Starting with the fastening facing you, hold the bandage up in front of you and let it hang down to the ground. (Make sure you have chosen a clean dry floor so that your bandages stay clean and put the dog away as bandages make tempting playthings. I have often seen a lovely white bandage being stuffed into a hole in the ground by a terrier on a mission.)

Using the correct type of bandage prevents problems. For example, elasticated bandages should not be worn overnight in the stable; when worn for this length of time they will feel tight and uncomfortable and a horse might become stressed and panic, trying to rip them off. On the contrary, exercising your horse in stable bandages, which are not elasticated and will not, therefore, move with the horse, may result in them working loose and sliding down his legs, possibly tripping him up.

Hold the bandage with both hands, fold the Velcro/tapes towards you and begin rolling, keeping the bandage tight and neat as you do so. If you are a skilled bandage roller, rolling the bandage up along your thigh looks impressive, and is actually a quick way of doing it; in this instance the tapes and rolling direction would be away from you.

Bandages need a pad underneath them to ensure that the bandage does not slip, and to even out the pressure on the leg. Today pads are often made of thin foam covered with material to prevent sweating and have largely replaced the Gamgee cotton padding that comes on a roll and was cut to size. Wrap the pad around the leg in the same direction as that in which you will be bandaging. If you wrap it in the opposite direction, it will bunch up as you bandage. Bandage towards the back of the horse, i.e. on the offside, bandage clockwise and on the nearside, bandage anticlockwise. This looks neat and ensures that the fastenings are secured towards the back of the horse.

Types of bandages
EXERCISE BANDAGES

Exercise bandages protect the horse during training and also support the legs and are an alternative to boots. Whether you use boots or bandages is a matter of personal choice. They are made of an elasticised material designed to stay put during exercise. They can be used without a pad underneath if a horse is to be worked for just half an hour or so but if a work session is any longer, a pad will even out the pressure of the bandage and make it more comfortable for the horse.

To apply an exercise bandage with a pad, hold the pad in place with one hand and lay the end of the bandage at the top edge of the pad on the outside of the leg at a slight angle upwards so that you have a point sticking up. Hold this point in place with the thumb of the hand that is holding the pad, and begin to wind the bandage around the leg. After the first turn to secure the pad, fold the point over and cover it with the next turn of the bandage to secure it. Working downwards, continue to wind the bandage round the leg overlapping it by half its width each time. Bandage down as far as the fetlock joint, and then go back up again. When you run out of bandage, secure it with the Velcro fastening or tapes and, if the bandage has tapes, tuck the tape ends in to a fold to keep them tidy. If you are jumping or riding across country, it is a good idea to wind insulating tape over the fastening to make sure it does not come undone.

STABLE BANDAGES

Stable bandages protect the horse's legs in the stable or when travelling, give support to the limbs if a horse is injured, prevent swelling and keep the legs warm thus aiding circulation. They are made of wool or stockinette and applied over a pad long enough to cover from below the hock to the top of the hoof. Because stable bandages are on the horse for a long period of time, overnight for example, it is very important to bandage evenly down the leg to avoid pressure marks. They stay in place better than travelling boots when transporting your horse, and give support to your horse's legs which travelling boots do not.

Put stable bandages on in the same way as exercise bandages but continue to bandage down over the fetlock and coronet to cover them.

TAIL BANDAGES AND TAIL GUARDS

Tail bandages have two purposes: to keep the hairs of the tail lying smoothly after grooming and to protect the tail from being rubbed when travelling. A tail bandage should not be left on for more than a couple of hours. Because it is elasticized to keep it in place, pressure is put on the muscles, nerves and skin of the tail which could make a horse feel very uncomfortable after a while; it is, therefore, very important to put a tail bandage on correctly. If a horse has never had a tail bandage on before, take care introducing it; you do not want to end up with a horse that hates his tail being touched. To get him used to a tail bandage, you first need to make sure he is totally happy with you handling his tail. As part of your grooming routine, handle his tail after brushing it by holding the dock in one hand and gently sliding your hand down it a few times so that he gets used to not only the sensation of feeling slight pressure around his dock, but also the sensation of your hand sliding down, which is how a tail bandage is taken off.

To put on a tail bandage, stand directly behind your horse close to his backside. He should be used to you being around him by now but if he fidgets, move with him so that you stay in position behind him. If he will not let you lift his tail to start the bandage off, then you need to include lifting the tail in the grooming routine.

As with the leg bandages, check that the bandage has been rolled correctly with the fastening tapes or Velcro rolled into the bandage first thus ensuring that they will be in the right place for fastening the bandage once it has been put on. Hold the bandage in your left hand, and the dock with your right (or vice versa if you are left-handed). Unwind a few centimetres of bandage and lay it over the top of the tail with the roll of bandage towards you, leaving a point sticking up, as with the leg bandages. Hold the bandage firmly and roll it around the top of the tail a couple of times, securing the loose end by folding the point over (Figure 8.9). Continue down the dock, overlapping the bandage by half its width each time and ensuring that it is wound with even pressure all the way down until you are half a bandage width above the end of the dock. Feel for the end of the bones with your fingers. Then, continue back up the tail until you run out of bandage. Once you have finished bandaging, wrap the tapes around the tail leaving enough to tie a double bow so that it does not come undone and tuck the ends into a

Figure 8.9 Make sure the top of the tail bandage is secure to prevent it slipping down.

Figure 8.10 Fasten it with a double bow so that it does not come undone.

turn of the bandage (Figure 8.10). Finally, bend the tail into a natural position. If you drop the bandage and it unravels, rewind it and start again.

To take a tail bandage off, undo the tapes, place your hands around the dock and gently slide the bandage off down the tail.

A tail guard protects the tail on long journeys and is very useful if your tail bandaging is not too good. There are neoprene guards on the market which stay in place fairly well, but some do slide off easily, especially on a clean shiny tail. A leather tail guard is practical as it is easy to clean, is secured onto a roller by a strap to prevent it sliding off and is substantial enough to withstand the pressure from a horse that tends to lean on the rear securing bar in a trailer or against the side of a horsebox. For extra protection, a tail guard can be put on over a tail bandage. A tail guard on its own can be left on much longer as it does not exert any pressure on the dock.

As stated, a tail guard has to be secured to a roller; make sure the roller is securely fitted and, if the horse is wearing a rug, the roller is placed over the rug. Adjust the long strap that connects the tail guard to the roller so that the top of the tail is protected. Fasten the tail straps around the dock, wrapping the tail guard around it smoothly as you do so (Figure 8.11).

Figure 8.11 Do up the tail-guard straps around the dock but not too tightly otherwise your horse might object.

To take the guard off, undo the tail straps first, then the roller, to prevent it falling to the ground and getting trampled on.

BOOTS

There are many boots on the market to cover all situations. It is most important to choose boots to suit the purpose for which you need them. Your horse needs protection if he has poor limb movement due to weakness or poor conformation. A fit, balanced, straight-moving horse is far less likely to injure himself. It would be sensible when working on uneven surfaces such as a less-than-perfect arena or rough ground to protect your horse from strains should he stumble or miss his footing. Increasing a horse's workload will put extra strain on his joints and tendons and so it would be wise to give his legs some support while he builds up his fitness. However, if you have good surfaces on which to ride, leg protection is less of an issue. It would be very easy to wrap your horse up every day to protect him but if you become too reliant on leg supports, his joints and tendons will remain weak as they will not be exposed to normal stress and will not develop the necessary strength to cope with everyday work. Ideally your horse should be fit enough to work on good surfaces without extra protection but in different circumstances, such as a competition where he may be under extra pressure, or travelling, it would be sensible to protect him.

Types of boot
BRUSHING BOOTS

Brushing boots fit snugly, enclosing the whole cannon bone and protecting this part of the leg from knocks and grazes from the opposite leg. An old comfortable pair of brushing boots can protect a horse's legs when he is out in the field.

TENDON BOOTS

Tendon boots protect the tendons at the back of the forelegs and are usually used for jumping when there is a risk of the hind feet striking the forelegs. The cannon bone is left exposed. (Figure 8.12.)

FETLOCK BOOTS

These boots protect the fetlocks from knocks and are usually put on

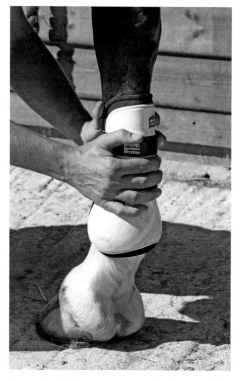

Figure 8.12 Putting on a tendon boot and checking it for security by giving it a good tug downwards with both hands. If it is too loose it will slip down.

the hind legs. There are many synthetic-material or leather fetlock boots on the market at different prices to suit most budgets.

YORKSHIRE BOOTS

Yorkshire boots are felt fetlock boots, fastened with a tape, that fold back on themselves to give a double layer of protection. They are light and soft to wear and are, therefore, a useful boot to use as an introduction to boots if your horse has never worn any before. They are washable and easy to use. The fastening tapes should be checked regularly for signs of fraying.

TRAVELLING BOOTS

These are soft boots made of padded material. Some are softer than others but I have found that more solid boots stay in place better; soft ones tend to slip down the leg when they have been worn a few times. They enclose the legs from the knee and hock joints down to the coronet and are shaped at the top to give protection to the knee and hock joints.

KNEE AND HOCK BOOTS

Knee and hock boots are specifically shaped to fit their respective joints, rather like the elbow and knee pads skateboarders use. They are designed to protect the joints from injury: the knees from a fall and the hocks from a blow when travelling, for example.

OVERREACH BOOTS

These bell-shaped rubber boots can either be of a pull-on design or fastened with Velcro. The pull-on ones stay on better in the field, but can be awkward to pull on and off your horse's feet. It depends on how well he stands still for you, and how strong you are at dealing with tough rubber. Soaking them in hot water for a few minutes helps with getting them on, but pulling them off when they are covered in mud can be tricky. It is easier to hose down your horse's feet with the boots still on to partially clean them first. The insides of the boots will need cleaning once you have removed them from your horse.

TURN-OUT BOOTS/LEG PROTECTORS

There are soft turn-out boots on the market designed to be worn for protection in the field and as brushing boots. They enclose the lower leg below the knee including the fetlock joint. Made of flexible material, they fit fairly tightly but do not interfere with the joint movement. If your horse is out in the field for a long time it is imperative that these boots fit him properly to avoid rubbing.

Although these boots are very useful, the best way to protect your horse's legs when he is in the field is to choose his companions carefully so that there is not too much rough play and to check the field for potential hazards frequently.

9 TACKING UP AND UNTACKING

IT IS VERY important to follow the correct procedure for tacking up and untacking to avoid potential problems. Many horse owners buy their first horses as adults and have often missed out on the basic horse-management training that youngsters helping in riding schools have access to. Out of frustration and impatience many people resort to bizarre techniques to get a saddle or bridle on a horse. Their method may work temporarily but, in the long term, they are producing a potentially unrideable horse, unless the intention is to always ride like an ancient Greek – bareback and without a full bridle. Being able to ride *au naturel* may sound romantic but, practically, do you want to, and should you, be riding down the high street like this? At shows and events, for reasons of safety (for riders and spectators) and control, riders must participate in tack that is not only correctly fitted but also correct for the particular equestrian discipline. If you are unable to train your horse to wear a saddle and bridle, it would be mad to even consider riding him without them.

If a horse does not readily accept wearing, and working in, tack, you will find him virtually impossible to sell because any potential purchaser would be put off by this, and his value will be reduced to meat money. Some horses resort to extreme, often dangerous, behaviour to avoid being tacked up, but this usually stems from rough handling at a young age. An immature horse can be spoiled for life by a saddle and bridle being slapped on carelessly, particularly if it is ill-fitting once it is on.

With time, patience and correct handling you can establish a good tacking-up technique which will make sense to your horse and give him an easier, less stressful life, with you and future owners.

143

If you have bought a horse with a tacking-up problem, go back to the beginning with him and treat him as if he is being introduced to tack for the first time. By doing this systematically you will ensure that you deal with any little signs of stress, discomfort or naughtiness as they appear, even if they are well-established problems.

Most problems can be sorted out in a few days, provided you allow enough time. It is far more important to spend an afternoon putting the bridle on and taking it off until you can achieve it quickly and quietly with a relaxed horse, than struggling to put it on once and going off for a mad hack from which your horse returns to his stable stressed and lacking in confidence and associating this anxiety with the unfortunate bridling session. There must be no time pressure; cancel all appointments and warn your partner that they may have to put the dinner on.

THE SADDLING PROCEDURE

The standard procedure for putting on a saddle is as follows.

- Place your saddle, saddle cloth and girth within easy reach of your horse's stable.
- Tie him up (if you have difficulties with this, see Chapter 3).
- Place the saddle cloth further forward than its final position.
- Holding the pommel with your left hand and the cantle with your right, place the saddle on top of the saddle cloth. (The girth should be attached on the offside of the saddle and laid across its seat.)
- Slide both the saddle cloth and saddle back into position. This ensures that the hairs of your horse's coat are lying flat thus preventing discomfort and rubs.
- Duck under your horse's neck and the rope to the offside and take down the girth. Come back to the nearside, reach under the horse's belly for the girth and do it up just tight enough to hold the saddle secure (Figure 9.1).
- Never leave a saddle on a horse's back unsecured. If he should move suddenly the saddle will fall to the ground and the tree could be damaged.

This straightforward procedure is, however, often complicated by problems, both small and large. For example: if your horse is too tall for you to get the saddle up on to his back without throwing it in the air, standing on a sturdy milk crate or grooming box will help; or, if a horse resents the saddle cloth being placed on his back, utilize the rug-training procedure outlined in Chapter 8.

BACK TO BASICS

If you are training a young horse from the beginning or have an older horse that resents wearing a saddle or is difficult to girth up, follow the procedure below. If your problems persist or become worse, seek advice from your saddler to make sure your saddle

Figure 9.1 When putting on a saddle, do up the girth loosely at first and tighten gradually to avoid making your horse sensitive to the girth.

fits well and/or ask the vet to investigate any underlying physical problem. It might also mean swallowing your pride and having some lessons from a good instructor who can tell you if your riding is causing your horse's reluctance to be tacked up!

Using a tail bandage to simulate a girth

After grooming your horse to make sure he is calm and relaxed, unroll a tail bandage and place it over his back in the position where a roller sits. Reach under his belly and take the ends of the bandage, gently pulling it taut and tie the ends together on his side in a reef knot that can easily be undone.

Your horse should not resent this. If he does, he may hump his back a couple of times as he feels the bandage around his middle but he should relax fairly quickly. Stroke him calmly and take his mind off it by recommencing

145

the grooming or picking out his feet. Lifting a foot will help him to relax and concentrate on something else. If you fuss or get anxious you will make the horse feel that the lesson is something to worry about and tension will set in. Treat all his lessons as part of the day's routine. The next step is to take him out for a walk around the yard or field wearing the bandage, then return to the stable and remove it. Repeat this exercise twice a day for two or three days until your horse is relaxed and shows no signs of stress.

Putting on a roller

The next stage is to repeat the same exercise using a roller. Use a pad under the roller for comfort and make sure the roller does not press down on your horse's spine but rests on the muscles either side of it, just behind his withers so that the roller girth goes around his belly just behind his elbows. If your horse is very sensitive around his middle, use an elasticized girth on the roller which has some give in it, that way, if your horse blows himself out against it, he feels less restriction than with a fixed girth. It can help to use a fluffy girth cover that gives extra softness and feels warm against your horse's skin; a cold girth can cause tension with some horses. Take the time to do it up gently in stages but do not take so long about it that your horse gets frustrated and bored.

Introducing the saddle

Now you move on to introducing the saddle. A good time to do this is after grooming when the horse's muscles are relaxed. Place the saddle cloth on your horse's back and then put the saddle on top. Slowly and calmly fasten the girth just tight enough to prevent the saddle slipping should your horse move suddenly. If he feels the saddle move he may panic. Leave the saddle on for a few minutes, but do not leave him unattended in the stable wearing items of tack, always keep an eye on him.

The other option is to put the saddle on in the arena after your horse has been lunged in a roller. Just replace the roller with the saddle at the end of the training session, and lead him around the school a couple of times to get him used to the feel of it on his back. Make sure he is happy to wear a saddle in these situations before proceeding further; if he is you can progress to lungeing him in the saddle from the beginning of the session. Make sure the girth holds the saddle securely without over-tightening it. By following this procedure, you should have no problems later with mounting and riding your horse.

Taking the saddle off

- Standing on the nearside of your horse, undo the girth and lower it gently.
- Go round to the offside and place the girth over the seat before lifting the saddle off. Return to the nearside and, holding the saddle with one hand under the pommel and the other grasping the cantle, slide the saddle off towards you and rest it on your left forearm.
- Take the saddle away to a safe place.

If you have been lungeing your horse in his saddle, for example, prior to untacking and he has a tendency to roll immediately the saddle is removed, tie him up first. If he sweated under the saddle and along the line of the girth and it is a warm day, sponge the sweaty area off. In cool weather, allow him to dry off, then brush the saddle patch so that it is clean. This makes sure your horse's coat and skin are clean and prevents a build up of dirt which could cause sore spots and rubbed areas.

Fear of the saddle

If you do the girth up too tightly your horse may come to fear the saddle; this is sometimes known as being 'cold backed'. This can manifest itself as a slight humping of a horse's back, or blowing out the stomach so that you cannot do the girth up. (Ponies are particularly adept at this and take it a step further: just as you put your foot in the stirrup to mount, they relax their stomach muscles causing the saddle to slip and you to end up on your backside.) In extreme cases, a horse will throw himself on the ground as soon as he feels the girth against his belly. Always do the girth up in stages, and walk your horse a few steps before tightening it up further. If your horse is already saddle-shy, retrain him from the tail-bandage-around-the-belly stage. Lungeing your horse first in a roller and then a saddle can help him to relax, as can using an elasticized girth with a fluffy girth sleeve, as mentioned earlier.

When I was a trainee in Germany one of my mares was extremely

147

saddle-shy. I was not told what to expect and so when I gaily plonked her saddle on her back and tried to do the girth up, she threw herself on the ground and laid there, eyes bulging. Luckily she did not land on the saddle; I eased it away and she stood back up as though nothing had happened. I was about to school her but thought it best to lunge her first. Having taken the saddle to the schooling arena, I lunged her for a few minutes and then placed the saddle on carefully. I did the girth up just as tight as was necessary to stop the saddle slipping. I led her around the school, stopping after every few steps to tighten the girth very gradually. It was about twenty minutes before she relaxed enough for me to mount, which I did very carefully and then walked her on while balancing on the stirrups, not putting any weight on her back until I was sure she was relaxed. As soon as I could sit normally, we commenced our schooling session. Over about three months she improved a lot but I always had to take things slowly.

If with a horse like this you just do up the girth quickly and get on, you run the risk of him rearing, bucking and throwing himself all over the place, you will fall off in the process or, worse, be fallen on, resulting in you being injured and the horse being traumatized. You will probably have great difficulty in ever getting a saddle on the horse again.

Biting and kicking

Biting and kicking under saddle are usually a result of an ill-fitting saddle causing discomfort when ridden. The horse resents the saddle being put on because he has a sore back. Biting can be caused by the girth being done up too roughly causing tenderness around the belly. Forgetting to loosen the girth after dismounting and leaving the horse for long periods tightly girthed can also cause this response. Particular care must be taken when training a young horse to avoid these problems being developed. Girth galls or rubs caused by dirty girths and saddle cloths or bad riding can all contribute to your horse basically telling you he does not want you around.

The first thing to do is to have your saddle checked for damage and correct fit and, if necessary, buy a new one that fits properly. Clean all your tack thoroughly and wash saddle cloths and girths. Treat all sores, taking advice from your vet if you are unsure of how to deal with the problem. (See Chapter 10 for information on treating minor wounds.)

If the biting and/or kicking has become a habit and continues after you have dealt with everything discussed above, retrain your horse from the tail-bandage-around-the-belly stage. If he tries to bite or kick you, avoid shouting at him, which will make him tense and more cross than he already is, remain calm and stay close to him. By standing close to a horse, you make it harder for him to take a swing at you. Tie him up before handling him and if you need to stop him swinging his neck or hindquarters at you, tie him up with two ropes (see page 65).

If you have inherited this problem with a recently bought horse, the best way to deal with it is to, again, retrain him from the tail-bandage-round-the-belly stage. This should work no matter how long the horse has had the habit. The older the horse and the longer he has been biting and kicking, the longer it takes to make an improvement but with patience and perseverance there is no reason why any horse cannot become more at ease with being girthed up.

If there is no improvement or your horse becomes worse, the vet must be consulted to investigate the possibility of an underlying physical condition. Also, make sure that you are not nervous and upsetting your horse; it is imperative to maintain a calm, authoritative attitude at all times when dealing with such issues in order to reassure your horse that you are his 'herd leader'.

Another tactic which works very well with a young horse is to let your horse watch you tacking up another horse that is calm and obedient and this will reassure him that you are not trying to kill him; he will see that the world does not collapse if he has a saddle on. This tactic might well not work, however, with an older, dyed-in-the-wool saddle hater whose attitude might be, 'Rather you than me mate.' In this case you will have to resort to your own 'bite/kick retaliation' techniques.

TYPES OF SADDLE

Ask a reputable master saddler, or someone who has expert knowledge of a style of saddle for a less-widely understood equestrian field, e.g. an endurance or Western saddle, to advise you on your options regarding a type of saddle and its suitability for your ambitions with your horse. Do make sure that the saddle not only fits the horse but also fits, and is comfortable for, you. Buying a 'horse friendly' saddle is all well and good, but if you are uncomfortable in it and cannot use your legs and seat effectively, then choose another one. A well-fitting, well-maintained saddle with a conventional tree and panels used for the purpose for which it was designed is a good long-term investment.

FITTING A SADDLE

A saddle should sit comfortably either side of the withers when it is girthed up and have good clearance at the pommel. You should be able to slide your hand comfortably down between the front panels and your horse's shoulders; this should not be easier or more difficult on either side but feel the same on both sides. The saddle should fit smoothly in this area and not look as though any part of it is causing pressure or pinching. A saddle causing a mild pinching of the shoulders can restrict the shoulder movement and the horse will move with short strides in front, but severe pinching could make a horse rear. (Figures 9.2a–d.)

a

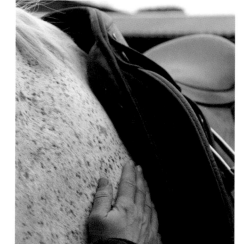

b

Figures 9.2a–d a) The front panels should lie behind the shoulder muscle; b) A well-fitting saddle should have good clearance at the pommel; c) It should sit evenly balanced on both sides of the horse's back; d) There should be no gaps under the panels.

c

d

If the saddle bounces around excessively at the back when you lunge your horse, it may be pressing down at the front, causing the back to lift and move. The discomfort triggered by this bouncing often results in bucking.

Look at the saddle from the side. If it appears to tip backwards, it will be lifting at the front and is probably too narrow for your horse. If this is the case, the weight of your seat will be tipped towards the rear of the saddle, causing the rear panels to put pressure on your horse's back. If when riding you are having difficulty sitting upright and find that your legs keep shooting forward, your saddle may be tipping you back (Figure 9.3). Ask someone to look at the way the saddle sits while you are in the saddle and how it affects your position and then you can decide if you need to call the saddler to fit it properly for you. There are various methods of padding a

151

Figure 9.3 The seat should allow you to sit upright in the saddle.

saddle including conventional flocking, air bags and various synthetic materials. The choice is wide but you must consider your purse plus your comfort and that of your horse. Many fashions come and go, but a master saddler who will give you sound advice is worth his weight in gold.

THE BRIDLING PROCEDURE

The standard procedure for putting on a bridle is as follows.

- Hang your bridle near the stable.
- Tie your horse up.
- Fetch your bridle and hang it over your left forearm.
- Undo your horse's head collar and fasten it around his neck.
- Make sure the noseband and throatlatch are undone before you put the bridle on.
- Place the reins over your horse's head and rest them near his withers.
- Stand on the nearside of your horse. Holding the cheek pieces in your left hand, reach under his jaw bone and pass the bridle into your right hand.
- Now holding both cheek pieces in your right hand, rest the bit on your

152

left palm and gently press it against your horse's teeth where the top set joins the bottom set; it is pointless pressing the bit against his gums. With your left thumb, tickle his gums to ask him to open his mouth slightly so that you can slip the bit between his teeth. As he opens his mouth, lift the bridle with your right hand so that the bit is raised in your horse's mouth and he cannot spit it out.

- Once the bit is in, use both hands to slip the bridle over his ears: reach up under his throat to his right ear with your right hand to slip it over this offside ear first to ensure that your arms are not all over his face; then place the bridle over his nearside ear. It is best to do the offside ear first in case he decides to move his head away and you cannot reach the ear furthest away from you.
- Pull his forelock gently clear of the browband. Make sure the browband sits comfortably below his ears and that it is not too small for him – a common cause of head-shaking.
- Twist the reins together, and pass the throatlatch between them to secure them before doing it up loosely. There should be a hand's breadth between the jaw bone and the throatlatch.
- Fasten the noseband according to the type you are using (see page 161).
- Twist the reins and fasten the throatlatch through them to keep them out of the way and put the head collar on over the bridle afterwards.

Figures 9.4a-e

Ideally the above bridling procedure will work every time but, as with saddling, problems are very common.

A horse may associate bridling with an unpleasant experience and perhaps one of the best ways to alleviate the fear of having the bridle put on, is to ensure that it does not automatically signify ridden work. It can be helpful, therefore, to accustom him to wearing his bridle at other times, just before feeding, for example, so that he associates his bridle with his something he enjoys. The bridle should be taken off before he eats but he should still associate the bridle with the pleasure of the feed. Alternatively, put his bridle on while you groom him, or lead him to the field in it. Wrapping grass around the bit can encourage some horses to take the bit happily and is an added incentive for accepting the bridle.

a

b

c

d

e

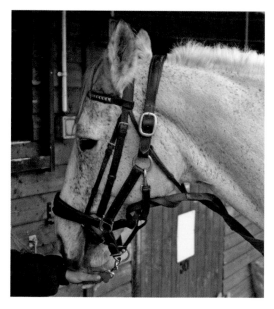

Figures 9.4a–e a) Holding both cheek pieces in your right hand, slide the bit into his mouth with your left hand, tickling his gums with your thumb to get him to open his mouth if necessary; b) Place the head piece over the offside ear first (this is the most awkward one) in case he pulls his head away; c) Place the head piece over his nearside ear after the offside ear; d) Gently pull his forelock clear of the browband; e) Twist the reins and fasten the throatlatch through them to keep them out of the way and put the head collar back on afterwards.

I had a young Thoroughbred called Stumpy Duncan. During his early training, I left him untied and with his reins around his neck for a moment while I fetched my riding hat from the tack room. I heard a commotion and returned to find him upside down in the corner of the stable with his head sandwiched between the wall and his water bucket. He had put his head down, trodden on the reins and done a back flip to end up in this position. Luckily the straw bed was deep enough to protect both Stumpy and the saddle from damage. Once he was upright again, I went to take his bridle off, only to find that his forelock came with it – a flap of skin lifted from his head like a toupee. The vet's visit left a young horse with several stitches in his head and I expect he also had a horrendous headache.

As soon as Stumpy had recovered, I tacked him up as normal as though nothing had happened. Because I was not anxious about bridling him, he was equally unworried about it then and showed no fear of the bridle in the future. The whole incident was dealt with quickly, quietly and without any panic. If you are over-cautious or nervous in such a situation, your horse will pick up on it and you will actually create a problem.

Many horse owners adopt strange techniques to make life easier, such as dismantling the whole bridle because the horse does not like his ears touched. Being in a hurry to get the bridle on, regardless of how you do it, just to ride out on a nice day may solve the problem temporarily, but in the long term you are perpetuating the problem by allowing your horse to dictate to you how he wants things done. If he does not like the bridling process, trying to find any number of ways round it is not the answer. Bribery works a few times, until the horse works out how to grab the titbit before you can get the bit in his mouth. The only permanent solution is to train him properly from the beginning, or to retrain him, in the following stages.

BACK TO BASICS

Getting a horse to wear a head collar or halter is the first stage in introducing head gear to your horse (see Chapter 3); once that is accepted, the bridle can be put on.

You do not need to start with the complete bridle, but it is important that you can slide the head piece over your horse's ears. If he is accustomed to being groomed and handled in this area you should not have a problem. If you do, see Chapter 1.

Introducing the bit

Use just the head piece attached to a simple snaffle, either a straight bar or jointed snaffle will do as long as it is easy to put into your horse's mouth. A rubber bit is soft and comfortable in the mouth but some horses treat this type of bit like a dummy and chew through it. It is sensible to get a horse used to the feel of a metal bit in his mouth as soon as possible in preparation for later schooling.

To place the bit into your horse's mouth, hold it across your left palm, leaving your left thumb free to tickle his gums (see pages 152–153). Make sure you can reach his head easily, standing on a box if necessary; if you cannot manage to put the head piece over his offside ear, have an assistant on that side to do it for you. It is vital that this goes well the first time to avoid problems developing in the future. If your horse becomes tense at any stage, stop where you are before continuing thus making sure that he is relaxed at each stage. If you remove the bridle when your horse is tense, he learns that if he is worried the bridle goes away. Horses can be very good actors at times, and I know several that would win an Oscar for their portrayal of an anxious horse to avoid all manner of situations from wearing tack to going in a trailer. It is therefore, important that a horse learns that, even if he is worried, what you are doing is not going to harm him, and that you will persist with whatever it is you wish to accomplish.

Throwing the head up

A horse may lift his head through fear, because of a bad experience or through naughtiness when he works out that you are not tall enough to reach his head. He may also get into the habit of tipping his head away from you so that you cannot reach his offside ear, spit out the bit and not let you get near him again. This behaviour must be stopped before it becomes a habit, otherwise you will have great difficulty getting anything on his head. If necessary, stand on a box or anything that keeps you within range of his head, he can only lift it so high (Figures 9.5a and b).

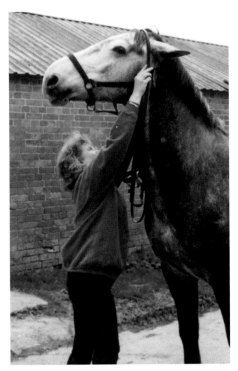

Figures 9.5a and b Many difficulties encountered when putting on a bridle can be overcome by making sure you can reach your horse's head, as demonstrated by Mary and Connor.

When working through this problem you must, as always, remain calm and relaxed and totally in control of the situation. If you panic or fumble, your horse will become even more nervous or annoyed and will try to take control again. Never resort to shouting at him; and hitting him, especially around the head, will just produce a head-shy horse.

Refusing to open the mouth

If your horse refuses to open his mouth, he will clamp his teeth together and purse his lips. It is amazing how much strength a horse's lips have in this situation! Again, do not become angry or upset with him. Persistent persuasion is the key; simply repeat the bitting procedure on page 156.

Not liking the ears touched

If your horse hates his ears being touched, it is a problem that is best confronted when you are grooming him (see Chapter 5) but if his ears seem to be particularly sensitive when he is being bridled, then the bridling should be tackled in the following way. Try not to handle or touch his ears any more than you have to as the bridle is put on because this will just make matters worse.

Remove the browband and noseband from the bridle so that you are left with just the head piece attached to the bit. The browband can often be the root of the problem in these cases; if it is not large enough for the horse it can press against the sensitive areas at the base of his ears and cause considerable discomfort.

To ensure that you do not have to handle your horse's ears, make sure you have the head piece loose enough to slip easily over your horse's ears but not so loose that he can spit the bit out. Again, make sure you can reach the top of the horse's head so that putting the head piece over the ears is not an extra struggle. If he tries to throw his head up, stop what you are doing but stay where you are and do not remove the bridle. As soon as he has relaxed, continue as described on page 153 until you have the head piece over his ears. Praise him, give him a titbit, and then remove the bridle again. Go through the whole procedure once more to make sure he accepts what you are doing and that will be enough for the first day. Subsequently, this needs to be repeated daily, morning and evening, in a very matter of fact way; if you carry on as though there is no problem, so might he.

Next, having checked that the browband is the correct size for the horse put it back on the bridle, together with the noseband, and try bridling him again to see how he reacts to the process with them in place.

If he continues to be extremely fussy and anxious about his ears and you recognize that his reactions are markedly different from simply not wanting the bridle on, have your vet check him for ear problems.

Backing away from the bridle

If a horse takes the bit in his mouth and shoots backwards before you get the head piece on, this could be a consequence of a fear of the bit or sensitive ears. A horse that is really afraid may go to the back of the stable when he sees you coming with a bridle. One of the causes of this type of fear is discomfort in the mouth from the use of the incorrect bit for your horse.

Put his head collar on and tie him up. When he is standing quietly

Figure 9.6 Four fingers, a hand's breadth, should fit between the throatlatch and your horse's cheek.

the action of the bit but it is not there to strap the mouth shut. He should have enough leeway to mouth the bit quietly when a noseband is correctly fitted. A drop noseband should have one finger's width between it and the nose bone (Figure 9.7), and a cavesson two fingers. A flash noseband should have one finger's width under the top and bottom straps.

Figure 9.7 You should be able to get one finger under the front of a drop noseband.

Are browbands and nosebands necessary?

Although your horse can appear 'undressed' without them, it is perfectly possible to use a bridle without a browband or noseband if your horse is ridden correctly into a contact. If a horse is ridden properly with seat, leg and rein aids, he should not open his mouth when a contact is taken. On the other hand, it does not help to ride your horse without a noseband if he persistently yaws at the bit; he must learn to accept the limits of a correctly fitting noseband and not be allowed to find a way to avoid taking a contact with the bit if he is being ridden correctly.

Rough rein aids can make a horse resist the bit, and the solution people often adopt to keep the mouth shut is a tight noseband but this is a situation that should be avoided at all costs, otherwise it is easy to slide down the slippery slope of progressively stronger bits and tighter nosebands. Always check your training technique is correct before experimenting with bits and other equipment.

CHOICE OF BIT

My advice would be to keep it simple. If your horse is correctly trained, he should work well in a snaffle, whether it is a straight bar, single joint or double jointed snaffle. My favourite is a loose-ring double-jointed snaffle with a lozenge in the middle and I find this suits most horses. Experimenting with multi-action bits, pelhams etc. should not be necessary if your horse works correctly. Horses do have different shaped mouths and so a bit should be chosen to suit them; thick bits can be too much of a mouthful for some horses and thin ones could be too severe for others. The bit should be wide enough so that if you slide it to one side, one bit ring lies against his face and the other ring has one finger's width between it and the horse's lips.

10 VETERINARY CARE

RECOGNIZING BEHAVIOUR THAT is not normal for your particular horse is the first indication that something is wrong, and assessing when your horse is off colour is so important to his well-being. You need to know your horse well enough to pick up small indications that something is amiss. He could be more grumpy than usual, be off his food or look depressed. Noticing small changes in your horse can expedite calling the vet for early treatment of symptoms. (Figure 10.1.)

All horses have their own little ways such as where they like to stand in the stable or field, how they greet you and normal feeding habits. If your horse usually whinnies when he sees you coming but on one occasion you find him standing dejectedly at the back of his stable, you can bet something is amiss.

My Thoroughbred, Stumpy Duncan, waved one front foot continually at me one evening when I went to check him over. On inspection, he had a cut right under his pastern, the only sign

Figure 10.1 A healthy horse will be interested in what is going on. Get used to what is 'normal' for your own horse then you will be sure to notice if anything is wrong.

of any injury being a couple of specks of blood on the shavings in his bed (which fortunately were new and white). This wound could easily have been missed and become infected had he not alerted me to it.

Get into the habit of assessing the whole of your horse whenever you are handling him. For example, if when you open his mouth to put on his bridle you detect bad breath, this can indicate an infected mouth injury or bad teeth, which you might otherwise not be aware of. Unbeknown to the stable staff, Amadeus managed to catch his mouth in the stable and it was not noticed until he had bad breath. On inspecting his mouth there was a gash in his gum so deep that you could see his jaw bone. As soon as I saw it I called the vet whose prompt attention followed by diligent cleaning helped the wound to heal over the bone without any future problems. Simply by having a quick glance at your horse's mouth and smelling his breath as you tack up can detect any problems in this area early on.

SIGNS OF GOOD HEALTH

A horse that is happy and healthy should be his usual self and easy to handle and it is important to weigh up whether any small deviations from the norm are simply due to everyday changes or indicate poor health. For example, a horse that is relaxed and tired after work will naturally be more subdued than one coming fresh out of his stable. If your horse is happy with his work and training but is a little better behaved and quieter than usual, this does not necessarily mean he is off colour. If, however, you have struggled with a difficult horse for months to find the key to successful handling and he is quieter and much better behaved than normal, you are more likely to think there is something amiss. As I have stated before, horses are very good actors and some know exactly how to manipulate a situation. Trevor can produce a dry cough as soon as the word 'show' is mentioned and also has perfected this cough during schooling, when he realizes I have got the better of him. Of course you stop to let a horse clear his throat when he coughs, but when it happens every time you pick up the reins, you smell a rat! This simply proves that truly knowing your horse is so important to assessing whether something is really wrong or not.

Signs of good health are as follows.

164

- Your horse's behaviour and level of alertness should be as normal. He can be upset by loud noises, excited by horses galloping around in the next field, and so on, and so these factors must be taken into account.

- If your horse is healthy, his coat will be shiny (good grooming plays a role in coat condition), his eyes will be bright and not runny (flies in summer can cause mucky eyes) and his nostrils will be clean. Dust can make horses cough and snort, but this does not mean they are ill. The membranes around his eyes and inside his nostrils should be pink and neither pale nor an angry red colour.

- A horse's legs should be 'clean' and cool, i.e. there should be no unusual lumps and bumps on, or heat in, his legs, and none of his feet should be noticeably hotter that the others. There can be a slight difference in hoof temperature if your horse has had one foot in a pile of droppings (which give off heat) and the others just on clean bedding, which is another good reason for skipping out regularly.

- A horse should be standing normally and not resting a leg in an unusual way (Amadeus frequently stands with his hind feet crossed. If he did not, I would suspect something was wrong!).

- If a horse is just standing quietly in his stable or field he should not be sweating unless it is a hot summer's day or if he has been worked, in which case he should be walked until he has dried off.

- The normal amount of food and water should be consumed but horses will drink more if they sweat during exercise and during hot weather.

- The level of breathing should be normal. You will see a gentle rising and falling of his ribs if you look towards the rear of his belly, and he should take between 8 and 12 breaths a minute.

- A horse's temperature should be 38°C and his pulse should be 36–42 beats per minute (see page 171). Next time the vet comes to the yard, ask him to show you how to take your horse's temperature if you are not sure how to.

- The droppings should appear normal and the usual amount of urine should be passed. Droppings may be looser if a horse is out at grass a lot or if he is anxious or excited: at a show for example. The colour of the droppings varies according to the diet. The urine should be pale yellow in colour. The number of droppings a horse does will vary with the individual, but as long as they are being passed, there is little wrong. On the contrary, when a horse stops passing droppings you should worry because this could be a sign of an impacted gut, which could result in colic. In this case the vet should be called.

SIGNS OF POOR HEALTH

- Unusual behaviour that is not caused by next door's donkey braying or other irregular occurrences such as fireworks.
- Listlessness or a complete lack of interest in the yard/field activities (but do make sure that your horse is not just having a rest). Lying down more than usual can be a sign your horse is off colour, but if he has had a couple of intensive training sessions or been to a show he may genuinely be tired. Amadeus likes to have a mid-morning nap; on one occasion the farrier had to shoe Trevor first because Amadeus was snoring away in the land of nod.
- Heavy breathing, sweating and restlessness can indicate colic, in which case do not hesitate to call the vet.
- Clear or white discharge from the nostrils can be a reaction to mouldy hay, and is usually accompanied by a dry cough. In this case, get better quality hay. You may need to damp it down until your horse has stopped coughing and the nasal discharge has gone. Haylage is an alternative to hay if your horse continues to have the same reaction to hay in the future. (see Chapter 6).
- Yellow discharge from the nose accompanied by a deep, rasping cough indicates a respiratory infection, and the vet should be called. Your horse will breathe faster than normal and appear to struggle to fill his lungs with air.
- Heat and/or swelling in the limbs indicate strain or injury. Take into account the work your horse has been doing and whether he might have landed awkwardly over a fence or been running about like a maniac in the field and slipped. If he is out with other horses, has he been kicked? This will give you an idea of the type of injury caused, such as a bruise or a strain.
- Changes in eating and drinking habits such as excessive thirst, or

reluctance to eat can be signs of a fever; take your horse's temperature and call the vet if it is high and you think he may be ill. On the other hand, if the horse has been working very hard and sweated a lot, he may need the extra fluid and be too stressed to eat until he has spent time relaxing first and so, again, it is important to assess the situation properly.

- The absence of droppings can indicate early signs of colic. Persistently loose droppings can be a sign that your horse needs worming but bear in mind that some wormers will cause the droppings to be loose for a day after administration. Infrequent urinating and dark-coloured urine could be a sign of dehydration; make sure your horse has access to fresh water at all times. If the urine has blood in it, call the vet.

- A raised temperature can indicate a virus such as a cold. Your horse can appear under the weather, as we would, in this instance.

FIRST-AID KIT

A first-aid kit containing items for both for you and your horse is essential. Necessary items are listed below.

Clean tea towels

Sponge

Cotton wool

Scissors

Vet wrap (adhesive bandage)

Melonin dressings (large and small available from the chemist)

Thermometer

Hibiscrub

Antiseptic spray

Hydrogen peroxide

Salt

Zinc cream

Set of four stable bandages and pads

Clean plastic pot or bowl for mixing diluted Hibiscrub, salt water etc.

Small bucket (kept clean solely for first-aid use)

Animalintex

Spare hoof pick
Antibiotic powder
Vaseline
Plasters for cuts
Antiseptic cream such as Germoline

WHEN TO CALL THE VET

The vet should be called if your horse has any illness or injury that you are not sure about or that is too severe for you to deal with. Your first-aid kit is exactly that, a kit for the initial treatment of wounds and problems before the vet arrives. Anything that cannot be treated with your first-aid kit needs the vet's attention. As a matter of routine, the vet should give your horse his annual flu and biennial tetanus vaccinations. These are good opportunities to ask him about any worries you may have, and to have your horse's teeth rasped at the same time.

Colic

If you notice any signs of colic such as restlessness, pawing frantically at the ground, lying down and standing up repeatedly, sweating, swishing the tail, or general signs of stress and discomfort, call the vet immediately. If your horse has eaten anything he should not have done, such as some rotten apples or unsoaked sugar beet (see Chapter 6), look out for the above symptoms. The consequences of colic can be fatal, especially if the gut is twisted.

High temperature

A high temperature of more than 39°C (the normal temperature is 38°C) could indicate an infection such as strangles and immediate veterinary attention is essential.

Coughing

A persistent, deep, rasping cough that sounds painful is a sign of a respiratory infection and the vet should be called. This is usually accompanied by a thick, yellow/green nasal discharge (see page 178).

Wounds

Any wound longer than 2 cm (about 1 in) that may require stitching or that is in an awkward place to clean should be treated by the vet. Puncture wounds need particular care; they can be very deep and need thorough cleansing to prevent the risk of infection. Wounds over joints are always potentially serious, especially if the joint capsule has been penetrated. Wounds that you are not absolutely sure about, and that cannot be cleaned and dressed with your first-aid kit require professional treatment. It is better to deal with a wound early on rather than worry about it for a couple of days. Delaying proper treatment will only make matters worse.

Back and neck injuries

Back and neck injuries are usually a result of a heavy fall. Muscular problems can be caused by poor riding and/or badly fitting tack, especially saddles. Whether you call the saddler or the vet first (or a good riding instructor) very much depends on the history of the problem.

Heat in the foot

Heat in the foot can indicate an abscess, which can cause the horse a huge amount of pain. The horse will be extremely lame when walked about. The vet will need to drain the abscess and give the horse antibiotics and pain killers. Heat could also indicate problems such as laminitis (see page 181).

Lameness

If the horse is lame when trotted up, and you suspect he has been injured either by stepping on a sharp stone (bruised foot) or by a kick on the leg (bruise or cracked bone) call the vet. If it is a simple injury, the vet may show you how to deal with it, so that next time you will know what to do yourself. It is always better to find out from the vet than to do the wrong thing because someone has misdiagnosed the problem, which will invariably end up in the vet being called anyway.

Long-term lameness or unevenness in the steps can be a sign of problems inside the foot, such as laminitis or bone disease, in which case the vet will take X-rays to make a diagnosis. Some lameness problems are caused by poor shoeing (see Chapter 7) but a good farrier can work wonders if he has access to the vet's records and X-rays because he can then judge how to shoe the horse appropriately.

Teeth rasping

If your horse is not accepting the bit and is fighting the contact or dropping feed out of his mouth when he is eating, or appearing to chew on one side of his mouth, which may coincide with him hanging on one rein, it is likely that the horse has rough edges on his teeth and they need to be rasped. This can either be carried out by your vet, perhaps at the same time as your horse's annual jabs are due, or a qualified horse dentist. With the latter, a word-of-mouth recommendation by someone who has used and trusts a particular dentist is a good idea.

To check if your horse's teeth are rough, carefully slide two fingers up inside his cheek and feel the outer surface of the teeth, taking care that he does not nip you. It is fairly easy to feel a rough edge where the top teeth meet the bottom ones. This is caused by the two surfaces not being flush and the teeth wearing unevenly. It is easiest to make this check after riding, while your horse still has his bridle on. Hold the cheek piece of the bridle with one hand to keep his head still, but do not grab his nose tightly because you will alarm him and he may throw his head up, and use the free hand to feel for the rough edges.

FIRST-AID PROCEDURES PRIOR TO THE VET'S VISIT

Everyone should know basic first-aid procedures in order to cope with a situation until the vet arrives. If you have followed the guidelines in Chapters 1 and 3, your horse should behave well when the vet comes. As long as you remain calm and in control of the situation, your horse will cope well with any treatment he has to have. Remember that nervous owners make nervous horses. There are, however, always the exceptions that prove the rule. I had booked the vet to administer Amadeus's flu jab and Amadeus sensed something was afoot. I went to the car park to meet the vet and on returning to the stable, Amadeus was nowhere in sight. The door was open and he had vanished! I heard a movement from an empty box on the other side of the barn and lo and behold there he was, hiding right up against the wall tucked in the corner where we could not see him from the doorway. Even the vet was taken aback and said that he had never known a horse do that! Consequently Amadeus received his flu jab where he was, and was then returned to his own box.

Taking the temperature and pulse
TEMPERATURE

To take your horse's temperature, place the thermometer in the horse's rectum. Most modern thermometers are digital and do not have to be shaken down like a mercury thermometer before being inserted. Smear it with Vaseline so that it goes in easily for a few centimetres but keep hold of it! I heard about someone who let go of the thermometer and had to call the vet out to extricate it – not a pleasant job!

PULSE

Take the pulse under the jaw where the facial artery passes over the jaw-bone. This is the best place to actually feel the blood pumping. Place the first two fingers of one hand on the jaw-line and press gently until you can feel the pulse (Figure 10.2).

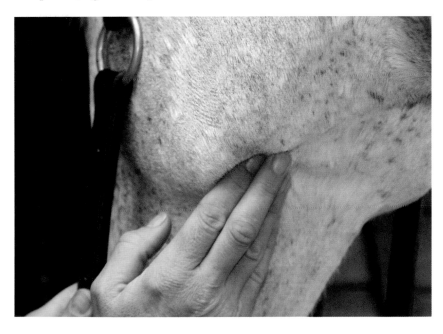

Figure 10.2 Taking the horse's pulse by pressing the facial artery against the jaw-bone.

If you do not know what a pulse feels like, take your own by placing the first two fingers on the artery on the inside of the opposite wrist and press the artery against the bone in line with the base of your thumb. You should then be able to identify your horse's pulse.

Wounds/Bleeding

For small injuries less than 2 cm (about 1 in) in length, trickle water from a hose over the wound, placing the end of the hose above the wound and not spraying the water directly on it, which might be extremely uncomfortable for the horse. If the wound is large, apply pressure by bandaging a padded dressing over the wound to stem the bleeding. Apply additional pressure by hand. Call the vet.

Administering medicine

Most medicine is put in the feed, but it may need disguising with something tasty: you may have to resort to putting the medicine into carrots or apples! Sugar beet is very good for disguising powder.

Cold hosing

Cold hosing at least twice a day can help to reduce pain and swelling from a bruise (possibly inflicted by a kick from another horse) or strain. Aim a gentle spray of water above the injury and let the water run gently down the leg over the site of the injury (Figure 10.3). Often a minor bruise or strain will improve after a couple of days of rest and hosing. Stable bandages will help to reduce the swelling. If the swelling does not go down, call the vet.

Figure 10.3 Aim a gentle spray of water over the injury and let it trickle down the leg

Treating leg bruises, strains and wounds

Trickling water over the affected area from a hose is the best way to treat these complaints. As stated above, running the water over the area, rather than directing the spray directly at it, is less likely to hurt the sore spot. A hose also keeps you at a safe distance from a possible kick, which is not so easy when using a bucket and sponge, and the running water from a hose is going to be cleaner than that in a bucket.

If your horse keeps picking up the leg you are trying to treat, ask an assistant to hold up the opposite leg so that he has to stand on the one you are treating.

If you have to treat hind-leg wounds with cotton wool, approach the leg by sweeping your hand over his quarters, down the thigh and on to the area you need to clean so that he thinks you are grooming him. With a foreleg, stand at the shoulder and work down his leg. Sweep the cotton wool over the wound in one swift movement, giving a quick dab as you go. Bear in mind that it may be sore and he is likely to flinch but this is understandable and should not be confused with bad behaviour. If he is misbehaving, a firm 'No!' and a swift tug on the lead rope will be required. If he is very unhappy about the wound being touched, use an antiseptic spray from a safe distance to coat the wound.

Poulticing

Poulticing is a common treatment for puncture wounds to the foot and for deep cuts which could become infected. The theory is that the poultice draws out pus and dirt to the surface of the skin, cleaning the wound. The danger with poulticing is that if it is not done properly dirt can remain in the wound causing a deep infection. I know of a horse that had a cut on his leg which was poulticed to help clean the wound, but instead of just doing it for a couple of days, after which the vet should have been called, it was poulticed for well over a couple of weeks. During this time a deep tissue infection developed which was so severe the horse had to be put down. I have been wary of poulticing ever since, and would rather call the vet to have a wound cleaned and dressed properly in the first place. Puncture wounds in the foot can be poulticed but make sure you keep the foot well dressed and clean. Any dirt left on the foot when you apply the poultice can work its way into the foot and in this moist environment an abscess can form, which will erupt at the nearest 'soft' exit point such as the coronary band.

Wiping the eyes and administering ointment

If your horse does not like having his eyes attended to and gets worked up when he sees a piece of cotton wool in your hand, you will have to use subterfuge. Put a head collar on him and tie him up as normal. If your tying-up training has not reached this point, then either place the rope out of the way over his neck, so that you can take hold of it if he tries to leap away, or let it hang to the floor where you can put your foot on it. Keep the cotton wool in one hand and a body brush in the other; groom his face a little before attempting to wipe his eyes and then surreptitiously wipe an eye with your cotton wool, which should already be primed with water or suitable ointment. If you are accurate you should be able to get the ointment into the eye but often ointment comes in a small tube from which the ointment can be squeezed into the corner of the eye. If you are using cotton wool, use a new piece of cotton wool for the other eye so that you do not spread germs from one eye to the other.

Another tactic is to hold the head collar lightly with the hand nearest the horse, and sneak the cotton wool towards the centre of his nose between his nostrils because horses seem to have a blind spot right in front of their faces. Raise the cotton wool to his forehead between his eyes, and then wipe one eye from the inner corner to the outer. He should let you do this with no problem at all. If, however, you approach his eye from the side, he can see the cotton wool coming as his vision to the side and behind him is very clear, and he will most likely shy away from you.

WORMING

If your horse is not wormed regularly, he can develop all manner of internal problems through worm damage. If you keep your horse at livery, the yard most likely has a worming programme, which ensures that horses are wormed on a regular basis, usually every eight weeks, with a rotation of different brands depending on what worms are prevalent at certain times of the year. For example, horses should be wormed for bots around Christmas time once the frost has killed the last of the bot flies.

If you are worming your own horse(s) and you keep them at home and have total control over your fields and their management, i.e. the removal of droppings on a regular basis to reduce the risk of horses picking up worms from each other, worming can be done every 8–12 weeks depending on the brand of wormer used. Read the labels on different brands to work out a suitable programme, or ask your vet for advice.

There are optimum times of year to effectively tackle each type of worm and a suggested programme is as follows.

- Treat for roundworms each time you worm (most brands of wormer deal with roundworms)
- February Treat for small redworm larvae (Panacur)
- March Treat for tapeworm (Pyratape)
- April to August Use a routine wormer (Eqvalan). Change the brand used each year on a three-yearly rotation (e.g. Eqvalan, Pyratape, Panacur, then Eqvalan again).
- September Treat for tapeworm (Pyratape)
- November Treat for small redworm larvae (Panacur)
- December (Christmas time) Treat for bots (Vectin)

Treat a new horse with a five-day course of Panacur Equine Guard followed by a double dose of Equitape on the sixth day to eliminate any worms he may have *before* turning him out in your field, he can then follow the normal worming routine.

Administering wormers

Try to do this with as little fuss and bother as possible. If you are using a wormer in a syringe and you approach your horse's mouth from the side, he will see the wormer coming towards him. Keep the syringe below his nose, then slide it into position between his lips and up the side of his mouth and he should be no problem. Some horses let you get this far and then object to the paste being squirted in. Do it as smoothly and as quickly as you can and, to prevent him spitting it out down your arm, place one hand under his chin and raise his head so that he should swallow the paste. If he does spit some out, retrieve what you can and wipe it along his lips. Give him his dinner immediately after the paste has been administered and hopefully he will lick most of the paste off without noticing it. If squirting the paste into his mouth proves to be a real problem, squirt it into his dinner instead and disguise it with something very tasty. Worming powders or granules that can also be mixed in with feed are other alternatives.

COMMON AILMENTS

Common ailments often occur because of poor stable management: irregular visits from the farrier and not observing early signs of illness or injury can result in lengthy (and expensive) veterinary treatment. You have a responsibility to be observant and caring at all times. Preventing problems is much more sensible than having the worry of treating a sick horse.

Thrush

This can result from a horse standing in wet bedding but it is more commonly caused by not picking out the feet correctly (see Chapter 5). The signs of thrush are a soft, mushy frog which can develop cracks and fissures as the rotten tissue disintegrates, and in bad cases a foul smell will emanate from the feet. This can be detected in the early stages by smelling the feet, but do not get your head that close to the feet if the horse has been known to kick.

PREVENTION

Make sure your horse has a clean, dry stable or field shelter so that he is not standing in wet bedding for long periods of time. His bed must be deep enough to allow any liquid to soak through to the floor, to ensure that he stands on the dry surface of his bed. Skip out frequently and pick his feet out on a regular basis, especially first thing in the morning otherwise he will have muck-packed feet all day. Ask your farrier to trim diseased tissue away as soon as it is discovered so that you can clean the frog properly and maintain healthy feet.

TREATMENT

To treat thrush, arm yourself with a hoof pick, water brush and half a bucket of salty water. Hose the foot first to remove excess mud, pick out the feet carefully making sure all dirt is removed and scrub with the salt water, brushing from the heel to the toe, thus washing any dirt away. Once the foot is scrupulously clean, dry it with a clean cloth. Spray the infected area with an antiseptic spray such as gentian spray, which is purple in colour and available over the counter. If this does not work after a couple of days, you will need to ask your vet for a stronger spray. If you can, get hold of hydrogen peroxide from the chemist. I explain it is for my horse and not because I want to go blonde; chemists often look at me oddly because my hair is quite dark, and so I feel it is best to clarify the matter! Hydrogen peroxide is most effective as a disinfectant. It should be diluted according to the instructions. It will fizz slightly as it gets to work in the hoof. One of the most effective ways of applying it is to get an empty syringe from the vet (without a needle) and squirt it into the cracks in the frog and into the clefts. If you do not have a syringe, put the diluted peroxide into a clean plastic pot and trickle it onto the diseased area, making sure it gets right into all the nooks and crannies. This procedure must be carried out twice a day. If symptoms persist, seek your vet's advice.

Cracked heels and mud fever

With **cracked heels** the skin becomes chapped, sore and splits or cracks. It is a skin irritation that is, more often than not, caused by not grooming the legs properly and is not helped by the horse spending a lot of time out in wet conditions. **Mud fever** is a skin irritation which is usually caused by incorrect grooming and care rather than the mud itself. There is a quote in my old and battered *Pony Club Manual of Horsemanship* which, when referring to the treatment of mud fever, says, 'Call your vet and feel thoroughly ashamed'.

PREVENTION

Correct care of the legs is absolutely essential to prevent such ailments developing in the first place (see Chapter 5) and you must make certain that your horse is not standing for hours on end in wet conditions. Even if he is out at grass all or most of the time, careful field management can ensure that he is not spending too much time in a poached paddock up to his fetlocks in mud. A clean dry field shelter or stable where he can stand in the dry is essential.

TREATMENT

Clean the affected area thoroughly with antiseptic lotion. Dry thoroughly with a *clean* towel or cloth, and dress the affected area with zinc cream. Repeat this daily until the symptoms have cleared up completely. Avoid putting the horse back in the same wet conditions.

Coughing and nasal discharge

Clear or white nasal discharge can appear if your horse is recommencing work after time off. His airways will not have been used to their full extent and the exercise can make the accumulated mucus work its way out via the nasal passages. This discharge should disappear after a day or two.

If the discharge is accompanied by a dry, shallow cough, this means that the horse's airways are being irritated by the dust from the schooling arena or that from the hay and/or bedding you are using, which may not be of the best quality. If the cough is not treated at this stage because you feel that it is not too bad at the moment, within a few days you will have a sick horse with a hacking cough and a discharge of unpleasant yellow mucus.

PREVENTION

The cure is to remove the cause. Change the bedding, get better quality hay, and water the school to lay the dust. You may need to damp the hay or use haylage as a dust-free alternative. The changes may cost you more but respiratory conditions caused by poor stable management can take a long time to cure and there will be vet's bills to pay. In a bad case, your horse may have to be moved to a more airy stable, with rubber matting, or spend more time out in the field.

TREATMENT

If you act immediately, the preventative moves above should cure the cough at the early stage. If things have gone beyond this stage, you need to call the vet who will probably administer antibiotics. To help clear his sinuses, you might have to get your horse to inhale menthol (Vic Vapour Rub or Olbas Oil) mixed with a bucket of hot water to help clear his sinuses. The bucket needs to be only about one third full. Most horses like the smell and will happily hold their noses in the warm vapours, though some may try to drink it. Having plenty of time in the fresh air is the best way for a horse to spend his convalescence.

Girth galls and sore skin

Girth galls are raised patches of injured skin, which usually occur in the girth area behind the elbows where the skin is very soft. Sore skin occurs in the saddle area where the horse has been rubbed by a saddle or roller.

An ill-fitting bridle, or one that is dirty and the leather hard and stiff, can rub the horse behind his ears, in the noseband area, particularly under his chin, and at either end of the browband, at the base of his ears.

PREVENTION

Make sure all your tack fits properly and that you keep it clean and supple. Leather that is well cared for and cleaned and soaped thoroughly is soft and pliable. Today there are many items of webbing tack on the market, which vary in quality. Make sure you buy the softest webbing you can as the harder the material, the more likely it is to rub. The edges of webbing tack can sometimes be quite sharp and actually cut the skin. I have cut my fingers on sharp-edged lunge lines when I have omitted to wear gloves.

Using a well-fitting saddle cloth under the saddle can help but make sure it stays in place and does not wrinkle up as the wrinkles can also rub the horse's skin. If you are starting to work your horse after a rest period, use a padded sleeve over the girth to prevent girth galls; his skin will be extra sensitive if he has not worn a girth for a while.

TREATMENT

Remove the cause. Change your girth, bridle, or saddle depending on what has been rubbing him. If the rub or girth gall is bad, you will not be able to put a saddle or roller on him until the area has totally healed, which can take a couple of weeks or so. Treat the area with a good old-fashioned remedy: salt water. Bathe the area twice a day until it looks less sore and then dress it with zinc ointment to help the skin become less dry and to heal. Wait until it is completely healed before using different, or at least cleaner, tack again.

If a bridle has rubbed your horse, you will not be able to put it, or even a head collar, on him if the rub is very sore. You may need to tie him with a neck strap while the wounds heal. Clean and oil the bridle thoroughly before using it again, and make sure it fits properly.

Sweet itch

Sweet itch is a skin irritation caused by an allergic reaction to midge saliva. Horses and ponies turned out by ponds or streams often suffer more owing to the number of insects. The midges pierce the skin along the crest of the neck and top of the tail where the blood vessels are near the surface. The irritation causes the horse to rub against trees, fence posts, or anything available, making the skin sore and raw, exposing the underlying tissue, which the midges relish, and thus a vicious circle is set in motion.

PREVENTION

The overfeeding of protein can be a contributing factor to the discomfort of sweet itch. Altering your horse's diet to one lower in protein reduces the protein content in the blood, which is then, it is to be hoped, less tempting for insects. Try to avoid turning him out when there are a lot of midges around, i.e. the late afternoon and early evening. Buy him a fly rug with a head and neck cover and belly protection so that the midges cannot get to him. Groom him thoroughly and wash his mane and tail with a mild shampoo to prevent the build up of dirt and grease at the base of the mane and around the dock, which can also attract insects. Dirt harbours germs, which contribute to infection once the skin is rubbed raw. Fly repellents vary in effectiveness, and the only way to find one that works is by trial and error and many people have their own remedies: oil of citronella mixed with cold tea is, I have heard, useful and a friend used to use vinegar mixed with water, though her horse did smell like the local chip shop! Feeding a horse garlic can also make him less attractive to flies.

TREATMENT

There are many ointments on the market to ease the path of sweet itch and relieve the irritation. If in doubt as to the best one for your horse, ask your vet. Douse your horse with fly repellent before turning him out. Work him properly so he actually sweats slightly when he is exercised. This keeps the skin clean as the sweat helps to remove dirt from the coat, provided you are diligent with your grooming!

Laminitis

Laminitis can affect all horses and ponies and usually occurs in the front feet, but it can appear in all four. It is caused by an interruption to the blood supply to the feet which results in necrosis (disintegration) of the laminae in the foot. It is not just caused by too much rich grass, but can also be a result of prolonged work on hard ground, gorging on hard feed (either by being overfed high-protein food or by breaking into the feed room), or toxaemia (after a mare has given birth). Your horse will stand pointing his front feet and taking his weight on his heels. He will be unwilling to move, and may shuffle along if he does. In bad cases, the pedal bone rotates downwards and can pierce the sole of the foot at the point of the frog. The coronet may sink inwards, and the toe of the foot may turn upwards. Laminitic rings will appear on the hoof wall.

PREVENTION

Make sure that any changes in a horse's diet are made gradually (see Chapter 6) and ensure your feed room is secure. Never leave feed bags lying around the yard just in case your horse gets out of his stable and fancies a midnight snack. When turning your horse out into a field that has been rested and the pasture is lush, do not leave him out all day; restrict his grazing to an hour or two.

Work your horse sensibly, especially if the ground is hard, and make sure you warm him up and cool him off by walking him for at least ten minutes at the beginning and end of each schooling session so that his blood circulation has a chance to remove any toxins from his body.

TREATMENT

Remove the cause (unless it has already been consumed). Call the vet who will administer pain killers and drugs to help the flow of blood improve. Support the frogs of the affected feet with a rolled up bandage secured in place by an adhesive bandage such as Vetwrap. Do not force the horse to move around. Cold hosing of the feet can give some relief from the pain. The treatment is long-term and the feet will need regular trimming and surgical shoes to support the frog. Supplements such as biotin will help healthy, new horn to grow.

11 CLIPPING

EXPERIENCING CLIPPING FOR the first time can be a frightening experience for your horse, particularly if it is done incorrectly and so it is very important to introduce him to clipping in a way that will avoid problems.

The simplest way to get your horse clipped is to ask someone who is a very experienced clipper to do the job for you. Another solution is to ask them to teach you how to clip and then to buy your own clippers. Clipping your own horse is convenient: you can do it when you need to, and it is often easier to do yourself simply because your horse knows and trusts you. If he is wary of strangers, or takes a dislike to the person you have picked to clip him, you might not have any choice. On the other hand, an experienced person will get the job done quickly, a definite plus point if your horse is not too keen on standing still while someone takes ages to clip him.

There is, however, nothing like the satisfaction of clipping your own horse and seeing a good result at the end of it. You may be slow at first, so just clip a small area (see the listing of clip types – in order of body area clipped – on page 197–199). You may need to expand this area if your horse still gets too hot, so progress to the next clip on the list. This is much more sensible than tackling a blanket clip, for example, the first time you use your clippers.

TO CLIP OR NOT TO CLIP?

Clipping is usually done during the winter months. The horse grows a thicker coat as protection from the winter weather but this can cause him to become too hot when he is ridden (this is not to be confused with the anxiety-induced sweating caused by poor riding technique). This coat growth is triggered by the shortening of the days, not by the worsening weather.

Most horses need their first clip of the year during October, followed by a second around the New Year. Your horse should not be clipped after February as his new summer coat starts to grow when the days become longer again; this will be made plain by the amount of hair he sheds when you groom him.

The more time your horse or pony spends at grass and the lighter his work load, the less he should be clipped. Removing too much coat will leave him cold and miserable if you do not rug him up adequately (see Chapter 8). Remember, the more you clip off, the more rugs you will need to keep your horse warm in the field and in the stable. On the other hand, a woolly-coated horse that is getting too hot when he is ridden will sweat excessively if he is not clipped and he will take ages to dry. If your horse is working comfortably without being clipped, then you do not need to remove any coat at all. Breeds with finer hair, such as Thoroughbreds, will not need to be clipped unless they are doing fast work. My Warmblood, Trevor, has a much finer coat than my Lipizzaner, Amadeus, so I clip them differently as a rule.

A clipped horse is easier to keep clean as the sweaty areas will dry more quickly, and mud is less likely to cling to a short coat. Washing and drying a horse after exercise is far easier than with a long-coated horse (see Chapter 5).

Clipping makes your horse look smart, but it should not be done just for that reason. Competing horses are often clipped all over for appearance sake, but Amadeus, a dressage horse, can be prone to bouts of bucking if he has a cold backside and so I just give him a blanket clip which keeps his back and quarters warm and increases my chances of staying on board! Leaving a saddle patch of hair is a good idea as it acts as a natural saddle pad affording the horse's skin some protection from being rubbed by the saddle.

Take into account your horse's individual needs. If he feels the cold, it would not be a good idea to clip too much hair off as he will lose condition quickly, and you will need to increase his feed to maintain his weight (see Chapter 6). Older horses often feel the cold more than youngsters and generally will not require much coat taken off. A horse's temperament also has a bearing on the type of clip he may need. If he is rather excitable, beware giving him a full clip and then riding him out on a frosty morning;

you may get more impulsion than you bargained for! Take care when doing up the girth on a clipped belly: the skin will be exposed and therefore more sensitive to the feel of the girth if you do it up too suddenly, particularly if the girth is cold. If your horse is always sensitive about the girth being done up, a clip will make him more so and he may show his displeasure by swishing his tail, giving you a nip or, at the very least, pull faces at you.

If you are riding a clipped horse, protecting his quarters from the chilly air with an exercise blanket helps his muscles to warm up before a training session and can protect him if you are out for a hack in inclement weather. A cold horse is a miserable one and may well misbehave, giving you a stressful ride, and a hot horse will become distressed and breathe heavily. It would be sensible to lunge your horse before riding him if he has just been clipped. The feeling of a chilly breeze around his nether regions can cause any horse to buck and squeal, so it is best to get this out of the way before you venture into the saddle!

PREPARATION FOR CLIPPING

Dress appropriately and have everything you need to hand, preferably just outside the stable out of the way of the horse. You will need the following.

- Rubber-soled shoes or boots.
- Overalls to protect your clothes from loose hair (waterproof ones are good as the hair does not cling to the material).
- Mounting block or grooming stool that is sturdy to stand on.
- Clippers.
- Extension lead.
- Dry bucket.
- Hay net.
- Head collar and lead rope.
- A shallow plastic dish (a freezer container is ideal) with about an inch of methylated, or surgical, spirit in it for cooling the clipper blades.
- Cloth for drying the clipper blades.
- Spray lubricant.
- Small brush for cleaning hair away from the air vents on the clippers so that they do not get hot too quickly.

- Body brush to remove loose hair from the coat once each area has been clipped.
- A rug to put on your horse so that he does not get cold; this can be folded accordingly to expose the next part of him to be clipped.
- Broom and barrow, or skip, to clear up the hair.
- Pieces of baler twine for measuring the height of the clip.
- Chalk for marking.

It is important to start with a clean horse. It can be very embarrassing to see a layer of grey grease appearing as the hair is clipped off especially if you have hired a professional person to do it for you; clipping always reveals your standard of grooming! Lumps of dried-on mud block the action of the clipper blades and can cause them to drag at the hairs rather than cut them. This is a very unpleasant experience for your horse and he will most likely wince as his hair is pulled. If he has too many similar unpleasant experiences, do not be surprised if he is not keen on being clipped the next time you try to do it.

The best time to clip a horse is after he has been exercised and he is relaxed enough to stand still for you during the duration of the clipping session, bearing in mind it could take you a while until you become more adept. Bringing a fresh horse in from the field on a blustery day and expecting him to co-operate is rather ambitious. A fidgety horse leads to crooked clip lines and a very unprofessional finish. Choose a quiet time at the yard so that you can get on with the job quickly and quietly. There is nothing more frustrating than lining the clippers up for a good sweep when someone stops for a chat and distracts you, or your horse moves at the wrong moment to see who is going past.

If the weather is inclement it is best to clip your horse in his stable. Bad weather will make him restless and he will become cold more quickly outside. Fork the bedding in his box to one side so it does not become full of hair, and tie up a hay net for him, which provides him with something to occupy him and also keeps his head and neck in a good position for reaching him with the clippers. Good lighting is essential; you must be able to see what you are doing otherwise you could get a nasty shock when your handiwork is revealed in broad daylight. If the stable is too dark, then you will have to clip outside. Choose a quiet corner of the yard where you will not be in the way and you are less likely to be interrupted.

Move the water buckets out of the stable to keep them clean and to remove the risk of marrying electricity and water; electrocuting yourself by dropping the clippers in a bucket of water is not a good idea! You will need an extension lead in good order, without any chewed flex or bare wires, and fitted with a circuit breaker. It should be plugged into a convenient socket, out of the way of neighbouring horses who may try to chew it and without having to trail it all over the yard ready for some poor soul with a full barrow of muck to trip over it.

Plug the clippers into the extension lead and, remembering that electricity and water do not mix, put the socket into a *dry* bucket (Figure 11.1). The bucket enables you to move the lead around the stable without the horse standing on the plug and socket and breaking them.

Clipper maintenance and adjustment

Figure 11.1 Place the extension lead in a clean, dry bucket to prevent your horse standing on the socket

Make sure your clippers and their flex are in good condition, and that your blades are sharp. Starting to clip and finding that your blades are chomping away without much effect can lead to a very long job, or failure to complete the clip. Blunt blades pull at the coat and the clippers have to work harder, causing them to get hot very quickly. The clippers will wear out sooner and worn-out clippers give a choppy, moth-eaten finish to a clip. The blades and clippers require an annual overhaul and it is best to do this once you have finished clipping for the year. The blades may need sharpening more often depending on how much clipping you do.

Adjusting the tension screw on the

186

clipper blades so that they work efficiently takes a bit of practice and, as each horse's coat varies in thickness, it is usually a case of trial and error to get it right so that the blades slide easily through the coat. If the screw is too loose the blades will struggle to clip; if it is too tight, the clippers will work, but become hot very quickly. If you switch the clippers off and feel the base plate of the blades it will be hot to touch and it is most unpleasant for your horse to have hot clippers against his skin. He will probably become fidgety once they get too hot for him and so watch his reactions as you work. If the blades are hot, clear the air vents with the small brush supplied with the clippers and cool them off in a shallow dish of methylated, or surgical, spirit for a few minutes. Dry the blades when cool and spray with lubricant before resuming clipping. If you do this frequently before they overheat, they will cool more quickly and you lessen the risk of burning out the clipper motor.

HOW TO CLIP

Introducing clippers for the first time

First, read the instructions! Make sure you are familiar with the sound of the clippers when they are running and practise using the tension screw, listening for a change in sound as you tighten it up. Switch the clippers on while you are grooming so that your horse gets used to the sound. I find that often it is the noise of the clippers that causes the problem, not the actual clipping, and so putting the radio on might help as the background noise disguises their sound.

Before commencing this next stage, you must remember to try to work calmly and confidently, if your horse becomes nervous you need to know that it is because of the clippers – so that you can deal with it accordingly – and not because he is reacting to your nervousness. Working with clippers is a new experience for you as well as your horse, try to adopt a good comfortable posture as you clip so that you do not become tense and tired because, again, your horse will pick up on the tension. Run the clippers along his shoulder just above the coat, pretending to clip. If he stands quietly, switch them off again and resume grooming. Repeat this exercise a couple of times. If he does not react adversely, you can go ahead with a simple clip, just on his chest and neck (see page 197). Again, food is an incentive for good behaviour: a large hay net while he is being clipped works well and having a clipping session before dinner time means that he gets his feed as soon as you have finished the clip.

If your horse is frightened when you switch the clippers on, find the smallest, quietest pair you can that will still clip the coat; I borrow the dog's clippers. Hold the end of his rope rather than tie him up so that you can move with him if he steps back and he cannot pull back on the tie-ring. Before switching them on, run the clippers over his coat either on his shoulder or the underside of his neck. Do this until he accepts it and stands quietly, then stop. If he becomes tense, keep still with the clippers touching him; once he relaxes, take them away and praise him.

Repeat the same procedure with the clippers running and clip a small area. If he is tense, keep the clippers on him until he relaxes, then turn them off and praise him. Do this in short stages each day. You will have a horse with small clipped areas for a few days, but hopefully they will all join up eventually! As stated, only attempt a 'bib' clip or a stripe up the base of the neck for the first couple of times.

When a horse becomes tense or misbehaves, most people's reaction is to take the clippers off. He soon works out that if he is tense or naughty the clipping stops and so he does it even more. Teach him that if he is calm and still the clippers stop, this is far more effective in my experience. Once your horse is happy with the small, quiet clippers, you should be able to progress to larger ones. If he becomes tense again, go back to the small ones.

As soon as you feel confident handling the clippers, you can start to take more hair off if you need to. Clipping should be done in a matter-of-fact way and it should not become a big issue. By all means praise your horse, but going overboard will make him think he has come through something really scary and he may be more wary next time.

Clear loose hair away from clipped areas with a body brush so you can see what you are doing. A dandy brush would be too harsh to use on your horse's skin. If you are taking a lot of coat off, place a rug over the area you have done so that your horse does not become cold – another cause of fidgeting, which leads to crooked lines!

Marking out the clip

Decide which type of clip is appropriate for your horse (see pages 197–199). Mark out the clip lines by running your finger nail against the coat to raise a line of hairs that you can follow.

White chalk on dark horses and charcoal on lighter colours can be useful. I have heard of water-based felt-tip pen being used to draw either a solid line or intermittent dots along the line of the clip - but make sure you clip the 'ink' off, and on no account use a permanent marker pen. Red lines on a grey horse do stand out! With practice, you should be able to get a matching clip on both sides by eye. Check from the front to see if the line of the clip looks the same on both sides of the chest (e.g. with a trace clip) and on both hind legs at the back.

To get the lines along the belly (as in a trace or blanket clip) at the same height on both sides, Use a piece of baler twine to measure where the clip line should go: place one end of the twine just behind the withers on your horse's spine; hold the other end and pull it taut down to where you want to clip the line. Tie a knot at this height. You can then check both sides of the clip by measuring with the twine. There is nothing worse than guessing and chopping off too much. If you do make a mistake, you may need to redesign your clip accordingly. I have done some rather unusual clips myself over the years!

Clip one side of the horse at a time to save you having to move around too much with the extension lead. A good place to begin is low on the shoulder, as this area is clipped with most types of clip. Also, as with most things you do around horses, begin on the nearside; this should help him relax because it is what he is used to.

Switch on the clippers holding them away from the horse to make sure he is not worried by the noise. If you followed the directions at the beginning of this chapter, he should be fine. Gently bring the clippers into contact with his coat, and confidently glide the blades up the shoulder against the lie of the coat. Follow the marked lines to outline the clip on the nearside and then complete the clip within the outline before repeating the whole procedure on the offside. Your horse is more likely to stand still at the beginning of the session so it is easier to get an accurate outline now rather than later on.

Clipping the neck

When clipping the neck, make sure you get a straight line along the crest where the coat meets the mane. Angle the clipper blades slightly so that the edge of the blade nearest to the base of the mane is pressed more firmly against the coat to help you keep the line straight (Figures 11.2a and b). Clip from the withers towards the ears.

If your horse is tall, position yourself on a mounting block or grooming stool (it must not wobble otherwise you could lose your balance) in line with the centre of his neck so that you can reach both ends of his neck easily. Standing too near the withers can mean you are over-stretching once you get near his ears and it is at this point he is more likely to move, you do, therefore, need to keep a steady hand and not fall off the mounting block. Even the odd snort from your horse can result in a wobble of the clippers and you can end up with a choppy line, or a chunk out of the mane. If you have any doubts about the steadiness of your hand, plait the mane so that it is easier to slide your spare hand underneath to lift it out of the way of the clippers. If you do not plait the mane, brush the mane over onto one side of his neck so you have a clear run with the clippers on the mane-free side, which is vital to a smooth finish. Take care on the side on which the mane lies naturally.

Clipping the head

If the head is to be clipped, do it next while he is still happy to stand quietly. Begin on his cheek as it is broad and flat and less fiddly. You can do this with the large clippers but small clippers should be used if possible because they are quieter and better for manoeuvring around the head.

Clip the side of his face up to where the cheek piece of the bridle would lie, i.e. a straight line from the corner of the horse's mouth up to just behind the base of his ear, moving the head-collar cheek piece out of the way. A blade guard can be used to avoid cutting the hair too short (Figure 11.3). A blade guard clips on to the underside of the clipper blades and protects the skin from too close a shave.

This is as far as you will get with a great many horses, and it is really all that is necessary. If your horse will not tolerate the clippers near his face, then leave it. You could trim his whiskers under his chin, either with small clippers, or scissors, and leave it at that. He will be quite smart enough.

Clipping the whole of the horse's face is only necessary for showing purposes, and so if you are only clipping the head because you choose to, make sure that the horse is happy with the procedure otherwise it is not worth putting both of you through the possible battle and upset. Remember that the horse's coat protects his skin from the elements and injury. Riding under thorny trees could lead to scratches on his face and so leaving hair at least on the front of his face is advisable.

Take care around the eyes and ears: do not clip the eye lids and do not remove the hair from inside the ears. To clip the ears, take the ear in your free hand and gently close the edges together. This deadens the noise and protects the inside of the ear from loose hair (Figure 11.4). Long hair along the edge of the ear can be removed by running the clippers along it.

Clipping the hindquarters

You might find it easier to bandage the tail before starting the hindquarters, but it is just as easy to hold the tail to one side with your free hand. Make sure the clipper flex is not trailing around your horse's hind legs just in case he moves and stands on it, or in case the feel of the flex against his legs spooks him. Begin clipping the line across the lower part of the buttocks. Do both hind legs while you are in the position to do so, so that you get the line at the same height on both sides. This is easier to see if your horse is standing square. If he rests a hind leg at the wrong moment, you will end up with one line higher than the other. Clip upwards towards his tail. If you are doing a trace clip, remove a wide strip of hair on each side of the hindquarters from the top of the leg to correspond with the line along the belly. The lower edge of the strip runs from the top of the thigh muscle at the back of the leg to the stifle joint. The upper line is horizontal and at the same height as the line along the belly. The whorl of hair above the stifle joint can be neatly clipped off in an 'arch' (Figures 11.5a and b). Once you have clipped the back end, move to one side and continue along his body according to the clip you have chosen to do.

Clipping the belly

To clip the belly, you have to work upside down (Figure 11.6). Make sure that you clip against the coat between the hind legs (how much you can do

191

a

Figure 11.2a and b a) Clipping along the crest: angle the clippers to get a smooth edge and make sure the mane is out of the way.

b

b) Take care when clipping along the crest that you do not cut the mane with the clippers otherwise your horse will sport a Mohican hair cut when the mane grows back.

Figure 11.3 Clip the face up to where the cheek piece would lie using the small clippers. A blade guard should be used particularly if your horse fidgets.

Figure 11.4 Fold the ear gently in half to keep it flat and to deaden the noise of the clippers slightly.

a

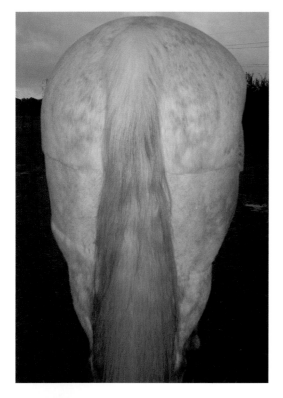

b

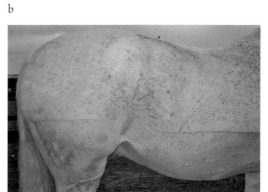

Figures 11.5a and b a) With a trace and blanket clip a wide strip of hair is removed around the quarters; b) the lower edge of the strip runs from the top of the thigh muscle to the stifle joint, clipping the whorl of hair neatly in an arch. The upper edge corresponds with the line along the belly.

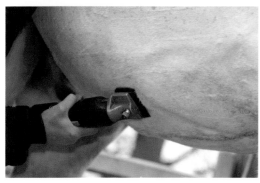

Figure 11.6 Clipping the belly requires being able to clip upside down.

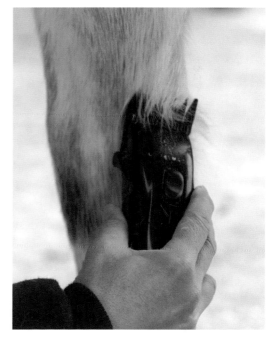

Figure 11.7 Trimming the legs with small clippers and a blade guard.

Figure 11.8 Trimming the legs with full-size clippers and a comb.

Figure 11.9 Clipping around the top of the tail leaving a triangle of hair.

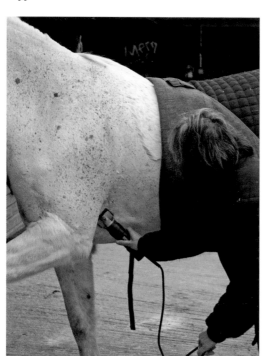

Figure 11.10 Clipping the elbow region.

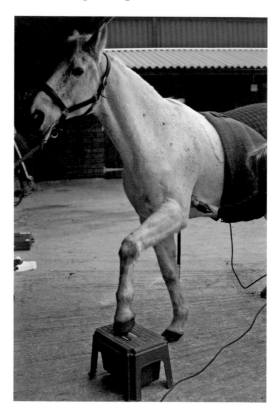

Figure 11.11 Stretching the skin flat is made easier if you have an assistant to hold your horse's leg for you. Amadeus has learnt to place his foot on a box to help out!

here depends on your horse's reaction to you wielding the clippers around the genital area in the stallion or gelding and the udder in the mare) and along the belly. The belly can be a rather expansive area, depending on how large your horse is, so you may need to have a rest to straighten out your back and neck. Clipping the belly is usually straightforward and another good place to start if you are new to clipping; no-one can see your mistakes unless they lie flat on the floor!

Trimming the legs

Trimming the legs is much easier than clipping them. You will need either a comb, or a blade guard to avoid trimming the hair too close (Figures 11.7 and 11.8). If you are using a comb, run it against the hair up the back of the leg and clip the ends of the hair that poke through the teeth of the comb so that you just trim the length of the hair rather than shaving it all off. This can also be done with scissors if you prefer.

Clipping around the tail

Again, if you have a tall horse, stand on something sturdy so that you can reach the area easily and so that you have an aerial view of your horse's rump. Starting a short distance down from the top of the tail run the clippers from the edge of the tail hair towards the centre of his back for 10–12 cm (4–5 in) on each side of his dock. The lines will meet in the centre of his back a few centimetres away from the top of his tail to leave a neat triangle of hair (Figure 11.9). You will need to do this if you are doing a blanket, hunter or full clip.

Clipping the elbow region and between the front legs

Clipping the elbow region can be the trickiest part of the horse to clip neatly (Figure 11.10). If you have an assistant, ask them to pull your horse's front leg forwards to stretch the skin taut under his elbow. If you are on your own, you can pull (gently) the skin taut with your free hand as you clip. I have taught Amadeus to stand with one front foot on a mounting block, which makes clipping his elbow area much easier, and is not dissimilar to the horse placing his foot on the farrier's stand when having his feet trimmed (Figure 11.11).

195

The skin between the front legs is also quite wrinkly and so you also have to pull sections taut on this area. You need to run the clippers from behind the elbows towards the chest against the hair. Again, this area is out of sight and so you can get away with a few missed patches! It is probably easier to work from the side and clip against the lay of the hair, although you do need to be a bit of a contortionist to see what you are doing.

Finally, clear up your mess. There is nothing worse than leaving loose hair to blow all over the yard, especially if the weather is wet. Loose hair sticks to wet ground and is a devil to sweep up! If you have clipped in the stable, remove all loose hair before putting your horse's bed back down. Then, if you have missed any, it lies on the floor under the bed and can be removed when mucking out the next day.

DEALING WITH A HORSE THAT HATES BEING CLIPPED

Some horses just hate being clipped and are frightened to death of the clippers. This is usually because of a previous bad experience but some horses are very sensitive to the noise of the clippers and break out in a sweat at the first sign of an extension lead. Some owners resort to sedation by the vet to tackle the task, but you risk the horse wobbling around or even falling over if he has too much, or still being aware enough of what's going on to kick the vet, you or anything else if he is not sufficiently sedated. This is certainly a 'quick fix' solution but I have never resorted to this.

Using a twitch is another way. You can make a twitch fairly easily by drilling a hole in the end of a 60 cm (2 ft) long piece of broom handle and passing a piece of thin soft rope through the hole, tying the rope to form a loop. This loop is passed over the horse's top lip, and the broom handle twisted to close the rope around the lip. This must be firm enough so that your horse cannot wriggle his lip out of the loop but it must be slackened off every few minutes to allow the horse's circulation to flow. When the loop is tightened, relaxing endorphins, i.e. natural painkillers, are released by the horse's brain to help him feel calm. This probably works in the same way as my method of digging my fingernails into the palm of my hand to help me cope with being in the dentist's chair: it takes my mind off the whirring and prodding!

I have only ever used a twitch to make the vet's job easier at the time of an emergency, never for clipping.

Sedating or twitching a horse in order to clip him does not tackle the root of the problem. Sedation is expensive and organizing a time and date with the vet that also suits someone brave enough to clip your horse under these circumstances can take some doing. It is far better either not to clip your horse at all, but to be particular about his care when he is sweaty after work, or to start from the beginning again to teach him to accept the clippers and clipping; this will take time, but is the best and only way in the long term. Remember that if a horse has a fine coat and does not get sweaty when he is worked, he will not need to be clipped anyway.

WHICH CLIP IS SUITABLE?

Neck and chest

Removing the hair from the underside of the neck and the front of the chest is a practical solution if your horse is taking a long time to cool down after exercise but still needs the protection of his coat in the field if he spends a lot of time outside. This is a good clip to start with and easy to do.

Begin with the chest as this is the furthest area away from his head, and allows him to get used to the clippers before you get too close to his head. On the chest there are two areas of hair, known as whorls, that grow upwards and outwards and you need to make sure you clip against the hair to achieve a smooth finish. Follow the grooves under the neck up to the jaw line, along either side of the horse's gullet and remove the hair along his wind pipe.

Belly

Clipping the belly, following a straight line between the elbows and the stifles, can make it a lot easier to brush off splashed mud, as the area will dry quickly. This can be combined with clipping the underside of the neck; this combination is sometimes called a bib and belly clip and is also suitable for horses spending most of their time in the field.

Neck and shoulders

This is one of my favourite clips because it is quick to do; it looks smart, and is easy to mark out. Clip a straight line from just behind the elbows up to the withers, like the front edge of a rug, and then clip off all the neck hair up to the jaw line. The head can either be left unclipped, or half-clipped. This is a useful clip for most types of horse and pony in average work such as hacking, or dressage and show jumping at riding club level.

Trace clip

With a trace clip, the hair is clipped away from further up the belly at the height the traces would be if your horse was in harness. The coat from the lower half of the neck is removed, the head either left unclipped, or half-clipped. The line of the clip extends around the hindquarters, exposing a strip from stifle joint up to this line. Again, this clip is useful for a horse with an average work load.

Racing clip

This is a more streamlined clip than a trace clip and easy to do if you are not very good at getting the lines even on both sides of the horse! Hair is removed from the lower half of the horse in a straight line from the stifle joint to the base of the ear. The coat on the hindquarters is left unclipped so that the horse does not get a chilly back. Clipping the head is optional. A racing clip is useful for most types of work.

Blanket clip

Hair from the neck, chest, belly and haunches is removed, leaving the shape of a blanket covering the top of the horse's back. The head is usually half-clipped. It is used for horses that are working at competition level when they would be too hot in the previously described clips.

Hunter clip

A hunter clip involves clipping the whole body except for a saddle patch. The legs are left unclipped to protect them from injury from thorns etc. but they can be trimmed. The head is either fully or half-clipped. A horse needing a hunter clip will be doing quite strenuous work and probably competing in dressage, show jumping, or eventing.

Full clip

The entire coat is removed from the body, head and legs. This clip is usually unnecessary unless you are showing or competing at a high level and need to look extremely smart. Exposing the saddle area and legs leaves these areas vulnerable to injury, such as scratches or cuts on the legs, or sore places under the saddle and they must be monitored carefully.

12 LOADING AND TRAVELLING

LOADING AND TRAVELLING your horse for the first time can be a very daunting experience. You have to cope with shoving your pride and joy into a vehicle that is going to sway and bounce along the road, frightening him to death, so that he emerges at the other end a nervous wreck and you cannot even get on him, let alone compete. Your finger nails are bitten down to the quick and you have palpitations, your hair is a mess and your white breeches are speckled with horse dribble and grease from the ramp springs. Nothing can be more frustrating that getting ready for an outing to find that your horse refuses to load, or takes so long to go in that you miss your class. Loading to come home can be as traumatic, if not more so, because you are both tired and everyone else has gone home and left you to it.

But it does not have to be like this at all; good training with careful preparation and a lot of common sense will help smooth the path.

Training your horse to load must be done in a safe environment and it is important to take the time to train him calmly, making sure that he is not frightened. If your horse has confidence in you at all times, loading him into a horsebox or trailer should be just another phase in his training. Gaining his trust is essential to overcoming problems caused by bad experiences that will take time and much patience to eradicate. It is, therefore, imperative that you get it right in the first place. If your horse is new to you, and you do not know how experienced a traveller he is, go through all the stages of training just to make sure there are no problems. If you have difficulties, then retrace your tracks and start again. Buying a new horse and expecting him to go with you to a show and perform well two days later is not entirely realistic unless you are extremely lucky, a very confident person in all situations or, of course, unless you have purchased a horse that loads well all ready.

Training horses to load happily is best tackled when the horse is young and impressionable but many older horses have not received this training and find travelling traumatic, and so it may take you a little longer to train them.

A good loader is a must for any kind of competition be they small local events or bigger competitions further afield. Even if you do not plan to compete with your horse, he will probably need to travel at some point in his life: going to new and exciting hacking destinations; on holiday; to the vet for X-rays or treatment; to a new yard; or to a new owner. Easy, stress-free loading and travelling will make your life together much safer and happier and so it is worth investing the time in training your horse to load and travel confidently.

If your horse sees loading as an enjoyable game, you should have many pleasant years ahead when you can load up and go wherever you like with him. You need to adapt your training strategy to match the character of your horse: a sensitive horse requires gentle persuasion, whereas a strong-willed animal might need a more dominant approach. But bear in mind that even a strong-minded horse should never be forced into submission because this causes tension and, although you might get a short-term result, in the long run it will be disastrous and you could end up getting hurt, particularly as you are in this instance working on the ground at close quarters with your horse. Calm firm handling is the best approach; it is essential to be in charge but you do this by winning your horse's respect, not by dominating or undermining him.

TRAINING EXERCISES

Leading between poles and jumps

You do not need access to a trailer or horsebox when you start your training. All you need to use initially is two poles placed parallel to each other 2 m (6½ ft) apart in your schooling arena. Begin by lungeing your horse in your normal fashion to relax him and to make sure he is listening to you. Once he is in a co-operative frame of mind, lead him in walk between the poles and halt between them. Leading your horse with a lunge line offers you a bit more leeway if you encounter any leaping around! After walking and halting between the poles three or four times, lead your horse around the arena to finish the training session. Over the next few sessions, build up to lungeing him between the poles in trot. He may peer at them with suspicion at first, but providing you stay calm he should relax quickly. The poles accustom him to going through a narrow gap calmly and straight.

You can advance this work by leading him between two jumps. Have two pairs of plastic blocks or straw bales with a pole on each pair to form a barrier. Place them about 4 m (13 ft) apart at first until your horse does this happily, then gradually reduce the gap to about 2 m (6¹/₂ ft). It must be wide enough for both you and your horse to pass through comfortably.

Walking and lungeing over different surfaces
WALKING OVER PLASTIC

The next stage is to give the horse a surface to walk on that is unfamiliar to him. Using the two poles on the ground, insert a sheet of plastic, which has the advantage of being portable and weather resistant, in between the poles, making sure that you secure both sides of the plastic under the poles. It may help to have two parallel poles in front of the plastic to guide your horse towards it. Lead him calmly towards the plastic; look ahead and walk calmly and confidently forward, you will thus reassure and encourage him to follow your positive lead. If he hesitates and pulls back, halt with him, keeping a quiet steady contact on the lunge line. If you pull him, he will pull back and become either anxious or cross, depending on his mentality. Remember that any indecisiveness you may feel he will read in your body language, and so be really calm and positive in your attitude and never get angry. When your horse relaxes, walk on again. If he follows you, speak calmly and nicely to him, and pat or rub him. If he is good, reward him; if he misunderstands or is difficult, be clear and determined!

Stay by his shoulder so that you can see his facial expressions, which are your early warning signal of any tension or adverse reactions. It is important that you walk over the plastic with him. He may stop and look at it, especially if he puts one foot on it and he hears the crackling noise it makes, and so you need to stand on it and shuffle your feet to show him there is nothing to fear. Once he starts to move forward he may race over the plastic at speed, so be ready to move with him. If you get left behind, he may well get away from you and head off around the school. If this happens and he is running about trailing the line behind him, just stay calm and approach him when he slows down or stops. If your reactions are quick, you may be able to creep closer to him, and catch the end of the line as he passes you. Do not pull it, but gradually take up the contact and bring him around on a circle, remaining calm, and use your voice to steady him. This is a very good reason for training your horse to respond to voice aids in your leading and lungeing training.

Repeat this exercise at the end of your next few training sessions until your horse walks over the plastic happily. He should follow you calmly, without you needing to take a firm contact on the lunge rein. If your horse feels you grab the line, he will probably pull back. Always keep a relaxed, kind contact on the end of the line, but be prepared to close your hand to take a firmer contact if he tries to jerk away, holding it just firmly enough to ensure that he cannot pull it out of your hand.

LUNGEING OVER PLASTIC

The next phase is to lunge him over the plastic. Do this in walk first at the end of a normal lunge session (see Chapter 14). Because you are not walking beside him now, he may lose a bit of confidence and so you should be prepared for him to scoot around the poles either to the inside or the outside. If this happens because he does not have the confidence to go over the plastic straight away, move one of the poles so that there is a small gap of ground between it and the plastic. Your horse should then go between the poles but he can now stay close to the plastic without actually placing his feet on it. Once he realizes it is not going to jump up and bite him on the knees, he should be happy to step on it again. You must take as long as is required to get your horse to walk over the plastic confidently; he must trust you at every stage, otherwise getting him into a trailer or lorry could be difficult. Go over the plastic two or three times, then lunge him away from it for a minute or two so that he can relax again, and then lunge him over the plastic again.

As every horse is different in his tolerance of new things, it is important not to push things too far and to stop when he has done well. Turning him out in the field to have time to think about and absorb the last lesson and, importantly, to relax, is a good reward for a horse after any training session.

WALKING OVER MARINE PLY

At this point it is a good idea to lead him over a sheet of marine ply, similar to that used for the flooring in trailers. As with the plastic, a pole placed either side of the ply will act as barriers, and two parallel poles in front of the ply will help to guide him over it in a straight line. Practise halting on it, and then walking off it again. When a horse puts a foot on a trailer ramp for the first time the sound may make him panic because it might be unlike any sound he has heard before. It can, therefore, be useful to get him accustomed to walking over a simulated ramp before trying the real thing.

'UNLOADING' OVER DIFFERENT SURFACES

If you have a rear-unload trailer, your horse will have to exit the trailer backwards, and teaching him to back over the pole-secured plastic and the marine ply will establish the technique before he gets in the trailer.

PREPARING A TRAILER OR HORSEBOX FOR SAFE TRAINING

When a horse is ready to progress to a trailer or horsebox there are some very important points you must be aware of: the chosen vehicle must be safe and in good condition in order that the horse does not have any unnecessary worries or frights; the horsebox or trailer must be big enough for your horse, many problems can be avoided if he has sufficient headroom and clearance in front and behind. It is also a good idea to train your horse to load in both a trailer and a horsebox because it is very likely that he will have to travel in both at some stage.

Make sure that you park your horsebox or trailer in a safe enclosed place; in the school is ideal, if you can get the vehicle in there, as you have space to lunge your horse to settle him before attempting loading. Initially, it helps to park near a fence to discourage horses that step off the side of the ramp and for the first few loading attempts a low ramp is less intimidating for a horse than a steep one.

If you are using a trailer, open the front ramp (if it has one) to make the interior look lighter, more inviting and less claustrophobic, and ensure that you have a clear passage through the trailer so that you can exit down the front ramp if necessary. If the trailer only has a back ramp, remove the central partition so that there is no risk of you becoming trapped. Many horses load better without the central partition as they feel less hemmed in. With a side-loading trailer or horsebox, make sure all partitions are fastened, or removed, so that they do not accidentally swing against your horse and frighten him.

Check the vehicle's floor; you do not want to load your horse only to have him put a foot through the floor and be frightened or hurt. All door hinges and partition fastenings must work easily. Getting a horse to load successfully is a waste of time if you have to struggle with bolts that are out of line or rusted solid because he could be out again before you have a chance to secure him.

If you will be travelling primarily on your own, you need to practise loading on your own but, in the early stages, it helps to have a calm, confident assistant to open and close the ramps for you, to be on hand for moral support and to help you catch him should he break free.

Have some treats in your pocket to reward your horse once he is in but avoid using food to actually get him in; this works a few times but you will then find that, instead of expecting a reward when he is in, your horse will demand it before he steps on to the ramp. Ponies are particularly good at developing giraffe-like necks, which allow them to reach a bribe while keeping all four feet planted firmly on the ground!

HOW TO LOAD

Attach a lunge line to a control halter or lunge cavesson so that if he does pull back, you have a better chance of holding on to him than you would with a lead rope. A control halter has a tightening action which comes into play should the horse select reverse gear and loosens as soon as either you ease the tension on the rope or he stops pulling. Always wear gloves to protect your hands. Rope burns are extremely painful and take a while to heal.

Approach the ramp in the same way you tackled the plastic and the marine ply but with your assistant, if you have one, standing to one side of the trailer near the ramp. Walk calmly and confidently up the ramp, expecting your horse to follow you (Figure 12.1). He should trust you by now and walk slowly up beside you. If he does, stand with him holding the rope in a relaxed manner.

If your horse stops to look at, or puts his feet on, the ramp and will not go any further, look straight ahead and keep a steady contact on the rope to stop him going backwards. If you have an assertive horse, carry a schooling whip so that you can tap him on his side to encourage him forwards, rather than have someone behind him brandishing a stick, because this generally causes more problems. Avoid trying to pull him in, as he will probably pull back with more strength than you can muster. If he goes backwards go with him, but avoid turning around and staring at him which may put him off. Keep looking forward into the trailer, thinking, 'what a lot of room there is, and what a nice place to go into'. If you are worried that it will all go wrong then your horse will not go in. Think only positive thoughts and just walk

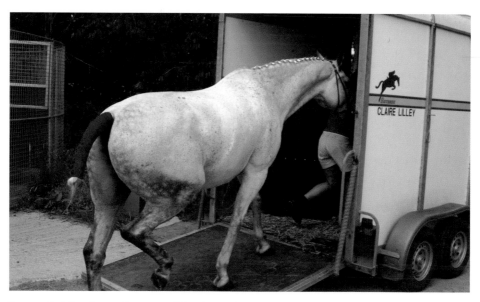

Figure 12.1 Lead your horse confidently up the ramp.

calmly up the ramp. Remembering to breathe can help to keep you relaxed. Even after a moment of hesitation like this, your horse should follow you in if he trusts you.

If, however, your horse refuses to budge and appears to be rooted to the spot, ask your assistant to place her hand on his haunches (making sure that she stands to one side of him and not directly behind in case he hits reverse gear fast) and gently rock him a little. This often encourages a horse to step forward again. If he stops again, repeat the rocking until he walks up the ramp. As soon as he takes one step forward, relax the rope. Your horse should then work out that it is nicer to go forward than backward. Praise him when he is good and, again, stand firm if he rebels. Patience is imperative; allow plenty of time to deal with a hesitant or difficult horse. If you are on your own and he refuses to move, use a schooling whip to tap him on the hind leg to 'unblock' him and get him to walk forward again. Touching him with the end of a lead rope or lunge line has the same effect.

If your horse leaps away from the ramp, do not let go if you can help it; instead, use short, sharp tugs to regain his attention. As soon as he stands quietly, repeat the loading procedure again. If you do let go, calmly retrieve him once he has stopped charging about. On no account start shouting or chasing after him as this will just make matters worse. When you have successfully loaded him once, praise him and finish the session for the day, and have a restorative cup of tea!

With a horse that rears, or raises his head so high he risks banging his head on the trailer roof, you will have to go back a stage and lunge him in a chambon first until he is calmly stretching down (Figure 12.2) (See Chapter 14.). At the end of the lunge session, leave the chambon on him, and lead him up the ramp, halt for a few moments, and either lead him out of the front again or back him down the ramp. (Figures 12.3a and b.) If your horse is familiar with stretching down he will keep his back relaxed and his hind legs moving. If he lifts his head he will feel the poll pressure of the chambon, and lower his head. A small handful of feed strategically placed at the front end of the trailer directly under his nose, will serve as a reward and also help to keep his head down. After loading him a couple of times in the chambon, then try using a head collar or control halter. He should be fine once he learns to keep his head low as he goes in. On no account strap his head down

207

Figure 12.2 Using a chambon prevents the horse throwing his head up in the air and limits his resistance to a bit of face pulling!

a

b

Figures 12.3a and b Loading with a chambon can teach your horse to a) relax and lower his neck as he enters the trailer and b) leaves it again.

forcefully. Most things will break, and you will end up with a frightened horse. A bit of gentle persuasion works best every time.

Until your horse will walk in and stand for the length of time it will take you to secure him with the partition, do not shut him in or tie him up otherwise he may panic. He must be allowed to stand quietly and calmly without you banging up the ramp or clattering the partition into place. One way to get him used to the ramp being raised and lowered, is to raise it in stages: a small amount at first, then lower it, then take it up a little higher, then lower it, and so on, so that he becomes accustomed to the ramp moving behind him before you raise it fully and fasten it.

When he has learnt to stand still inside the trailer your assistant will be useful for helping you with the partitions and the ramp. If you will be travelling him with the partition in place, then you need to put this back in the trailer if you have removed it. Repeat the previous loading training with the partition in place. If your trailer has a breast bar, put this back in so that your horse learns to walk up to it and stand, then release it and lead him out of the front again.

With central partitions that are in two halves, get your assistant to secure the back part, then you secure the front. Do this slowly and quietly so that you do not worry your horse. If you do not have an assistant, make sure your horse will stand quietly before you attempt to close both halves on your own.

Whether a horse should be tied up or not is a matter of preference. The partition ensures that he is secure and cannot go anywhere. If you tie him up, do not have the rope so short that his head is in an uncomfortably high position. Many accidents in horseboxes and trailers happen because a horse has panicked and fallen, resulting in a twisted neck because he cannot get free. Leaving him loose allows him total freedom to use his neck to balance. Just imagine how it would feel if you had to make a long train journey, standing up with your arms tied behind your back the whole time! You could secure him with a rubber rope as he is in an enclosed space (see Chapter 3). He should be tied up, however, while you move around to the back of the trailer to close and secure the tail bar (Figure 12.4). Talk to him as you do this so that he does not think you have disappeared.

Many horses load and travel well with the partition removed as the

Figure 12.4 A horse should stand calmly before you carefully move the partition across and fasten the tail bar.

trailer feels less claustrophobic. With more space they can straddle their legs easily to balance. Trevor used to crash about and trample on himself when travelling with a partition and so I removed it, after which he was easier to load and he would position himself diagonally across the trailer. I secure him with two rubber ropes, one clipped to each side of his head collar to prevent him from turning round – and pulling faces at the motorists behind. He now arrives at competitions calm, relaxed and not having sweated up. My attempts at smartening him up are no longer in vain and he has all his plaits intact when we arrive at our destination!

Give your horse a few minutes to get used to being inside the trailer with the tail bar fastened, reassuring him all the while before you lift the ramp (Figure 12.5). Once he is calm enough

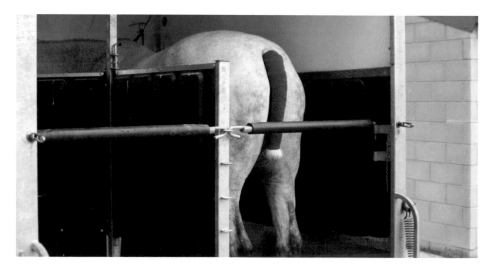

Figure 12.5 Make sure that a horse remains calm in the trailer once the tail bar if fastened before you attempt to lift the ramp.

to be shut in, the ramp must not be thrown up suddenly and slammed shut, which could upset him again, but should be gently and quietly closed and secured.

When raising the ramp, always stand to one side; never stand directly behind a trailer ramp because this means you will be underneath it as you walk forward to close it. If he should panic and step back, the ramp will slam down on you and you will be hurt. I learnt this from experience: a horse came out faster than he went in before I had the ramp fastened because I had not secured the tail bar; as I raised the ramp, he shot backwards, and my shoulder was clipped by the corner of the falling ramp breaking my collar bone. I was not directly beneath it, but neither was I far enough to one side. The horse was stressed, I was stressed and the whole outing had been a disaster. I then had to get back to the yard and do evening stables with one arm but luckily the farrier was there and he very kindly filled buckets for me!

With most horseboxes horses stand facing sideways and so you must practise moving your horse around into position. He will need to make a turn around the forehand and this needs to be done initially on the ground. Coil the lunge line to keep it out of the way and hold it near the bit. Make a fist with your other hand, and give short pushes against the horse's side where the girth would be. He should step away from the pressure and move his haunches away from you in a small turn. If he does not react, then push more firmly. If he still does not move, poke him with your thumb which will feel more pronounced. Praise him once he understands and responds, and then repeat the exercise with gentle pressure again.

If you have any problems loading, always go back to the beginning and start again.

Unloading

The way in which you unload your horse is as important as that for loading him and your trailer should still be in the school or enclosed area for this training. Some horses can become very excitable, and some owners very tense, at events, and in a hurry to get on with the day, and smooth unloading ensures this is not made worse.

After loading him successfully, and closing the ramp, let him stand for a few minutes. Talk to him from outside the trailer so that he knows you are still about. Then say nothing and pretend you have walked away; this begins the training for him to remain calm in the box at a show while you take the time to do everything you have to do before unloading, such as getting your entry number from the secretary, visiting the toilet, and getting something to eat.

When the few minutes are up, quietly open the front ramp, making sure no-one is in the way as you take it down, and go in to your horse. Untie him if you have tied him up, or clip your lead rope/lunge line on. Use a lunge line the first few times you unload him, just in case he dashes out, at least then you will be able to bring him around on a circle. Release the chest bar, securing the partition to give a wider exit if possible. He will have to stand quietly while you do this. As mentioned before, having a small pile of feed on the floor in front of the horse when loading him not only gives the horse a reward for going in but also teaches him to stand in the trailer rather than dragging you straight out down the front ramp. He must leave the trailer when you say he can.

Lead your horse out down the front ramp of the trailer staying by his shoulder (this is a reason why your horse should be accustomed to being led from either side), and looking ahead and watching where you put your feet. This is the moment when an over-excited horse could send you flying, and you could be trampled. Take things slowly. You do not want him to rush out and barge past you. I witnessed an owner at a show shouting, 'stand clear!' while she let the front ramp of her trailer fall to the ground, releasing a cantering horse that proceeded to run around the show ground until someone managed to grab him. I stood there in amazement as she said, 'Oh he always does that, it's the easiest way to get him out.'

If you have a rear unload trailer and have an assistant to help you, go in to your horse through the groom's door and make sure he is not tied up, but that you are holding the line as your assistant lowers the ramp.

If you will be going to shows on your own, it is important that your horse stands quietly tied up while you lower the ramp yourself before going in through the groom's door to untie him and back him out.

Your horse must learn to step backwards slowly down the ramp. To ask him to go back, stand in front of him to one side, and with your fist, give short pushes against his chest. He should yield to this pressure and step back. Repeat the pushes so that he goes back one step at a time and does not panic and shoot out too fast. Keep him straight and do not allow him to spin around and go out frontward.

In horseboxes most horses stand sideways and should be brought down the ramp forwards. They will also be far more comfortable coming down a steep horsebox ramp forwards.

As soon as your horse unloads safely and sensibly, reward him with praise and a favourite titbit for this good behaviour. Repeat this procedure two or three times a week until he will happily stand inside on his own with both ramps secured.

At shows, your horse will have to accept being tied up to the outside of your trailer and, once again, a full hay net tied next to him will help to keep him occupied. If you have already taught him to tie up in the yard, you should have no problem with this but if he resents being tied up, repeat the basic tying-up training in Chapter 3.

THE FIRST OUTING

What you do the first time you travel your horse sets the trend for future trips and so it is very important to get it right.

When your horse loads and unloads happily, go for a short drive taking your assistant with you. Make sure you are confident towing a trailer or driving a horsebox if you are travelling your horse yourself. Although a horse must be trained to load regardless of whether you tow or drive, if you are not confident it is worth hiring someone when you need them to travel your horse for you. Today you have to take a special test to tow a trailer and most people's driving licences only cover horseboxes up to a particular size, over which you need an HGV licence.

Remember to make your safety checks, tyres, battery, oil etc., before this first short trip and every future trip. I have seen horse owners plaiting up and getting ready at the yard, only to find that the horsebox will not start, so check that you will make it to the show before you get ready.

It is very important that you pull away smoothly and drive slowly to start with. Have your window open if you are in a towing vehicle so that you can hear your horse if he clatters about. It is important to be able to distinguish the quiet thumps as he shifts his feet to balance himself from the loud banging and crashing noises that tell you there is a problem. Avoid potholes and go slowly over speed bumps allowing your horse to adjust to the movement of the vehicle. Once he is settled, drive at the normal speed for the particular road. Driving too slowly will infuriate other drivers and driving too fast around bends and roundabouts, will throw your horse around in the back. Use common sense, therefore, but it is better to err on the side of caution. Always give yourself enough time to brake smoothly and gradually when approaching junctions, crossings, bends etc; braking suddenly will also throw your horse around. If you have any doubts about his well-being, pull over in a safe place, and check on him before continuing. You should not hear a sound from a well-balanced, calm horse if you drive sensibly. If he loads well before you actually take him out but refuses to load the next time, you need to scrutinize your driving! Take a mobile phone and details of your breakdown cover with you, in case of emergencies.

When you arrive back home, unload in the same calm and positive fashion. Relax and try to enjoy the whole process and make a fuss of him with his favourite food and treats when he goes back into his stable. This approach will keep you both calm when you go to shows, competitions or to the vet, or even on holiday together.

TYPES OF TRAILER OR HORSEBOX

There are many types of trailer and horsebox on the market. Traditionally, horses in trailers face forwards, and in horseboxes they face sideways or stand at an angle in a herring-bone fashion. There has been a lot of research recently about which way horses prefer to stand, many choosing to face backwards. Hence there is a growing market for trailers and horseboxes equipped to cater for travelling facing rearward. If a horse is left untied in a trailer, but with the central partition in place, he will most likely stand at an angle with his back side pressed against the outside wall, or sitting on the tail bar (hence the need for tail protection). Whichever way a horse faces, he will need room to straddle his legs in order to balance. Some horses travel well untied without partitioning, having the freedom to straddle and balance, which is helpful if a horse has panicked when travelling before, and has fallen over.

Travelling horses sideways in horseboxes is not usually a problem but, often, many relaxed horses travelling completely unfettered by rope or partition turn around to face backwards.

There are some very smart trailers and small horseboxes that are designed with low ramps and side loading to carry their charges facing backwards. In the end it is a matter of suiting your pocket and your horse! The most important factor when making your choice is that the vehicle is sound, safe and roadworthy.

13 IN THE FIELD

There can be no better scene than a small herd of horses quietly grazing together in the field, enjoying each other's company and the 'facilities' (Figure 13.1). Seeing your horse happy with his chums before you head home can bring a smile to your face and give you a warm sense of pride. However, turning up again later to fetch him in again when he does not want to come, or if he has been in a fight and needs medical attention can shatter this idyllic scenario.

Figure 13.1 There's nothing like a good roll!

FIELD MATES AND FIGHTS

A lot of bad feeling can be caused in a yard by an inconsiderate owner with a bossy horse causing injury to his field companions, with no regard for the large vet bills their owners are being presented with. If your horse is the bossy one, at least he will be the one with the least damage but you will not be popular in the tack room at coffee time! If you are sharing facilities, it is only common courtesy to sort out any problems as they arise. It is to be hoped that you have an experienced yard manager who can rearrange the horses into more companionable groups, something for which you will be grateful if your horse is the timid one of the group and coming off worst in the squabbles. There is nothing more frustrating than owning a horse you cannot ride for weeks on end owing to him being kicked in the field, or losing a shoe just before a show by galloping around in the mud when chased. In the worst situations your horse will make a bid for freedom by jumping out of the field (see page 226) to get away from being bullied.

Horses that all get on well in a group have usually been together for some time and have sorted out their pecking order. One horse will be the boss and one will be the lad at the bottom of the class, with the others slotting somewhere in between. Problems in a happy group can occur when a new member is introduced. He will have his own ideas about how important he is and will have to defend his corner because the others will try to put him at the bottom of the order. The horse all ready at the bottom of the pecking order may also want to upgrade himself and try to keep the newcomer down. Fighting often ensues, therefore, as the horses sort out the new positioning in the hierarchy. The worst fights happen if the new horse was boss in his old field and it stands to reason that he will fancy being in pole position again.

In the wild, the alpha horse will not only be at the top of the pecking order but will seek out the best places to graze and drink and the herd will follow. If your horse is boss horse in the field, the pecking order could extend to include you. A dominant horse will try to put you lower in his herd even if it consists of just you and him. As the trainer of the horse, you have to be number one (see Chapter 1). Changing his field mates or putting him into his own private paddock may help, as will keeping him stabled for part of the day. Horses that are out twenty-four hours a day can sometimes be difficult to train initially while you are setting the ground rules, and working a horse like this will be easier if you have all ready sorted out the hierarchy between you and earned his respect. If you are frightened of him, he is not going to regard you as herd leader and will be more likely to form a close bond with another horse, shutting you out.

Fights are common in a mixed group of mares and geldings. A wild herd will have a stallion, an alpha mare, other mares and foals, and geldings do not come into it of course. Young male horses will be kicked out to fend for themselves and form their own herd, often as a bachelor group while they are maturing.

A group of geldings will get along quite happily unless a mare is introduced and then trouble starts as the geldings compete to prove which one has the most stallion-like behaviour. The same applies to mares; they will live together quite harmoniously until a gelding comes along, more often than not ganging up on him and chasing him away, unless some of them are in season, in which case they will be vying for his attention!

Figure 13.2 Two heads are better than one when it comes to being on the look-out for danger! Friesian mares in their field.

For all the reasons above, it would not be wise to turn your horse out for the day in an unfamiliar field full of horses he does not know. Putting him in an adjacent field can lead to racing up and down the fence with all the horses getting over-excited and so it would be safer to turn him out in a field further away with just one horse either as a companion or as a neighbour. Choose one that gets on with most horses so that your horse can befriend him. Just leave them out for an hour or so before bringing them in again. If they get on, then the time can be extended gradually over a few days. If they have been in neighbouring fields and get on well over the fence, they should be happy in the same field. Most yards will turn horses out either individually in adjacent paddocks or in small groups of two to four (Figure 13.2). Sometimes if there are three horses, two will gang up on the other one, so if this happens, the arrangements must be changed.

If your horse goes out on his own, make sure that he can see other horses or else he will neigh the whole time to see if anyone responds and run about becoming stressed. The individual paddock system gives the horses companionship; they can nibble each other's necks over the fence (as long as the fence is not electrified) without the risk of fights and injury and it gives each horse the opportunity to move away from the other without being bothered should the other horse be a bit of a pest.

Some horses are much happier with just one field mate, which does not have to be another horse; a goat or a sheep, for example, can be a good companion. Remember though that horses spending all their time with just one other horse can become too attached to that friend, even to the point of excluding you from the group, which will give you difficulties when training. In this situation, it may be best to keep the horses in adjacent paddocks, so that they have their chosen company but do not form too close a bond. You must be your horse's best friend, not the horse next door.

When putting your horse out with a new companion, stay and watch them just in case they take a real dislike to each other. The usual greeting is to blow down their nostrils at each other, which is followed by squealing, especially with mares, and then by a warning strike-out with a front leg. Then comes the trot and canter around the field to see who can run the fastest, followed by a rolling match to see who can flip right over from side to side. They will then graze at a safe distance apart, keeping an eye on each other. If all is well, they will gradually sidle nearer to each other and settle down to some serious eating. If one of the horses is more playful than the other, the horse that wants to eat will kick out at the other when he wants some peace, as with my two: Trevor likes to eat and Amadeus is the playful one. Two horses that like playing will be fine together as long as they give up eventually and settle down to graze.

Figure 13.3 Play time: this Arab colt has found a stick with which to amuse himself.

Amadeus used to play some hair-raising games with my Lusitano, Leo: they would stand on their hind legs shadow-boxing, barge each other, squeal, kick out and so on, but never hurt each other. Leo was boss, and Amadeus, who was a three-year-old thug at the time, was number two. More gentle behaviour with horses of a quieter disposition ranges from ear-flicking, tail-swishing (horses often stand head to tail so that they each have a personal fly swatter) and strolling around the field in search of tastier grass. Other horses may be content to amuse themselves and even find 'toys' to play with (Figure 13.3).

CHECK YOUR FENCING

Before turning your horse out in the field, make sure that it is horse-proof. Where we live, on the edge of Salisbury Plain, an escaped horse can be lost for a couple of days over the army ranges, resulting in a helicopter search and a change to the army's firing schedule! Take time to check the field on a regular basis for loose rails and wobbly fence posts, make sure that the gate fastens securely and cannot be broken by horses pushing against it, and examine hedges for dead areas which become brittle and easy for horses to push through. If the grazing is good, your horse should not be tempted to look for pastures new but the grass is always greener on the other side of the fence and it is amazing how far a horse's neck can stretch when reaching for that elusive blade of grass!

TYPES OF FENCING

The choice of fencing depends on what already exists in your field and the amount of funds available to you. If you keep your horse at livery, have a look at the condition of the fencing when you are choosing a new yard. If it does not look substantial enough for your horse then go somewhere else. If you have a horse that tends to push into fencing, you should warn the yard manager.

Electric fencing

Electric fencing works well as a reinforcement to thin hedges or fences that have seen better days. It can also be a very effective deterrent to horses that push into and lean over fencing, chew it or try to jump out of the field. If you are using it on its own, choose the thicker, clearly visible tape and use at least two strands, making sure they are pulled taut enough to create a secure barrier and that the posts are strong enough not to bend when the electric tape is pulled taut (or when horses lean against them). Wooden fence posts are better if you intend to use this type of fencing on a long-term basis.

Loose trailing fence can get caught around a horse's legs, which can have disastrous consequences if it is live at the time. This happened to Amadeus when he was a foal. He still has the scars on his legs and is very wary of electric fencing to this day, which is not a bad thing, but it was not the best way to learn the lesson and it would have been better if the accident could have been avoided. That is the trouble with having an inquisitive horse!

Post and rail

Post and rail is the best fencing as long as it is not done with wood that is not really up to the job because it will be continually breaking as horses chew it and push against it. If you use cheap wood, you will be forever trudging around the field with spare planks, nails and a hammer making repairs.

Barbed wire

Barbed wire should be avoided if at all possible. Just leaning over it can cause nasty lacerations to your horse's chest but even worse injuries happen if a horse is chased into the barbs.

Stock fencing

Stock fencing consisting of a wire fence with *small* meshes, combined with a couple of wooden rails or a strand of electric fence is a good option, but the meshes should not be too big. Large meshes can trap hooves or teeth: Amadeus got his nose stuck in one as a foal and pulled out some of his baby teeth. No wonder his owner was happy to sell him on to me!

Hedges

You cannot beat a tall, thick hedge – preferably a prickly one – to keep your horse and his field mates secure. It also acts as a windbreak and gives protection from bad weather. Horses are far happier in a field that has trees or a field shelter to protect them from the elements.

CARE OF THE FIELD

Maintenance

Regular maintenance is essential to keep your horse safe and healthy.

The removal of droppings helps to cut down the fly population, control worm infestation and prevents the grass withering underneath piles of muck. Picking up the muck is a tedious but essential part of grassland management and if it is done regularly prevents bald patches in the grass. The job can be quite therapeutic in the summer: strolling round the field in your shorts, tanning your legs and getting a good aerobic work out pushing a full barrow back to the muck heap, but less fun on a rainy winter's day.

Running a chain harrow over the field on a warm, sunny day will spread out any remaining droppings and allow the sun to kill off any worm infestation. The field is then best rested while the remnants of the droppings are washed into the soil by the next lot of rain and will fertilize the grass growth. Harrowing and resting a field should take place every three months or so, when the grazing starts to look tired and in need of a chance to regrow.

Make sure the gate opens and closes easily so that you do not have to deal with a gate hanging off its hinges, a stiff bolt and a stroppy horse that wants to get to the grass.

Looking after your field is very important if you want to prevent your horse from standing in a sea of mud in the winter, and having no grazing in the summer. Limit turn-out in the winter to the bare minimum that will keep him happy, altering your stable routine accordingly. The less turn-out he has the more interesting work he needs to keep him relaxed and stress free. A dry pen with plenty of hay to eat is preferable to him standing in mud for hours on end, which can cause problems such as cracked heels and thrush.

In the spring, once the ground has dried out a bit, it is a good idea to have the field rolled to flatten out all the hoof marks and other holes and ridges that appeared in the field's surface when it was muddy, otherwise you will have hard, lumpy, rutted ground in the summer, which could cause your horse to trip or fall if he is letting off steam around the field. In the growing season, weeds grow as fast as the grass and so your field will need topping every 4–6 weeks or so to avoid having a field full of unwanted plants. Applying a fertilizer in the spring can give the grass a much-needed boost but watch the weather forecast and try to time it so that you spread it over the field before a day or two of rain, which will help it to soak into the soil. Remove the horses from the field while you fertilize.

Rest paddocks before they are totally bare, otherwise they just take longer to recover. Rotating grazing to give each paddock even use avoids having a field you cannot use for months on end.

Poisonous plants

Familiarize yourself with plants that are poisonous to horses. Generally speaking, if you have good grazing horses do not eat anything which is not good for them; they are only likely to do so if they are really hungry. One of the most poisonous plants for horses is ragwort (Figure 13.4). All ragwort must be removed from a field and it is vitally important that the whole plant is removed; the root must not be left in the ground. Most horses would not eat ragwort when it is growing in the field

Figure 13.4 Ragwort is extremely poisonous for horses and should be dug up as soon as you see it.

unless, again, they were extremely hungry because it is not palatable in its normal state but it becomes more palatable, though no less poisonous, when dried. Fields containing ragwort should, therefore, never be used for hay. Ragwort can cause liver damage and is one of the most frequent causes of poisoning, even death, in horses. Ragwort should be eradicated either by being dug up, as stated, or by using an herbicide. The Injurious Weeds Act (1959) and the Ragwort Control Act (2003) can be enforced by local authorities to make people remove ragwort.

Another nasty plant is giant hogweed which looks like a more robust and larger version of cow parsley. It is poisonous to horses if eaten and its sap is extremely irritant to both equine and human skin, so take care when strimming the edges of your field and cover up if you want to avoid severe blistering.

Other common poisonous plants are deadly nightshade, yew, buttercups, bracken, oak and acorns, privet and rhododendron (see the Allen Photographic Guide no. 34, *All About Poisonous Plants* by Sonia Davidson, published by J. A. Allen).

Water troughs

Horses must have access to clean, fresh water in the field, which can either be from buckets, which should be refreshed daily, or a trough. If you do not have a purpose-made trough, you can use an old bath but it is important that it has no sharp edges or exposed taps on which a horse may injure himself. Filling a trough with a ball-cock system is preferable because it will be continuously topped up when the water falls below a certain level and you do not always have to be on hand to fill it as you do if it has to be filled with a hose pipe.

All troughs should be sited for your horses' ease of access but not, if possible, under overhanging bushes or trees that may drop debris into it. Troughs must be cleaned regularly, before the water turns into a green soup, and to remove any debris and wildlife that is collecting on the bottom and in the water. Horses will not drink mucky, stagnating water and will go thirsty.

When the trough needs to be cleaned, empty out the water by either tipping it up (if it is not too heavy), unplugging the drain hole or baling it out with a bucket. If you have a ball-cock, tie it up with a bit of string to prevent the water streaming back in. Leave a small amount of water in the bottom and get to work with a stiff scrubbing brush (and a lot of elbow grease) to remove all the grime from the sides and bottom. Pressure-washing with a hose would be ideal, if you have access to a generator and the appropriate equipment. Tempting as it is to swill the trough out with disinfectant, this can only be done if you can rinse out any residue thoroughly otherwise you risk the horses refusing to drink out of it because it smells strange, or poisoning them.

Once you have scrubbed the trough clean, leave it to dry for several hours to help kill off water-borne bacteria, algae etc. (Your horse can drink out of a bucket for an afternoon.) To prevent a further build up of algae, there are eco-friendly pond products which claim to reduce build-up. If they are safe for goldfish, they should be safe for horses, but I have yet to try this myself and you should get professional advice before using it. Someone I know put a couple of goldfish in her water trough, which successfully kept the water clear but I can imagine what horses like Amadeus would think about creatures swimming around in their drinking water!

Another efficient way to keep your trough clean is to place a bundle of straw tied with baler twine in the bottom, which prevents the build up of green algae in the water. As it becomes sodden it sinks to the bottom of the trough. Not surprisingly, Trevor manages to fish them out and eat them and so I am constantly replacing the bundles!

Escaping from Fields

Horses usually only escape in search of better grazing or water and so if good grass and an adequate supply of fresh water are available all the time they should be happy to stay put. Horses and ponies will, however, go to great lengths to reach a tasty snack and will certainly go in search of water if they are thirsty.

If the above are taken care of, the fencing and general maintenance precautions discussed on pages 221–223 must be checked.

Some horses will try to escape just for the fun of it. Amadeus used to have a field mate called Bomber, a small Welsh pony as cunning as a barrow load of monkeys, and so they got on famously of course. Bomber could fit through small gaps in the hedge and Amadeus would try to follow. I still remember the sight of my horse with his head, neck and one front leg on one side of the hedge and the rest of him on the other side. When I called him from the gate, he extricated himself very quickly, and stood there, looking at me as if to say, 'Who? Me? I wasn't doing anything'. In the meantime Bomber had trotted merrily into the yard and put himself in a vacant stable.

JUMPING OUT

If your horse has a tendency to jump out of his field, firstly make sure that he likes his field companion, if he has one, and is not desperate to get away from him. Conversely, if he does not have a companion, your horse may not like being alone and jumps into a neighbour's field for company. Both these situations indicate that you have to do some groundwork in building your horse's self-confidence with a sensible work/care routine to ensure that he does not become stressed in situations that worry him. Find him a companion he is happy with, even if, as stated before, this is a sheep or goat.

You must be aware of any problems as soon as they occur. As prevention is far better than cure in these circumstances, try not to give your horse a reason to jump out. It is so important to observe your horse when he goes into a new field, and to make sure he settles before leaving him to his own devices. Turn him out in a paddock near the yard at first just for half an hour or so and bring him in before he becomes stressed. Putting him in the furthest field out of sight of other horses is a common cause of jumping out as he either searches for other horses or runs back to the safety of his stable.

TURNING YOUR HORSE OUT

In my experience more injuries happen to horse owners when they are turning horses out in a field or bringing them back in than in any other situation. Following a safe, sensible procedure for turning your horse out in the field either on his own or with other horses can prevent many problems, especially being injured yourself. Aiming him for an open gate and just letting go is not a good idea.

Take the horse to the field in a head collar and lead rope, or use a lunge rein if he might try to make a run for it. If he pushes and barges you when you take him to the field, lunge him in the school beforehand, and make sure

Figure 13.5 Leading your horse to the field. This pony is quite happy for his owner to take his lunch along!

you teach him to lead to and from the field before you start to turn him out (Figure 13.5). This does require the co-operation of other horse owners; it will not help if others let their horses out to gallop around the field while you are trying to establish a bit of discipline (see Chapter 2).

If you are turning him out with another horse, that horse should be turned out at the same time by a second person. Trying to turn two horses out together on your own can result in you being trampled on if you are not very careful (Figure 13.6). Always wear a safety hat and gloves as protection when leading your horse to and from the field if you have any doubt about his behaviour. Broken fingers are very inconvenient and being kicked on the head by a horse eager to get out into the field will give you a horrendous headache, at the very least.

Obviously a gate should be closed properly when horses are in a field but it is also a good idea to close the gate when the field is unoccupied: this informs other people that you have removed the horse, and he has not just escaped through the gate (mind you, he could have got out another way) and approaching a closed field gate also discourages the horse from galloping off as soon as he sees grass. Lead him into the field, and turn him to face the gate as you close it, leaving yourself enough space to step away from him. Quietly slip off the head collar and step out of the way, making your exit

Figure 13.6 Always get help when leading two horses at once otherwise you could be caught in the middle of a fight!

through the gate once he has turned and wandered (or galloped) off. The last thing you want is him barging back past you to the yard. Always remove the head collar. I have known a couple of horses with horrendous head injuries caused by the head collar getting hooked up on a tree branch. If your head collar is not easy to put on and take off, get another one that is. Head collars that unclip under the throat can be slipped quickly and quietly off over the ears, provided your horse is not fussy about his ears being touched (see Chapter 5)

If your horse tries to break away from you, make sure you have him on a lunge line so that you can bring him around you on a circle. Once he has settled, release him. Bribery with a titbit can prevent him from shooting off, but I do know horses that can whip a piece of carrot out of your hand and disappear in a spray of mud with an I'm-not-fooled-by-you look on their faces. If you and a friend are turning out two horses at the same time, co-operate with each other so that you release the horses together. Stand the horses slightly apart to ensure that they cannot barge each other and neither of you is flattened when they turn away. Just letting your horse go will probably result in your now ex-friend bring dragged through the mud desperately trying to get her horse's head collar off. If this does happen, it is safer for her to unclip the rope rather than get hurt, and wait until they have settled down before going to get the head collar off. Your horse should trust you enough to come to you in the field in this situation (see the Catching your Horse section on page 231). Watch the horses for a few minutes until they settle, and then leave them in peace to enjoy their playtime.

Inclement weather

Horses and ponies that live out will generally find themselves shelter from bad weather but there are those hardy souls that, even if they have a field shelter, will stand quite happily in the middle of the field. These animals also seem to be sensible when the conditions underfoot are bad and they do not charge about (unless they are frightened by something) because they are used to the freedom and do not feel the need to rush around all the time.

I know several horses that were quite hardy while living out but that became 'couch potatoes' once stabled. The lure of a warm dry bed at the first sign of drizzle was just too much to resist. If you observe a yard full of horses on a day when it is pouring with rain, they settle themselves down for a snooze in the dry and are only too happy not to be outside. Horses that are stabled the majority of the time do become less 'street wise'.

If your horse is stabled for a large part of the time, take care when turning him out in bad weather. Pay particular attention to the ground conditions. If it is wet and slippery and your horse is the type to rush about when turned out, he could slip and wrench a shoulder, for example, or even fall over. I knew of a horse that slipped, fell on his side and caught all four feet in wire stud fencing. Fortunately he did not panic and lay still while his owner extricated him one foot at a time and was not hurt but this incident could have had disastrous consequences. Free time in the safety of a school is better than nothing.

In summer many horses find the heat of the day too much to bear and are happier being turned out at night when it is cooler and there are fewer insects around. The disadvantage with this is that your horse will be out grazing for twelve hours or more and so if you are watching his waistline, make sure he is in a small paddock with grazing that is not too rich. Some horses will pace themselves with the grazing but there are others that gorge themselves, which can result in them being too tired and full to work the next day; they just want to sleep. If your horse lives out all the time make sure his turn-out/work ration works well enough for you to maintain your herd-leader status.

Horse walkers

If you cannot turn your horse out in bad weather a horse walker is extremely useful but it should not be used as a substitute for a proper work/exercise regime (Figure 13.7). If you do not have the luxury of a walker, a short time out in an enclosed pen can be better than nothing, unless your horse is quite happy to remain in his box (Amadeus is a real fair-weather horse and would rather stay in than go out in the rain at any time). Horse walkers are also useful for supplying a horse with a little controlled exercise when he is recovering from an injury, for example, working off a little of his energy before he is turned out to prevent injury or even keeping him occupied while you are mucking out.

Figure 13.7 A horse walker is useful for allowing your horse to stretch his legs if the ground is unsuitable for turn-out, or if he is too fresh to go directly in the field because he may injure himself. Putting him on the walker or lungeing him first may help him settle before putting him in the field.

CATCHING YOUR HORSE

Catching your horse should be very easy if you do it correctly but if a strict routine is altered, problems can arise. For example, trying to catch a horse five minutes after you have put him out, because you forgot the farrier was coming, is a recipe for disaster or, if he knows he goes out in the field in the mornings while you muck out, he will understandably become tetchy if he has to stay in and do nothing. Have a routine but make sure that if it is altered, there is a good reason for it; do not keep a horse in at the time he normally goes out just because you do not feel like walking to the field. If the vet or farrier is coming then the horse will just have to wait. Horses should be able to accept a flexible routine from time to time and not become little dictators when it comes to going out and coming in. If you are trying to load your horse to go to a show, for example, at the time he usually goes out, he may try to demand to go out in the field, which will be very stressful for both of you. And the consequence of this is that when he is finally turned out he might be difficult to catch again. Amadeus got away from me once when I was trying to load him for a show as he was determined to go to the field. The gate was open, he broke away and went rushing off neighing to his friends only to find he was all on his own; it was six in the morning and no-one else was around! He trotted back to me meekly, went into the trailer without a fuss, and off we went to the show. He never tried that again.

Knowing how to approach your horse safely without alarming him is essential. Yelling at him from the other side of the field will warn him of your approach but if he would rather stay out than come in, he will suddenly become as deaf as a post and you will probably be in for a long wait before he acknowledges your presence.

The way to catch your horse is to have your head collar and rope over your left arm, carrying it close to your body so that he does not see it waving about, which could put him off being caught. Have a titbit in your other hand but on no account give it to him until you have caught him, otherwise he may pinch it and run off again. Approach his shoulder on the nearside in the usual way but if your horse is wise to this and sidles off just out of reach, it may be a good idea to try approaching him from the offside. Stroke your horse's offside shoulder and if he accepts this, slip the rope over his neck, and

231

reach under his neck to get hold of the end of the rope. Walk around the front of him and quickly and quietly slide the head collar on over his nose, flip the head piece over his poll, and do it up. Begin to lead him towards the gate and give him his titbit. Once you are out of the gate, make sure it is secured properly before leading him to his stable.

If he is out with other horses, make sure they are caught at the same time if there is likely to be a problem such as them all wanting to come in together and trampling you in the process. You may have to deal with this yourself or ask the yard staff to help you if the other owners are not available at the time. Horses owned by different people do know their owners or handlers and will not generally move to come in unless their owner or handler approaches them. If the horses in the group are used to each of them being caught at a different time, catching your horse should not be a problem but it will always be safer if the horses are not overexcited and your horse is not in the middle of the bunch. However, if a new horse is introduced to the group, this routine can be upset by the newcomer wanting to come in first all the time. If this happens, go and get some help. If there is no help around and you are stuck with someone else's horse getting in the way, your best option might be to bring him in, then go to get yours, and put the other one out again, provided he has another friend in the field, or you know that he will be all right on his own.

Refusing to be caught

Your horse should be pleased to see you when you go to the field. If you have a good relationship with him, catching him should not be a problem but, having said that, all horses can be mischievous and play games at times (Figure 13.8).

If he does not want to be caught, then you have to go back to basics and establish the ground rules (see Chapter 1) before trying to catch him in the field. Try to remain calm at all times and act as though you have all the time in the world. He certainly will not come to you if you are stressed.

The following are a few options to try if your horse does not want to be caught.

When we first moved to Wiltshire, Amadeus would not let the staff at the local livery yard catch him. They tried enticing him to the gate by placing his lunch by it, with the aim of catching him while he was eating. He remained at the furthest point in the field until they became fed up and went in for a coffee. They returned a few minutes later to find him in exactly the same place, but the feed had miracu-lously disappeared. They left him out all afternoon until it was time for the

Figure 13.8 The expression of a horse not wanting to be caught: Trevor in an uncooperative mood.

girls to go home. They locked up the yard, and made a big show of getting into their cars and shouting goodbye to each other. No sooner had they done this than Amadeus came belting down the field to the gate neighing franti-cally because he did not want to be left out all night on his own! This resolved the problem; he was easy to catch after that and would actually neigh for someone to come and get him when he was ready. He still does this to this day.

On moving yards this year, both the horses have tried it on both with the staff and the students. Trevor would not be caught recently, and would kick up his heels and gallop off every time anyone approached. I went into the field as though going for a stroll. He looked at me, and went to shoot off but, on realizing who it was, changed his mind. I ignored him, walked past his nose and went to sit on the fence. After a few moments he came to see what I was doing and so I stroked his nose without attempting to catch him. He moved away slightly and then came back; this time I stroked him and put his head collar on. Mission accomplished in five minutes (Figure 13.9).

When catching horses that do not want to be caught, the best way to gain their attention is to pretend that you have all the time in the world and are not remotely interested in them.

Amadeus let one of the students catch him, but then refused to move. He wanted to go out of the gate at the other end of the field (goodness knows

Figure 13.9 Bringing Trevor in from the field – finally!

why) and not towards the stables, he therefore planted himself on the spot. The poor student tugged on the rope and so he hopped in the air to frighten her then held her hostage with his nose up in the air and an obstinate expression on his face. Consequently she rang one of the staff on her mobile phone to be rescued! Of course, he followed meekly behind the tutor while the student was near to tears. 'Problem? What problem?' he seemed to say, looking smug.

Horses know if you are anxious to catch them. One of my first horses was a Welsh cob. I had just bought him and thought it would be nice for him to have a bit of grass and so I turned him out in a huge field containing sheep plus several horses, and never saw him again for four weeks, except from a distance. I sat tearfully for hours in the field with a bucket of food. He would raise my hopes by coming within a few yards of me and then shoot off again. I eventually caught him with the help of the farmer and the other horse owners who removed every animal from the field and then cornered him with four pairs of people with lunge lines. Consequently I returned him to the dealer I had bought him from. I had made the mistake of turning my horse out before he got to know me at all and so it most likely was not his fault he did not want to come to me but mine for expecting the happy-horse-and-owner relationship immediately. Horses will not want to be caught if they have no respect for you or do not like you, hence the need to establish a good relationship from the outset.

Some horses, especially bossy ones, will intimidate you by turning and kicking out, or coming at you with their teeth bared (or both). This type of behaviour firstly needs sorting out in the stable (see Chapter 1) before you turn the horse out. Grazing your horse in-hand can help but do not allow him to trample and push you, or drag you around. A good time to graze him in-hand is after he has been worked. Grazing helps him to relax and can be looked on as a reward for good work. By you staying with him, he should accept you as a 'grazing buddy'.

Your horse should not go out in the field seeing it as a way of getting away from you. Firstly make sure you build a relationship with him by caring for him and working him properly so that he both respects and likes you. Take a radio or a good book, and sit down in the field for half an hour or so as though you have every right to be there. Once you have read for a while, your horse should become curious and come to see what you are doing. Pretending to graze by pulling at the grass with your fingers can make you appear to do the same as him, one way of getting him to accept your presence. Then leave the field without even attempting to catch him. Once he stays close to you and lets you touch him without him becoming tense, he should be easy to catch.

14 LUNGEING

LUNGEING IS AN art, involving knowledge of how your horse moves, and which equipment to use and for what purpose. Done well, lungeing can make a huge improvement in your horse's way of going but done badly, it could stop a good horse ever reaching his full potential. These skills are worth learning, as there is no shortcut to teaching your horse to be more athletic, and to stretch and use his back correctly. It takes time to develop correct muscles. Being able to observe your horse from the ground allows you to assess his conformation and musculature. His physique should change from month to month with progressive training continuing through his whole career.

The most important reason for lungeing your horse is to strengthen his whole body. He will benefit from being trained from the ground so that he is free to improve his own balance without the added weight of a rider. Skilled lungeing will improve his concentration and his willingness to listen to you, his trainer. From a safety aspect, this is crucial to achieve before attempting ridden work, whether with a young horse or one in need of reschooling. Most horses will benefit from one or two lunge sessions each week as part of their all-round training, for whichever discipline they are used: jumping, dressage, carriage driving, and so on.

If you have had a bad day at work and feel stressed at the thought of a schooling session with a horse that is not in the mood, a lunge session is a good alternative to attempting ridden work which could just create tension between you both.

THE EFFECT OF STRETCHING

In order for a horse to move well his back muscles have to be relaxed, i.e. extended. If your horse can stretch forward and down with his neck fully extended when he is moving, then his back muscles are relaxed, allowing his dorsal spine to lift. His spine is supported from underneath by the abdominal muscles. (Figure 14.1.) As his spine lifts, his pelvis coils under, and his hind legs come under his body. His hind leg joints become more able to flex and carry weight. By extending his neck, and supporting his forehand with the muscles surrounding his withers, the horse is able to move freely through his shoulders and relax through his poll, jaw and mouth.

This ability to stretch through the back is the foundation upon which training your horse to work into the bridle is based. Stretching can be achieved by simply lungeing your horse over a pole on the ground. He will lower his neck to look at the pole as he approaches it, and then have to flex his leg joints to clear the pole. His back will relax, and his stomach muscles contract. Lungeing in a chambon prevents him from contracting his back

Figure 14.1 Amadeus stretching forwards and down in a chambon. Note the freedom of his shoulder movement. You can clearly see the definition of his back, neck and belly muscles.

237

muscles and trailing his hind legs encouraging him to relax and stretch his neck correctly. A horse cannot hollow his back with his neck stretched down. Circle work on the lunge requires lateral bending of the horse's spine, which he cannot do with a tight hollow back. Conversely, a horse with contracted back muscles goes along with his head up, his back dipped, slack stomach muscles, flat loins and his pelvis pushed away resulting in his hind legs appearing to paddle along behind, rather like a duck swimming in a pond. Forcing the hind legs under to force the pelvis to tuck before the horse has developed strong abdominal muscles by stretching can cause neck and shoulder problems.

A correctly stretching horse should never be behind the vertical. If he is, then his poll muscles are under strain and the angle between the jaw and jowl is too tight thus restricting space for the tongue. Bear in mind that a horse's tongue begins far back in his mouth, and if he has no room to relax it, mouth problems such as teeth grinding or sticking the tongue out of the side of the mouth or over the bit are common. Strapping such a horse's mouth shut with a tight noseband will not work; once the noseband is taken off, the problems will worsen. The only remedy is to go back to stretching with the nose forward and down to the ground on the lunge so that the horse relaxes through his back and neck again. A relaxed mouth is a sign of a correctly moving horse but a certain amount of mouthing is considered good because it causes a moist mouth. Changing nosebands and bits in an effort to stop the mouth problem are futile if the problem lies in the mechanics of the horse's back movement.

Strengthening your horse is achieved firstly by allowing the horse to stretch correctly through his back with his nose reaching forward and downward towards the ground. Your horse must be allowed the freedom to use all of his joints and stretch down in a *natural* way, i.e. as though he were looking for grass. The ideal is that he stretches down with no auxiliary equipment at all.

Once your horse can stretch on the lunge and is relaxed and supple, the next stage should be to encourage him to work in a rounded outline. In order to do this, he must learn to move with a lifted back that can swing, i.e. appear to bounce up and down behind the saddle area. A swinging back is supported from underneath by the abdominal muscles which you can see as a visible line along the lower sides of his belly. As a result of working with his hind legs underneath him, he should arch his neck forward from his withers with his poll being the highest point and his head should be vertical to the ground. To work on the bit under saddle he needs to understand working into a rein contact on the lunge to make sure that he is physically and mentally prepared for ridden work.

TOP-LINE MUSCLES

The biggest muscle in the horse's back is the longissimus dorsi. Its fibres contract in a sequence causing a 'ripple' effect. It has a right and left side so that each side of the horse can move independently. This muscle acts as a stabilizer for the lateral movement of the horse's spine as he moves otherwise he would wiggle along like a snake. The top line of the horse begins at the poll and is connected all the way along by muscles and ligaments and it is a support system for the underlying spine, allowing the spine to flex up and down, and from side to side. (Figure 14.2.)

LOWER MUSCLES

In order for the horse to lift his back and carry a rider, he needs the muscle structure below his spine. The rectus abdominis supports his torso, the protractor muscles down the front of each thigh swing his hind legs forward and the scalenus muscle at the base of the neck flattens out the curve at the lowest point of the neck vertebrae causing the base of the neck to lift. The action of these muscles is what gives the horse his 'round' appearance from his ears to his tail (Figures 14.2 and 14.3). As the base of the neck lifts, the complexus muscles become visible on either side of the neck, rather like a long sausage running up the centre of the neck. His back should appear slightly humped, and should move up and down in a subtle way. If you run your hand across the back muscles of a correctly trained horse, you should be able to feel the edge of this slab of muscle, rather like a saddle blanket of muscle. A horse with a violently bouncing back is often mistaken for one with a supple, swinging back, but in fact he shows weak loin muscles. The back muscles are not strong enough to control the movement of the back

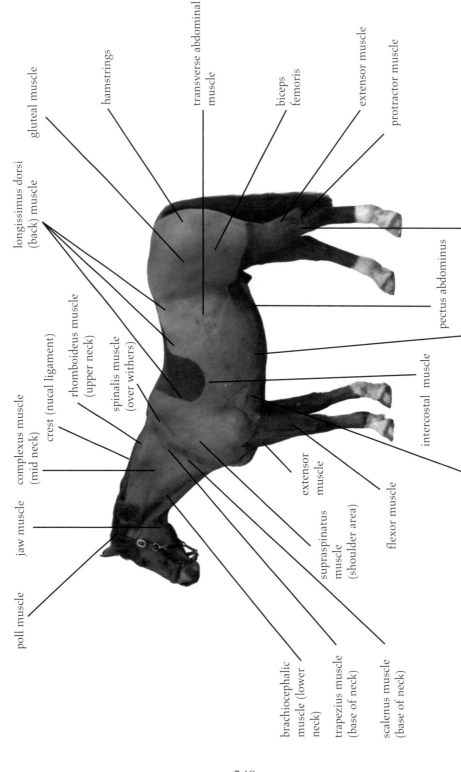

poll muscle

jaw muscle

complexus muscle (mid neck)

crest (nucal ligament)

rhomboideus muscle (upper neck)

spinalis muscle (over withers)

longissimus dorsi (back) muscle

gluteal muscle

hamstrings

transverse abdominal muscle

biceps femoris

extensor muscle

protractor muscle

flexor muscle

pectus abdominus

abdominal muscle

intercostal muscle

pectoral muscle

flexor muscle

extensor muscle

supraspinatus muscle (shoulder area)

brachiocephalic muscle (lower neck)

trapezius muscle (base of neck)

scalenus muscle (base of neck)

Figure 14.2 Important muscles of the horse.

Figure 14.3 Trevor working in a rounded outline on the double-lunge; his steps are shorter and higher than in Figure 14.8 because his frame has shortened. Note the 'tucking under' of his pelvis, causing his back to rise and his neck to arch as he accepts the contact with the bit.

and, in this case, you would feel the spine with your hand and the back muscles would be soft rather than firm. Contracted back muscles on the other hand feel tight and as hard as rock, which you would feel on a tense horse with a hollow back; the hind legs of this horse would, again, be out behind in the paddling-duck position. The tail is a good indicator of tension in the back: the tail bones are the last section of the spine and so if a horse is working with a relaxed swinging tail it is almost certain that the rest of his back is working as it should be.

Trying to acquire a rounded outline from your horse by restricting his muscles and forcing him into an unnatural shape that he cannot cope with creates tension and stress and you will make more problems for yourself later on when you start your horse's ridden work. An understanding of the biomechanics of the horse and which muscles you are trying to work at any one time is essential in order to train him sensitively and with an awareness of any potential problems before they arise. A young horse needs time to establish his outline and balance. Forcing him to look like the shape of an advanced horse with a more collected outline will probably cause him many joint and muscular problems in quite a short space of time, let alone mental anxiety. There are many horses, of no more than seven or eight years old, whose working life is virtually over and they are worth no more than meat money, simply owing to poor training. Similarly, working the horse in a deep outline incorrectly and for extended periods of time can be extremely damaging to his back and neck muscles.

LUNGEING EQUIPMENT

You will need the same clothing and equipment as for leading in-hand (see page 47) plus some extra items.

Lunge cavesson and lunge line

A lunge cavesson is designed for lungeing or in-hand work. The lunge line is attached to a ring on a secure nose piece to give you control without having to connect the line to the bit. It is particularly sensible to use a cavesson if you are new to lungeing and only just familiarizing yourself with handling a lunge line. Controlling your horse with half-halts (in the form of small tugs) on the line work very well provided the cavesson is fitted snugly and not likely to twist around on your horse's head. Many horses will panic if the cavesson slips around and a cheek piece touches an eye.

Bit connector

Lungeing from the bit requires skill and sensitivity and if you are using this

method, which with some strong-minded horses is preferable, it is best to use a bit connector to which to attach the lunge line. Attaching the line to the inside bit ring is fine if your horse is not likely to pull away but if he does, the bit may be pulled through his mouth. A bit connector helps to keep the bit evenly placed in the horse's mouth, and acts on both sides of the bit at the same time when you use half-halts on the lunge line to keep him steady in his work (Figure 14.4).

Figure 14.4 A bit connector prevents the bit from being pulled through the horse's mouth to one side.

Lunge whip

This needs to be light enough to hold comfortably and long enough so that you can touch your horse on his shoulder or hind leg easily from a safe distance. You do not want to be running towards him every time you need to use it. Most of the time gestures with the whip will suffice though your horse needs to know you will use it if necessary. Some horses are very good at sliding away from the end of the whip just as you get into position for a good shot!

Roller

It is better to use a roller than a saddle for lungeing because you will be able to see your horse's muscles working clearly; a saddle sits on the part of the horse's back you need to watch. A roller also gives the horse more freedom to move than a saddle, particularly if you suspect your saddle does not fit your horse properly and is affecting his back movement. The roller must be padded where it sits on the horse's back either side of his spine so that it does not press on the bony processes of the vertebrae. It needs to be done up securely so that it does not slip and frighten the horse or cause him to be rubbed. Attachment rings on the roller are used for the attachment of side reins, or for passing lunge lines through if you are long-reining your horse.

HOW TO LUNGE

If your horse leads in-hand correctly (see Chapter 2) you should be able to proceed to lungeing. If you get any problems with lungeing, repeat the leading in-hand stage to make sure you are in control, and that your horse understands you.

Position yourself and the horse near a corner of your schooling area so that you are enclosed by fence on two sides; this gives you both a feeling of security. The middle of a large field is not the place to start because if your horse takes fright, or just decides to get away from you, he has the room to do so, and pursuing a horse at full pelt around a large field in the heat of summer is not a lot of fun. A trailing lunge line could get caught around a horse's hind legs and cause him to panic. A corner of a field or schooling area with the two sides that are not fenced barricaded with straw bales is a better option. Although the barrier is low, it helps to keep your horse in a confined area. Bales of straw or shavings (and in some cases poles or logs on the ground can be a sufficient boundary) are safer than using jump stands with raised poles, just in case your horse does run off through them. He could try to jump the raised poles and knock them all down, frightening himself even more and giving himself a complex about jumping, which does not bode well for future jump training. In addition, the lunge line could get caught on a jump wing causing further problems.

The area you mark out should allow you to lunge your horse on a 15 m circle.

Begin by leading your horse around the schooling area carrying a lunge whip behind you instead of a schooling whip, then move further away from him, lengthening the lunge line as you do so, ending up leading him parallel with his shoulder at a distance of about 5 m (16 ft). Then stand on one spot, pivoting around your left heel to bring the horse on a circle around you. Turn to face his belly, and point the lunge whip towards his hocks, keeping it low, do not brandish it about or you might alarm him.

After a couple of circles in walk, making sure that he is relaxed and listening to you (you will know if he is by his attitude and the fact that his inside ear should be angled towards you), proceed to trot. Work him at a steady working trot so that he is putting a bit of effort into it, which will build up his stamina and help to keep his attention. He should be relaxed enough to keep a steady rhythm with his back swinging. If he goes too fast he will become tense, and if too slow he will not be working his muscles.

When you want to bring him back to walk, the easiest way is to remain facing his belly, shorten the line and bring him onto a smaller circle. He should then walk of his own accord.

To trot again, let the line out and step away from him as he moves away from you, sending him around on a circle large enough to allow him to trot.

To bring him to a halt so that you can change direction, bring him onto ever decreasing circles in walk until he stops near you. This should already have been established with your leading work. If your body language says 'Stop', he will. Stand up tall in an assertive way, and stay still so that you are also 'in halt'. Praise him when he has done well and then repeat the walk-trot-walk circles on the other rein. If the lunge line is connected to the centre nose ring of the cavesson or to the bit connector you will not need to alter it but if it is clipped to the bit, change it to the other side.

When giving your horse verbal aids, use the same words he is already familiar with from his leading training, adding in 'Trot', 'Steady' and so on as you need to. Bring his first lunge session to a close by leading him around the school to relax before finishing the lesson, which should be about fifteen to twenty minutes long, excluding the time it takes to lead him around before and after. As soon as your horse is happy being lunged in an enclosed space, try lungeing him in a bigger area; move your circle around the school so that you are not grinding around on the same spot. Apart from preventing the surface from being dug up, it gives an added dimension to the work to keep both you and your horse thinking about what you are doing.

TRAINING AIDS

Ground poles

Simply placing a pole on the ground for your horse to walk over will encourage him to stretch his neck down and promote flexion of his joints as he lifts his feet over it, helping him to keep a rhythm in his gaits. As he lifts his feet and lowers his neck, he has to employ his stomach and back muscles more, strengthening his whole body. Pole work is by far the easiest way to improve the way your horse moves and help him concentrate on his training, and is often a far simpler solution to solving training problems than resorting to 'quick fix' gadgets.

EXERCISE 1

Place one pole on your circle for your horse to step over (Figure 14.5). This is also a good exercise for you as you have to line your horse up with the centre of the pole each time. Make sure that you can do this in walk before attempting it in trot. Once you achieve this several times in walk, try it at a steady trot. You will have to move about a bit yourself to get in the right place, and may need to lengthen or shorten your lunge line as you do so. If you have any problems, move away from the pole and lunge your horse without going over it.

Figure 14.5 Place one pole on a circle for your horse to step over.

EXERCISE 2

As soon as you have mastered one pole, place another on the opposite side of the circle and lunge him over the two. This is far simpler for your horse to master initially than a row of poles, which might panic him and make him try to jump them. This exercise can be done in walk, trot or canter.

EXERCISE 3

Next, add in two more poles to make a star shape (Figure 14.6). Spaced evenly around the circle, the poles help your horse to get used to stepping over a sequence of poles in a rhythm without them being too close together and worrying him. This exercise can be done in walk, trot and a steady canter.

EXERCISE 4

As soon as the previous exercise is successfully executed, place three of the poles in a fan shape with the centre of each pole about 4 m (13 ft) away from the next (Figure 14.7). Try this exercise in walk before proceeding to trot as it requires good co-ordination both from you and your horse.

Figure 14.6 Poles laid out in a star shape.

Figure 14.7 Poles laid out in a large fan shape. Leaving a space for a trot stride between the poles prevents the horse from rushing.

The chambon

The best way to encourage your horse to stretch down, in my opinion, is to lunge him in a chambon if he is too tight through his back to do this of his own volition.

With a chambon, there is no restriction on the horse stretching down (Figure 14.8) It only comes into effect, if correctly fitted, if he tries to lift his head unnaturally high.

Figure 14.8 Trevor's top-line muscles of the neck and back are being stretched and the lower neck muscles are relaxed. The belly muscles can be seen tightening to support the spine from underneath.

The chambon consists of a head piece which should be shaped to sit comfortably over the horse's poll and not interfere with the sensitive area around the ears. The head piece has a strap attached to it with a ring on each end. A cord attaches to the bit each side and passes through the rings on the head-piece strap. This cord is then attached to the girth between the horse's front legs by a connecting strap. The strap should be fitted so that the cord attachment is just taut when the horse is standing with his neck in a natural position; it should only act if he tries to raise his head too high and is not designed to hold his head down. The cord should loosen as soon as the horse lowers his head and neck.

248

Any gadget which holds the head down can damage ligaments and strain neck muscles or, at the very least, cause incorrect muscle development in the horse, which can take months of remedial training to resolve.

The chambon works by applying poll pressure from the head piece and contact with the bit if a horse lifts his head too high but, as soon as he relaxes and stretches, the chambon becomes inactive. This encourages him to move with a softly swinging back, free gaits and in a calm, relaxed manner. He should stretch down naturally. Lungeing a horse in a chambon over a single pole on the ground can encourage him to stretch down and to activate his joints (Figure 14.9)

top-line muscles of the neck stretching

loins lifting

pelvis tucking under

poll joint supple

the horse should have a relaxed mouth and chew quietly at the bit with his mouth closed

tail carried in a relaxed manner

nose stretching forwards and downwards

increased flexion of the joints

lower neck muscle relaxed

stomach muscles supporting the horse's back from underneath

Figure 14.9 Action of the muscles when stretching forwards. Lungeing over a single pole on the ground can encourage a horse to both stretch down and activate his joints.

Side reins
SIDE-REIN HEIGHT AND LENGTH

It is most important to fix the side rein(s) at the correct height on the roller and at a suitable length to suit the conformation and muscle structure of the horse. The side reins should be parallel to the ground when the horse is reaching forward to, and working correctly on, the bit; his nose should be vertical and his poll the highest point, and the side reins should be adjusted to correspond to the height of the horse's neck so that they stay parallel to the ground. If they are too high the horse will lift his neck as before and if too low the horse will drop his head behind the vertical and overbend, looking back at his knees; this is not stretching but avoiding using the back muscles.

A horse with a low-set neck will need the side reins fitted lower than those for a horse with his neck set on high. A horse should be able to have his neck arched forward from his withers with, again, his nose vertical to the ground. On no account should the side reins be so short that they pull his head behind the vertical. This strains his poll area, restricts his jaw movement and can impair his breathing, and makes him tighten his neck muscles and fight the contact. Your horse must always appear to ease his neck forward into the reins in order for the rest of his body to work correctly.

Having the side reins too low can pull his neck down at the withers, putting him on his forehand. The only exception to this is when a horse is likely to rear: putting the side reins on too high with such a horse could result in him throwing himself over backwards and so, in this case, side-reins set a little too low will help keep his front end on the ground! Fixing the side reins too high can allow your horse to become tense through the underside of his neck and resist the bit contact with his jaw, giving the appearance of an upside-down neck. This can cause him to move with a tight, dipped back, and trailing hind legs, which could have disastrous results when you come to ride him. He should be working with engaged hind legs, and a lifted back, only then are the side-reins effective.

It is not only the conformation but also the experience of the horse that must be taken into consideration. A novice horse working in a lower frame will require longer side reins than an advanced horse that is able to work in collection in a shorter frame and that will be happy with shorter ones. (Figures 14.10a and b.)

poll the highest point

top-line of the neck arches forwards and upwards

loins lifting

pelvis tucked under

a relaxed mouth accepting the bit

tail carried in a relaxed manner

lower neck muscle relaxed

increased flexion of the joints

stomach muscles support the back from underneath

Figures 14.10a and b Action of the muscles when working in a correct outline on the bit. a) Lungeing in side reins. Amadeus is stepping energetically forwards but is not lifting his back and relaxing into the contact; b) Lungeing in side reins over a pole with the lunge rein inverted has the desired effect. The horse's poll should be the highest point and his nose on or just in front of the vertical.

TYPES OF SIDE-REIN

To help your horse establish a steady contact with the bit, plain side reins are the best and these can be made of leather or webbing. There are various other options on the market, some with rubber-ring inserts and some with elastic inserts. These can be useful for sensitive horses that have been frightened by being held in too tightly by a strong-handed rider, as a small amount of give in the rein can help them gain confidence working into a contact again. But if there is too much give, as sometimes happens with elastic inserts, a difficult horse will work out that if he pulls against the side reins the give develops a yo-yo effect with his neck. The horse will remember this and, when you come to ride him, he will probably keep pulling your arms forward. If you have a weak position in the saddle it is likely he will find your point of no return and you could end up on the ground.

By training him with plain side reins, your horse will learn to take a comfortable contact with the bit as the reins give him a clear boundary within which to work, just as you should when you ride him. A horse working correctly through his back and neck will find a soft steady contact within the parameters of the rein contact himself.

METHODS OF ATTACHMENT

Side reins can be used singly when the outside side rein is attached as normal but no side rein is attached on the inside; the lunge line is the only inside rein and is attached to the bit. If you are not confident about having the lunge line attached to the bit, attach it to the inside ring on the lunge cavesson nose piece.

Some horses can panic if both side reins are put on at once and throw their heads up, pulling themselves in the mouth. Using just the fixed outside side rein is, therefore, a good way to introduce side reins to your horse; you can reassure your horse with small half-halts on the lunge line. Just closing your fist and softening it again will usually suffice. Inverting the lunge line by passing it through the bit ring and fastening it to the girth can help to flex the horse a little to keep him under control (Figure 14.11).

When using both side reins, each rein should be attached to the bit and attached to the roller at a height which allows the horse to carry his head

Figure 14.11 Lungeing Amadeus with the lunge line inverted to help me ask him to flex and to stop him running off (he was very spooky that day). A normal side rein is on the outside.

vertical to the ground and his neck in a comfortably rounded outline so that his gait is not inhibited and his shoulder movement is not shortened. His muscles should look as though they are working, but he should not appear to be uncomfortable.

LUNGE TRAINING

Circles

Loosen your horse in walk, trot (and canter if he is at that stage). These circle patterns can be executed with no training aids. To familiarize yourself with the different sizes of circle, pace them out yourself on the ground before bringing out your horse. The largest circle will be 15 m in diameter, then 12 m and finally 10 m. For some of these exercises you will need a larger area to lunge in, either square or rectangular at least 20 m x 30 m. If your horse is new to lungeing then begin with ten minutes in total, changing direction after five minutes. Half an hour is plenty for a fit horse and make sure you change the rein frequently, at least every ten minutes. If you have worked him on one rein once, and on the other twice, make sure you do the reverse on the next session to ensure that his muscles are worked evenly on both sides, even if one direction is easier than the other. He needs to get the feeling of what to do on his good side to help him improve on his worst rein.

Always introduce new exercises without any training aids attached at first but if your horse comes out of the stable really full of himself and you risk losing control, a loose chambon is useful. It will only act if he throws his head up high and will not therefore cause him to panic but just give him something to be aware of.

First of all, work your horse in a steady trot, or walk if he is calm enough, on a 15 m circle. If you need the circle to be bigger, then walk a small one yourself rather than lengthening the lunge line. This keeps you close enough to him to touch him with the whip, as well as staying near him so that he concentrates on you. Giving him the full length of the lunge line not only provides him with the chance to look around at the countryside, but he will also be far enough away from you to ignore you. A relaxed, supple horse will be able to work on a circle, stretching down on his own, and not be crooked through his body. Young horses will tend to look to the outside and scramble around the circle by falling on their inside shoulder. Crafty horses may take advantage and either run in at you, or pull away (see page 259). A chambon will help with crookedness problems by encouraging your horse to tuck his pelvis under so that his hind legs are under his body enabling him to take weight on them. This enables him to ease weight off his front legs thus improving his balance and making himself more manoeuvrable and being able to bend through his spine sufficiently to follow the line of the curve of the circle, which causes the ribs on the inside of the bend to be pushed closer together.

If you find your horse sticks his neck to the inside to avoid bending his spine, then use just one side rein on the outside to keep his neck in line with his body. This helps his inside hind leg step forward under his belly, causing him to bend correctly. A correct bend along his spine helps him to take a contact on the outside rein without hanging on it. You will need to fasten your lunge line to the inside bit ring so that you can act as the inside rein, asking him with half-halts to flex his poll slightly to ensure that his forehead is facing directly around the line of the circle. His forehead should line up with the front of his chest if he is bending correctly along his spine. There should not be excessive bend in a horse's neck on a circle. If there is, have a look at the horse's hind legs, I am sure that they will be flung away to the outside of the circle and not taking any weight. Your horse's neck position is an indicator as to what is going on with the rest of him. If he can stretch down correctly, then he should be able to work into a pair of side reins, which should be of the same length. If you have an advanced horse and are working specifically on small circles, you may need to shorten the inside rein a hole or two to allow him to flex his head slightly to the inside at the poll; this must not be abused. Having the inside rein too short causes tension and resistance in the jaw and poll which could, in turn, cause tension in your horse's back and inhibit the engagement of his hind legs. Small-circle work must be interspersed with large circles to prevent tension and to keep the gaits of your horse true and rhythmical.

EXERCISES
Exercise 1
Position yourself and your horse in one corner of the school. Lunge him at trot on a 12 m circle and then continue on a straight line, travelling with him up the school. After travelling a few metres, bring him around on another 12 m circle. Repeat this sequence all around the arena until you are back where you started. Repeat on the other rein. This can be done in walk, trot or canter. You may like to trot the circles, and walk in between and then canter the circles, trotting in between, and so on.

Exercise 2
Lunge your horse on a 15 m circle maintaining a steady rhythm in whichever gait you have chosen to work in. Remaining on the spot, with your leading heel, i.e. the same heel as the rein on which you are working, pushed into the ground so that you do not move, shorten the lunge line to bring your horse in on a slightly smaller circle. Each couple of circuits, make the circle a little smaller, until it is 10 m. Giving half-halts on the line are important to flex his poll slightly, regulate the rhythm and test his brakes. If your horse becomes tense, let him out again gradually. Spiralling in and out in this way helps him to bend his spine, step under with his inside hind leg,

and tuck his pelvis under. This is one way of introducing your horse to collection, or taking weight on his hind legs. Repeat on the other rein.

Transitions

Trying to ask a fresh horse to make walk and halt transitions is futile. Most horses do not want to come out of their stable and halt. It is better to let him trot on a large circle and then make walk to trot transitions as soon as you can to get him to concentrate; you can then begin your training session. Leave halt transitions until the end of your session when he is more likely to listen.

Transition aids are given with your voice and your body. Using your voice to ask him to walk, trot or canter should suffice. Horses are perfectly able to learn word commands provided you say them in the same tone of voice each time, but do say them as though you mean it; a timid whisper will no doubt be ignored but neither is there any need to bellow at him. Stand up tall at all times and try to develop an air of authority: friendly but firm should be your attitude. By remaining quiet in your movements, your horse will easily notice if you move the whip slightly, brace your body (a very effective half-halt when it is coordinated with a small tug on the lunge line) or soften your muscle tone. Your body tone should fluctuate between standing to attention and standing normally (without slouching). Planting the heel of your leading foot into the ground makes you like an immovable post so that you can hold a steady contact on the line without leaning back or pulling; you are pulling if you cannot soften your fingers at any given time.

Ask for a transition at the moment when it looks as though it is going to work and not when your horse is going too fast or is unbalanced. If the transitions are well prepared for, they should be easy for him.

When you ask for an upward transition, there is no need to rush towards your horse brandishing the whip. A common mistake is to let the lunge line go loose in an effort to encourage the horse forward, but all this will do is to abandon the rein contact and confuse him. Stand up tall, keep your elbows by your sides as though you were riding him, give two or three half-halts by means of small tugs on the lunge line in order to get his attention and say your command word. At the same time, sweep your whip forward towards his inside hind leg to encourage him (the whip is a substitute for your leg aids). Once he has made the transition, maintain a steady contact with the bit with gentle half-halts, using a closing and relaxing motion of your fist, or firmer tugs if you feel him resist you. Otherwise keep your hand quiet and still so as not to disturb the steady contact once you have it. Too much fiddling with the line will make your horse tense in his mouth or unsteady in his head carriage. He will become shy of the rein contact and may well avoid it by tucking his chin in. If this happens, keep your rein hand still and encourage him forward to the contact with a smooth sweeping motion of the whip. Half-halts prevent you getting into a pulling match with your horse. It is far easier to stay in control in a relaxed manner by using short spells of any gait rather than endless circles in canter which get faster and faster, ending up with your horse getting away from you.

For downward transitions, again prepare him with two or three half-halts, co-ordinating the last half-halt with your command word. If he does not make the transition, continue for a few more strides, repeat the preparation and ask again. As soon as he responds correctly, reward him with a 'Good boy' but keep the praise short and clear. As before, maintain a steady contact on the lunge line after a successful transition.

EXERCISES
Exercise 1
Frequent transitions will make sure that he responds when requested at all times, e.g. one circle in trot, half a circle in walk, one circle in trot, and so on. This exercise can progress to counting the number of walk steps between the trot transitions, say six walk steps, then trot a circle, walk five steps, then trot etc.

Exercise 2
Once you and your horse are confident with transitions from walk to trot and trot to walk, proceed to transitions into and out of canter. To ask for canter from a steady trot, give a few half-halts on the lunge line to prepare your horse and keep the circle to about 15 m so that you can touch his inside hind leg with the lunge whip if you need to reinforce your aid for the upward transition. Follow this sequence: canter for two circles, trot again for

one circle, canter for three circles, and trot again for one circle. If your horse does not understand the canter aid at first, try cantering alongside him for a few steps, and then resume the circle. A good friend of mine does this with such success she does not need to say anything, she just moves her own legs in trot or canter and her horse copies her. You may need to walk a small circle yourself so that your horse is working on a larger circle in canter to help him balance.

PROBLEM SOLVING

Rushing and running away

If a horse starts to go too fast, slow him with short sharp tugs on the lunge line so that he feels them through the lunge cavesson. The horse should be wearing the lunge cavesson over a bridle with the noseband removed. Then you can cue half-halts on the cavesson and have the side reins attached to the bit. Place one pole on the ground and lunge him over it several times to help him focus on something other than rushing off. If he still does not listen and is playing around, now may be the time to introduce one side rein on the outside attached to the roller and the bit. If you feel confident working with the lunge line clipped to the bit, you can act as the inside rein and can give smaller half-halts directly to the bit. The outside side rein will give enough contact to ensure that the bit will not become crooked in the horse's mouth.

Using the side rein will ensure that the horse now starts to move in a rounder outline because he will have to use his muscles and work hard instead of just running around acting the fool. Place a single pole on the track at 90 degrees to the fence/wall, halfway along one side of the school. You need to keep him on a small circle, about 12 m in diameter, to settle him down and as soon as he is settled, let him out onto a 15 m circle. Lunge him over the pole every now and again; you will have to move your circle around the school to do this. Repeat the work on the other rein. Once he has behaved well and is a bit tired, finish the session by removing the side rein and allowing him to stretch down. Finally lead him once around the school as you did in the first stage of lungeing.

Another way to deal with rushing or running away is to try attaching your lunge line to the girth, then threading it through the bit ring to your hand. This gives you the chance to flex your horse quickly so that he cannot fix his neck and pull away from you, but you must be careful not to pull his head around. Make sure you relax the rein as soon as he responds. Once he has settled, attach the lunge line normally again.

PULLING THE LUNGE LINE OUT OF YOUR HAND

Some horses learn to jerk the lunge line out of your hand. Rather than trying to hang on and risking broken fingers, or a wrist, and a horse trailing the lunge line behind him, do not put the lunge line on him but put the side reins on and 'mock' lunge him by standing exactly as you would when lungeing and guiding him around you with the whip. Within a few circuits of the school his attention should be redirected to you and he will listen to your voice when you ask him to slow down and stop. As soon as he stops, stroke him gently to calm him, clip the lunge line back on and you should be able to lunge him normally.

If your horse does rush around the school, control your anxiety otherwise he will sense your nervousness and become anxious himself. Whatever worries you have, such as being concerned that he might fall over or break a leg, remain calm, stand tall, be in command and mentally will him to slow down. Telepathy does work with horses; your posture and mental concentration on what it is you want them to do will help you to control them without uttering a word.

If he still refuses to slow down or stop, turn your back on him and stand quietly out of the way, ignoring him. Put your whip down and fold your arms so that no signals are given. Empty your mind of everything he is up to and think about something else such as what to cook for supper or the cobwebs on the school roof, anything to totally switch your attention to something other than the horse. Once he realizes you are not interested any more, the pounding hooves will stop; resist the urge to look round at him and he should come up to you quietly. Amadeus sneaks up a few steps at a time and then stops to see what I do. He absolutely hates being ignored and so this is by far the best tactic with him.

Wait until your horse is very close and then quietly turn to face him. Do not stare him in the eye as this could be taken as a threat and he will run off again. Stroke his forehead gently; clapping him loudly on the neck is not a comforting gesture and he may take offence. Always be very quiet with praise when your horse is good, even talking to him in a whisper, because this has the added benefit of calming you down as well.

Finally, when calm and order are restored, clip the lunge line on and lunge him again. Finish on a good note with stretching exercises on the lunge.

Laziness and refusal to co-operate

If your horse goes to the opposite end of the speed scale and moves too slowly when you lunge him, sweep the whip in towards his haunches; you need to be close enough to flick him with the end of the whip. It is futile hitting the ground with it because you will just fray the end of the lash and have no influence over your horse. In order to get him moving and then to keep him moving, you will need to move alongside him, either in a brisk walk or slow run. Run alongside him in a straight line, and then walk on a small circle yourself, keeping him trotting in a circle around you. Before he loses momentum, go off on a straight line again to refresh the trot. This can be quite exhausting (for you, not him) so take frequent breaks in walk, keeping him going with quick flicks with the end of the whip if necessary. Make sure you both enjoy each session and keep the time short, no more that fifteen minutes, so that you finish on a good note with him feeling energized, not worn out and bored. You may be better lungeing a lazy horse in a chambon to encourage him to stretch and move. Side reins may put him off the idea of moving forward initially, but he should progress to accepting them after about a month of stretching work.

Leaping and spooking

A spooky, nervous horse is best lunged in a chambon, which will encourage him to work through his back rather than jump in the air. It is less restrictive than side reins, which a nervous horse may resent and react to by throwing his head in the air and jabbing himself in the mouth. If a horse throws his head in the air when wearing a chambon, the head piece gives subtle poll pressure and contact with the bit at the same time. The horse finds it difficult to work with his head up in the air with the lower muscles in his neck tightening and quickly works out that if he relaxes his neck and back, the chambon becomes loose and non-restrictive. As soon as the horse experiences the preferable sensation of stretching down, he should calm down within a few minutes and be able to walk and trot with a relaxed demeanour, using his back, stomach and hindquarter muscles properly.

At the end of the session, remove the chambon and your horse should be happy to stretch down on his own. You may need a lunge session each day or every other day for a week or two to establish relaxed work, depending on how quickly the horse calms down.

Spinning round

If your horse becomes afraid, or simply fed up, he may spin round to face the other way. This can also happen if you are lungeing him on his stiff side, and he will try to go the other way. If he succeeds, stay as you are, calmly bring him onto a smaller circle until he walks and then bring him closer still so that he halts. Once he stands still you can calmly move around to the other side of him and start again.

If he spins quickly and ends up with the line wrapped around his body, he should stop. Try not to panic, move quietly towards him and walk around him, unravelling the line as you go. Provided you are calm, he will stand still. Once you have sorted out the line, resume what you are doing in a calm manner.

Cutting in

If a horse cuts in, keep the lunge line low and sweep the whip towards his shoulder with an underhand flick, like an underhand badminton serve.

Attaching one side rein on the outside will help as it gives the horse some support on that side. Repeat the work on the other rein with just the new outside rein attached; he must be worked in the same way on both reins even if he finds one way easier than the other. It is a mistake to keep going for longer on the difficult rein than on the good rein as the horse will get annoyed and anxious because he finds it hard. Give him a break by working him on his easier rein so that he relaxes and is then more able to accept working on the more difficult rein again. Once he is happy working with the outside side rein attached, attach the inside side rein to get him used to having the contact with both reins. At this stage, you can either continue with the lunge line attached to the bit, provided you are subtle enough not to interfere too much with the side-rein contact and just concentrate on guiding the horse around the circle or on a straight line if you are moving around the school, or, if you prefer, you can attach the line to the front ring of the cavesson.

If your horse is very sensitive to the rein contact attach the side reins to the side rings of the cavesson, but this is not a good idea with a headstrong horse that will probably ignore them altogether.

Running at the trainer

If your horse runs at you, threatening your authority, you must be brave and stand up tall. Move quickly to one side of him so that you are level with his belly to head him off, preferably so that you have your line and whip in the correct hands. (Most remedies for lungeing problems involve being quick on your feet.) Make a very fast movement towards his quarters with the whip sending him forward and onto a circle, touching him with the lash if you can, just so that he knows you can still touch him. Resist the temptation to hit him hard on the backside because, if he is all ready tense and angry, this could infuriate him. Your half-halts will need to be firm ones to grab his attention so that he does not rush off but dig your heel into the ground to anchor yourself in case he tries to. He may well stop and run at you again, so employ the fancy footwork and move in line with his belly again. If you are quick enough the first time he tries to charge, he should not do it again. You need the element of surprise. Getting upset and yelling will not help but developing a tiger-like growl can be very effective. A horse's temper tantrums are best dealt with coolly and calmly so that you regain his respect quickly. Once he realizes he cannot upset you, he should calm down and you can then quietly resume the exercise for a minute or two before stopping and praising him. Rewarding a horse for being calm works much better than getting angry with him when he is cross.

Another way to deal with your horse running at you or falling in is to make a small square of poles and stand in it, lungeing your horse around the outside. He is not allowed into your space and placing a physical barrier between you acts as a visible deterrent.

15 LONG-REINING AND DOUBLE-LUNGEING

LONG-REINING AND lungeing with two reins or one long line (double-lungeing) are valuable skills to master when it comes to controlling and working your horse on the ground. Long-reining is useful for work in straight lines when working on transitions from walk to halt, reining back and piaffe and passage. Long-reining is often used to prepare horses for driving and for walking young horses out before they are trained under saddle. I do not use them for the latter because there is a great risk of being towed along by the green horse in this instance. Double-lungeing can help to develop the engagement of your horse's back and hindquarters by encouraging him to step under from behind more, especially when working with one rein passing around behind him. This helps him to develop collection, i.e. to take more weight on his hind legs.

With experience you can achieve the 'feel' required to guide your horse on long-reins, learning how to use the rein contact as necessary in exactly the way you would when riding. In order to long-rein and/or double-lunge your horse, it is important to have mastered normal lungeing first. Bear in mind that all horses are different. You may find it easier to control your horse on a circle than on a straight line, in which case it may be beneficial to double-lunge before long-reining on straight lines. You can use either two separate lunge lines, which can be a bit of a handful, or one continuous line, which is about the length of $1^{1}/_{2}$ lunge lines and is less cumbersome. I have patented a design for an easy-to-use continuous line, the Feeline which is sold as part of my lungeing kit that is on the market. The Feeline has a clip at each end to attach to the bit and a sliding clip on each side to attach to the roller (Figure 15.1). If you use two separate lunge lines they have to be

Figure 15.1 My Feeline has a clip at each end and a 'sliding' clip on each side for quick and easy attachment to either the bit or the roller.

threaded through the rings on the roller, which takes longer to do. Also, they are less easy to remove should you need to disconnect them in a hurry.

Even if one long line is used, attached to the bit on both sides, I refer to 'reins' plural in the same context as when riding: two reins are always referred to even though they are buckled together.

Equipment for long-reining and double-lungeing

Gloves, stout footwear and a hat are advisable as with all in-hand work for your own safety (see equipment list on page 47). You may need a long schooling whip, driving whip or lunge whip to encourage your horse. A lunge whip could be awkward to handle bearing in mind you have long-reins to cope with but it enables you to be far enough behind the horse's hind legs to be out of range should he kick out. If you are using a schooling whip on the side of your horse's haunches furthest away from you, stand slightly to the other side of his haunches so that, again, you are out of the firing line should he kick.

Kit out your horse in his lungeing gear of boots, roller, and bridle (see also pages 48 and 242) and a cavesson if you prefer to attach the reins to this rather than the bit.

LONG-REINING

When you long-rein, you walk behind your horse with a rein in each hand. This can either be with two separate lines, one in each hand or one continuous line that attaches to both sides of the bit. This training can be useful for teaching your horse to drive and accustom him to you being behind him. At first, he will be unsure of where you are and tend to tip his head in order to look at you, which can make it difficult to guide him in a straight line. It is better to walk slightly to one side of his haunches until he is used to you being there because firstly, he can see you, and secondly, should he kick out you are not in the direct firing line of his hind legs. Only when he is relaxed with you slightly to one side should you move directly behind him. When you first move directly behind him, it might be a good idea to do so for just a few moments and then move to one side again so that he can see you. Gradually work up to spending longer behind him as you need to. (Figure 15.2.)

Figure 15.2 Long-reining with the rein-handler positioned to one side of the horse. Herman – with Maria handling the long reins and me assisting – is wearing side reins to help to maintain a round outline. Note how light the contact is on the long reins as we guide Herman around the school.

265

How to long-rein

The long reins are attached to the bit rings, and then pass to your hands. Putting them through, or clipping them to, the rings on the roller can help to prevent them dropping too low down, when you run the risk of the horse putting a leg over the rein. It would not be wise to use a saddle for this work in case your horse reacts adversely, such as rearing, falling over backwards or galloping off and the saddle is damaged in the process. This has happened and so it is wise to use a roller to ensure you do not have to replace your expensive saddle.

Before attempting to long-rein him, work your horse on the lunge as normal to settle him. At the end of the lunge session, change your lunge whip for the schooling or driving whip, if one of these is less cumbersome to hold than the lunge whip, and stand on the nearside of your horse by his shoulder. Keep hold of the line, pass the other end of the line over his neck, go around the front of the horse and clip it to the roller and the offside bit ring or, if you are using separate lines, pass the second one through the offside roller ring and then clip it on to the offside bit ring. Feed the line out as you slowly walk into position just behind his haunches on the nearside.

With the schooling whip in your right hand, pointing forward on the outside of his right hind leg so that you can easily give him a quick tap on the leg if you need to, ask him to walk on using your chosen voice command, which should have been established in his earlier lunge sessions. He may peer at you strangely out of the corner of one eye as you are working him from an unfamiliar place but he should get used to this after a couple of attempts to get him to walk forward. If he does not, then a small flick with the whip will help. Practise walking and halting a few times. To halt, stand tall, stop walking, brace your position, and maintain a steady hold on the reins but do not pull. If you resort to pulling, your horse may well set his neck and pull against you, which could result in you being towed along unceremoniously. If this happens, half-halt with your whole body a few times until he stops. Think, 'stop, and stop, and stop', and 'play' him into the halt like a fish on a line rather than trying to make a dead stop. Plant both feet firmly on the ground, and brace your legs, back, stomach, biceps, and shoulders so that you feel like a concrete block at each half-halt. Once your horse feels you are immovable, he will stop. As soon as he has stopped, soften the reins, and your body tone, and reward him with your voice.

If you get into difficulties and he does make a run for it, hold the rein nearer the bit on one side and bring your horse around you on a circle. This is when one continuous line has the advantage: it does not drape along the ground and it is easy to control the far side of the line, which acts as your outside rein. It is, therefore, simple to bring him in on a small circle with the line either over his back, or around behind his haunches and you have no trailing reins to worry about. Just shorten the line so that you keep a contact with the bit. While bringing your horse around on a circle use half-halts to gain control; repeat the half-halts until you have sufficient control to stop him.

Once you have resumed control, make sure you can perfect the walk and halt transitions and do not proceed to trot unless you know your horse will stop. Your horse must be able to work in a steady collected trot for you to keep up easily. You do not want to be sprinting along behind him; besides this being exhausting, you may trip up and stomach-surfing in the dirt is neither fun nor elegant!

CONTROL EXERCISES

Control exercises such as long-reining your horse around obstacles, through poles etc. at walk is interesting for you both and safer than careering along at speed. It is a good way to practise working directly behind him when going between obstacles, and slightly to one side of him as you make large turns.

As soon as you can turn your horse in either direction, progress to practising figures of eight in walk. If you can manage, try them at a steady trot once you have mastered them in walk. Make frequent transitions to walk to test that your horse will slow and stop when asked. If he starts gathering speed, bring him around on a circle in the way described earlier. When he is working in trot, you will have to jog along behind to keep up but it will keep you fit! As you change direction in the figure of eight, make sure that you tell him clearly which way you want him to turn by feeling on the new inside rein with a closing and softening of your fist but make sure that you keep a contact on both reins. On the turn, the outside rein must ease slightly to allow him to turn in the new direction but do not soften the contact too much or you will pull him round with your inside rein and he may spin right round and stare you in the face.

DOUBLE-LUNGEING

Stand in the normal lungeing position in the middle of the circle. Attach one rein to the inside bit ring, or inside cavesson ring, and the other rein to the outside bit ring, or outside ring on the cavesson; this outside rein passes either over the horse's back or behind the horse. You then have a rein in each hand. If you use a continuous rein, attach each end to the bit or cavesson and position the outside rein in the same way as above. This training can encourage him to work with engaged hindquarters, to develop collection, and to improve transition work.

Lungeing and long-reining can be adapted to each individual horse and help you develop your awareness of the sensitivity of the horse's mouth and his reactions to your rein aids. It is a good way to encourage the horse to step under his body with his hind legs without forcing his muscles into a false roundness, which can cause all manner of physical and mental problems for him. Problems can occur, however, when using 'quick fix' gadgets that apparently cure everything. A good basic rule is to avoid using anything if you do not fully understand its effect on your horse. It is much better for you and your horse if you keep training aids to an absolute minimum. Physical development takes time and cannot be artificially achieved. Learning to handle, lunge and ride your horse correctly, with an understanding of how he moves and which muscles he uses is essential to having a fit, well-trained horse that will enjoy a long useful life.

How to Double-lunge

Equip your horse as for long-reining. Loosen him up by lungeing him normally with no training aids so that he can stretch and relax in walk, trot, and canter if you wish, on both reins. If you have one long line, attach it to the inside bit ring and coil it up so that you are using it just as a normal lunge line. If you are using two separate ones, leave one close by so that you can utilize it later.

Double-lungeing is not complicated but following a few basic ground rules will help you to become proficient in a very short time.

STAGE 1

Have the inside rein connected to the bit and passing directly to your inside hand as with normal lungeing. The outside rein is clipped to the bit, and clipped, or passed through, the outside ring on the roller before coming over the horse's back to your outside hand.

Commence lungeing as normal. If you are in any doubt about the sensitivity of your hands, then connect the double-lunge rein to the rings of a lunge cavesson in order to perfect your technique before attaching the line to the bit.

The outside rein controls the straightness of your horse, helping to keep his neck in line with his body and controlling his outside shoulder. With the outside rein passed over his back to your hand, all you have to worry about is keeping an even amount of contact on each rein. Keep the spare line coiled in your outside hand (the one holding the outside rein) so that your inside hand is able to feel the contact easily without extra rein to hold. Hold the outside rein steady to support your horse, and increase the contact slightly on both reins at the same time when you want to stop or half-halt. The rein aid works in conjunction with bracing your body. Just pulling on the reins will have too sharp an effect on your horse's mouth. With one continuous line, it is possible to hold the reins in one hand so that you can be sure of an even contact, leaving your other hand free to hold the lunge whip. If you need to make sure you have the line under control, lunge without the whip at first.

Position yourself level with your horse's belly in the lungeing position and ask him to walk on a circle around you. As he walks on, step further away from his belly, lengthening the reins by letting them slide through your fingers until your horse is on a 15 m circle around you. If you prefer to be closer to him at first, then walk a small circle yourself to stay with him. Practise walk and halt transitions and half-halts, bracing your back, stomach, arms and legs exactly as you would when riding these movements.

Repeat the same procedure on the other rein. Change the connection of the lunge lines so that your new inside rein passes directly to your inside hand and the outside rein lies over the horse's back as before.

You should have mastered walk and halt transitions after a few sessions and you can then progress to walk and trot transitions. Leave canter work until you feel confident working with the double-lunge but if your horse trots or canters without being asked, there are a couple of things that will help you keep him under control and settle him quickly.

Keep an even contact on both reins. Pulling on the inside rein will turn his neck in too much, and he may well pull away from you; if he does, shorten your outside rein to regain control of his neck. The advantage of having the reins attached to the bit is that you can alternate between a firm and soft fist on the inside rein to ask him to soften his jaw and stop pulling. If you hang on like grim death he may panic and dash off. Shorten the reins and gradually bring him on a smaller circle around you, half-halting as you go, and saying 'walk' calmly to him. Panicking and screeching at him will only make things worse. Remain calm and exude an air of quiet authority, even if you feel tense inside. Once your horse is calm and has stopped, praise him for stopping, repeat the exercise for a few minutes and then quit while you are ahead; that way your nerves stay intact, your horse can have a quiet think about the lesson, and you can have another go tomorrow. If you get problems, revert to normal lungeing to make the necessary corrections for a couple of weeks, and then try again.

If he spins round because you are pulling on the inside rein, keep your hands up so that the reins do not trail on the floor. They may wind around his body, but he should stand still as he will be trussed up like a chicken provided you keep calm and do not panic! Just walk over to him calmly, talking to him, and slowly unravel the reins. The easiest way is to walk around behind him to straighten out the reins, gather them up, and go back to the inside. Your outside rein should still be over his back, so it should be straightforward to retake the reins and start again.

STAGE 2

When using the Feeline fasten one end clip to the bit and connect the sliding clip to the roller (Figure 15.3a). Place the rein on the horse's back (Figure 15.3b). Go around the front of the horse to the other side (Figure 15.3c). Pick up the rein, and connect the *sliding clip* to the bit and the *end clip* to the roller (Figures 13.5d, e and f). This is your inside rein. Fastening it in this way helps you ask for a little flexion when you are lungeing. You are now ready to double-lunge on the right rein (Figure 13.5g). Begin with the inside rein inverted and the outside rein passed over the horse's back at first (Figure 15.3h). Whether using the Feeline or separate reins hold the inside rein in the same hand as the direction in which you are moving, and the outside rein in your other hand. With the inside rein inverted like this, you can feel gently on the inside rein to encourage your horse to flex laterally a little at the poll to help him bend around the circle. Having the rein attached to the roller and passing via the bit to your hand helps to prevent the horse resisting your rein aid as the rein acts on the bit in a sliding action. The outside rein controls the speed and amount of bend, and prevents his whole neck swinging in, which would allow his back end to swing out, and he would not have the correct lateral flexion to the inside.

It is important to be able to soften and firm your fists to feel the contact, thus helping your horse relax his jaw when working, and important only to do this when you feel your horse tensing against the bit. Altering the pressure of the bit very slightly encourages him to chew and not to set his neck and jaw against you. With double-lungeing you can feel the reactions of your horse very clearly in your hand and can respond immediately. Inverting the inside rein is extremely helpful if you have a stiff, resistant horse that is likely to set his neck and gallop off. By having the facility to ask for lateral poll flexion, as above, it is easier to keep your horse on a circle, and encourage him to flex. Again, you must on no account pull his head in with your inside rein in case he spins round. Keeping an even contact on both reins is important in order to keep his neck in line with his body, which helps to strengthen the correct neck muscles along his top line and the deep internal scalenus muscle at the base of his neck. Jack-knifing his neck will prevent these muscles from working and cause him to overbend and drop his poll.

Always work your horse evenly in each direction, even though he may find one easier than the other. Working him on his good rein gives him a break from the effort needed to work on his stiffer side. Resistance can simply be caused by tight muscles rather than naughtiness, though horses find bending through the body and flexing at the poll much harder when they are tense or stressed. Relaxation is necessary to permit bending through the body.

a

b

Figures 15.3a–h a) Clip an end clip to the bit and the sliding clip to the roller. b) Place the rein on the horse's back; c) Go around the front of the horse to the other side; d) Pick up the rein on the offside;

c

d

e

f

e) Clip the sliding clip to the bit; f) Clip the end clip to the roller; g) You are now ready to double-lunge on the right rein; h) Double-lungeing with the inside rein inverted and the outside rein over the horse's back.

g

h

STAGE 3

Warm up as before with the line used as a lunge line attached to the bit. Follow Stage 1 with the inside rein running from the bit to your inside hand and the outside rein over his back. Remember to work in both directions in walk and trot, making good transitions. Then ask him to halt and pass the outside rein behind his hind legs, positioning it just above his hocks (Figure 15.4). Begin in walk first so that he gets used to the line before you commence trot work. Having the line behind his haunches encourages him to step under with his hind legs and is very useful for developing half-halts and transition work. Having worked through the previous two stages you should now be familiar with using your inside and outside reins evenly. This even contact must be maintained with the rein around his haunches. Practise having the reins in one hand so that you can feel the horse take an even contact on both sides of the bit; it is also easier to cope with a whip if you have one hand free. The rein contact should only be strong enough to keep the offside line in contact with your horse's hind legs, just above his hocks as stated, and your inside rein guides him round the circle. If the contact is too strong with the inside rein, you will cause too much bend in your horse's neck and if it is too strong with the outside hand, the line may slip up under

Figure 15.4 Double-lungeing with the rein passing behind the horse.

274

the horse's tail. If this happens, keep a steady contact on your inside rein and just loosen the rein around the haunches until it slides back into place, then take up an even contact again.

It is a good idea to practise without a lunge whip at first until you have gained confidence with handling the reins; a schooling whip pointed at your horse's hindquarters may prove beneficial and will be less awkward than a lunge whip. By this stage your horse should be responsive to your voice aids, but the outside rein can help you. If you ask your horse to walk on, for example, and he does not, tug the outside rein slightly against his hind legs to persuade him to walk on. If he goes too fast, half-halt with your body and both reins. You should now see the effect of having the outside rein behind his quarters: as you increase the pressure on both reins, his pelvis should appear to tuck under, you should see his back lift up and his neck will arch forward to the bit. Once he has responded to the half-halt, ease the contact on the reins but do not let them go slack. Maintaining a slight contact with both reins shows him how to half-halt correctly and in balance, with all four legs placed vertically under his body: his hind legs under his pelvis, and his front legs under his shoulders. If he is a little resistant to the bit, you could invert your inside rein as before to help ask for flexion. These half-halts are the foundation of good transitions, which in turn lead to collection. To start with, perfect your transition work from halt to walk, walk to halt, walk to trot, and trot to walk. Then try transitions within each gait, e.g. medium walk to collected walk and vice versa, working trot to collected trot and so on.

Once your horse is working happily in walk and trot, canter work can be introduced. The motion of the haunches lowering can cause the line to slip up under his tail and so it is important to keep a 'soft' outside rein, and not to pull. Lifting your hands too high can have the same effect and so keep an eye on your hand and arm position at all times. Aim for a slow, collected canter to help your horse take his weight back onto his haunches. As his haunches lower, his forehand will appear to lift, if he is working correctly.

DEVELOPING COLLECTION

A horse should reach forward to the bit once his posture and balance are correct. Collection begins with the pelvis being tucked under, the back being lifted and the neck being arched and reaching forward into a rein contact. It has nothing to do with holding the head and neck of the horse forcefully in position and compelling him to go forward. In these circumstances he will of course not want to go forward because he cannot if he has tense disconnected hind legs with stiff joints. The hind legs begin at the point of croup where the spine connects to the pelvis (sacroiliac joint) and so a horse that is unable lower his haunches from this point will not be able to flex his stifle or hock joints either because all these joints work together. If the pelvis cannot tuck under, the back legs cannot bend and come under the haunches thus they cannot take weight and the horse cannot be balanced. He can certainly not work in collection.

Faulty collection

Horses that are forced into attempting collection before they are ready often show typical faults. The hind legs step so far forward under the belly that they no longer carry weight. This is the result of a horse being forced to work with his hind legs underneath him before the rest of his body is able to conform. Because his legs are so far forward, he can lower his haunches without coiling his loins and, as stated above, if the sacroiliac joint is not flexed, neither are the stifles or hocks. These straight stiff legs in their unnaturally forward position make the horse look as though he could fall back on his tail and if the forelegs also slant back behind the shoulders, not supporting the forehand, the fore and hind feet look like they are hobbled together.

A horse displaying these faults will appear to be rounded, but the neck will develop a dip in front of the withers, the nose will lie behind the vertical and he will move with a shuffling gait. This is just sacrificing correct training for a 'round' top line. Poll problems are common in horses with this false roundness and such horses will need to be retrained from the beginning so that their spines can again be supported from underneath by the proper muscular development.

A horse that is held in with tight reins and forced up to the bridle will take short tense, not collected, steps. The structural problems are the opposite of those listed above: the pelvis will be tipped away, causing his back to hollow, and the hind legs, although equally stiff and straight, will be out

276

behind pushing the horse along without taking any weight at all and, once again, the sacroiliac, stifle and hock joints cannot flex. The horse carries himself on his front legs, with all his weight being taken on his forehand.

A horse moving in this way will resist the rein contact by contracting his top line muscles and lifting his neck. The muscle below the neck (brachiocephalic) will bulge and there will appear to be a triangular dip at the base of his neck because the muscle in front of the withers (splenius) is not supporting his neck. The muscle along the middle of the neck (complexus) will be thick at the head end and non-existent at the shoulder end. His poll will be tight and he will lean against the bit with a locked jaw. Quite often these horses are ridden or lunged in draw reins to lower the neck but if the neck is lowered in isolation, the back remains tense and the hind legs disengaged; forcing the neck to be 'round' does not help the horse to use his back. Once the draw reins are taken off, the horse will lift his neck even higher because the muscles he has been using to fight the reins will have become stronger and so his whole body shape becomes even more 'upside down' than before: he will move with a sagging middle, his nose up in the air and trail his hind legs. Again, the only way to help this situation is to go back to correct training.

POLE WORK

Double-lungeing over poles can be extremely beneficial for strengthening your horse's muscles and mobilizing his joints, while reminding him to work with his hind legs underneath him (Figure 15.5).

As with all new pole exercises, start with one pole on the ground and line him up with the centre of the pole. Make sure that you can keep the outside rein in place above his hocks and a contact with your inside rein, whether you have it directly to the bit, or inverted. Maintaining an even contact with the reins is very important to make sure your horse can use both hind legs equally and reaches the pole(s) straight on. His neck must be straight, and he must be allowed to extend his neck forward, so that he has the freedom to move his shoulders correctly, and to work evenly with his front and hind legs.

Figure 15.5 Double-lungeing over raised poles encourages both working through the back and activity of the joints, and is much safer than trying to run along behind.

Double-lungeing gives you the sensitivity to feel how much rein contact your horse needs, and enables you to adjust his outline to that required for maximum schooling benefit. Make sure you are happy in walk before attempting trot work. Single poles are simpler to use. If you are attempting a sequence of poles, keep it to a maximum of three so that you can concentrate on controlling your reins both before and after the poles. It would be inadviseable to canter over poles because, as canter puts a horse's hind legs under him, he might jump the poles. You would also have to be extremely careful to keep the rear line in place just above his hocks so that he could not accidentally catch a leg up in it.

16 LOOSE SHOOLING

WHAT IS LOOSE SCHOOLING?

Loose schooling is allowing your horse to work free without a lunge line. But it must be work: loose schooling should never be an excuse not to work a horse properly or to just let him run amok around the school because you cannot be bothered to get your tack out. Loose schooling is about developing communication between you and your horse. If your preliminary work has been thorough and sound, making sure that your horse always understands you, then he should listen willingly when free in the school. It would not be wise to try it with a new horse who barely knows who you are as it is more than likely he will charge around calling to other horses and would probably be hard to catch again. If you have been having problems catching your horse in the field, then establishing the ground rules in the school is a safer option than in a large open space. Exercises in loose schooling begin with simple walk-when-I-walk, stop-when-I-stop exercises, building to the more advanced free jumping of single jumps and, later, grid work.

Your horse can either be worked free, i.e. without side reins, so that he can stretch and loosen his muscles or he can be worked with side reins so that you can keep a little control over him and ensure he uses the correct muscles throughout his body. They should be fitted so that he can arch his neck forward to the bit with his nose just vertical, or just in front of the vertical, and at the correct height on the roller to keep his neck in a comfortable position, allowing him to remain relaxed and free through his shoulders. Running about with his head raised and the lower neck muscles tight results in his hind legs trailing out behind him, and short tense steps

279

will not be beneficial to his training at all. If this happens, it is better to train him on the lunge first, either in a chambon or side reins until he is calm, and then spend a few minutes with him working free at the end of the session.

Some horses do take advantage of you when they are let loose and so if your horse is one of these, rather than risk losing his attention totally it is again advisable to loose school him in side reins. A chambon is not necessary as your horse should stretch of his own accord.

To make loose schooling sessions more gymnastic, poles on the ground or raised poles, such as cavalletti or heavy poles placed on plastic blocks (though these must be filled with sand or water to stop them moving out of place), are most useful. Loose schooling also gives you the opportunity to watch your horse from a distance and observe how he copes with such obstacles on his own, which can reveal a lot about his character.

It is important not to overface your horse and always begin with simple exercises to build his confidence. *Never* use side reins or any other attachment on a horse when he is jumping. He needs to stretch his neck over the jump and to use it to balance, and requires the freedom through his back and shoulders to launch himself off the ground. When landing, he raises his neck; if his neck is tied down he cannot lift it and will most likely have a terrible fall.

WHERE TO LOOSE SCHOOL

The most important aspect of loose schooling is choosing an enclosed area, such as an indoor school, in which to do it. An outdoor arena must have a fence high enough to discourage the horse from jumping out. They can jump amazingly high from a trot when the lure of a nice cosy stable overrides any interest in your plans for the day. If you do not have access to such a safe arena, then the following work can also be done on the lunge. To prevent your horse getting into the corners of the school and potentially spinning around in the opposite direction, place a pole across each corner.

It is important that the school surface is sound. A deep, loose surface could cause your horse to fall over, and if he steps into the deeper holes of an uneven surface, he could be injured. If your school has a well-worn track around the edge, you run the risk of your horse getting stuck in the groove, which could place him off-centre when going over poles or jumps.

The door or gate must be properly secured, not fastened with a loop of old twine over the gatepost. This could break if your horse leant against it, which can happen easily if he makes a dash for the exit. Gates are often lower than the surrounding fence and so if your horse is likely to jump out, keep him on the lunge.

Make sure the arena is clear of spare jumps and other equipment. Even if you think they are safely stowed in the corner, your horse could accidentally (or deliberately) run behind them; it is amazing how small a space they can fit into when they want to. Leaving jumps piled in the centre of the arena is a recipe for disaster. It is essential that you have clear space to move about with your horse. If you are running along looking at him, you will not always see foreign objects and could find yourself face down in the sand.

When loose schooling you need your horse's full attention and so choose a quiet day. A windy day is likely to make him livelier than usual and easily distracted, and horses in the next field would definitely be a distraction; he might want to join them.

EQUIPMENT FOR LOOSE SCHOOLING

You need to be equipped as for lungeing with a hard hat, stout footwear, gloves etc. (see page 47). Your horse requires protective boots, a cavesson or bridle (without the reins attached), so that you can lead/lunge him before and afterwards, and a roller with side reins attached ready for use should you need them. As with lungeing and long-reining, it is not a good idea to use your saddle just in case he should have a fall and damage it. Training aids are not necessary for stretching and loosening up. You need a decent lunge whip with a long lash to sweep towards your horse to guide him but do not crack it like a circus ringmaster; a lazy, difficult horse may need to be fired up but most horses are frightened of a cracking whip, unless they have been specifically trained to accept it, and avoid cracking it at all costs with more sensitive horses.

If you have any doubts about loose schooling at any stage, put your lunge line back on and lunge as normal.

HOW TO LOOSE SCHOOL

Loose schooling is best attempted after several months of training from the ground with leading and lunge work thus ensuring that you have already established that you are not only in charge but also the person your horse can trust and turn to if he is afraid. If he has no respect for you and is in the habit of charging, barging etc. then avoid loose schooling for your own safety. I know of a situation where a young colt foal was encouraged to put his front hooves on his owner's shoulders. This was fine while he was small but later his owner had problems with him trying to mount her when he was loose in the school and his hormones took over. She had him castrated, and buckled down to some serious training pretty quickly!

It is a good idea to start by lungeing your horse first as usual using side reins and then to introduce a few minutes of loose schooling afterwards. Remove the lunge line but, initially, leave the side reins attached and, if you are lucky, he will not notice you have taken it off and continue to circle around you. If this is the case, carry on with this 'mock' lungeing by standing in the middle of the school pointing the lunge whip at his hindquarters as normal and using your voice aids for walk, trot, halt, etc. If when lungeing you have established that you lower your whip to the ground when you bring your horse into halt, he should respond to the whip being lowered when he is off the lunge. At a later stage, try doing this without the whip and see if it still works when you just lower the hand.

Detach the side reins and see if he stretches down and relaxes as you send him on the circle again. At this point he may realize he is free and head off around the school, but just stay level with his belly so that you are still close enough to keep in contact with him and he still notices you are there. If you walk off and leave him to it, he will be confused as to what you expect from him. You are still the trainer and your posture and attitude must remain consistent, as must the work; make sure that you always do the same exercises in both directions. (Figure 16.1.)

After he has worked successfully for a few minutes, give him the verbal

Figure 16.1 Loose schooling Trevor in the indoor school.

cue to halt, stand still and he should stop. Walk slowly up to him, if he has not already come to you – as my horse does when he thinks he has finished – attach the lunge line and lead him back to the stable.

Leading exercises can be done when your horse is loose. Practise the walk/halt/walk exercise described in the leading in-hand chapter, touching his neck to reward him when he stops with you. Having a packet of Polos will help motivate the correct response but do not be too free with them or you will end up with a horse that does nothing unless he gets a titbit, which can lead to nipping. Save the treat for the end of the session just before he returns to his stable.

Have your lunge line in your hand and at the first sign he may not be paying attention clip it on again rather than waiting until he has sneaked away from you altogether.

Once you are successful in walk and halt, try working him at a steady trot; jog next to his shoulder so that you can see his facial expressions and he can see you. My horse will play this game in walk but does not see the point of trotting; he just stands still and watches me jog around the school but joins in with the walking again.

Like dogs, horses are capable of learning simple verbal commands, 'stay' and 'come', for example, which can be useful when working a horse loose and, again, the discretionary use of treats can help with this training. I know a New Forest pony that can 'fetch' on command and retrieves gloves, sponges and so on, but he may well become a kleptomaniac as he tends to 'fetch' everything he can reach!

LOOSE SCHOOLING OVER GROUND POLES

Place a pole on the ground halfway along one long side of the school at right angles to the wall and place two poles parallel with the wall, one on either side of the jump, to act as a barrier, raising the two pole ends that meet off the ground using a couple of plastic blocks.

Start by leading your horse over the pole to show him what is required, after that lunge him over it a couple of times in walk and then at a steady trot. You must remove the side reins completely for this so that there is no danger of anything becoming detached and tripping your horse. If this is successful in both directions, detach the lunge line and go though the same procedure. If he goes over the pole willingly, repeat the exercise standing in exactly the same place as you were when lungeing him. If he is unsure of what he is meant to be doing, run alongside him at the same distance from which you would normally lead him. Repeat on both reins. If you do not make a point of working your horse equally on both sides, you may find that he not only leads and lunges in only one direction, but will also be more difficult to ride one way than the other when you come to work him under saddle. Another case of bad training I came across was that of a horse that was only ever led from one side and when ridden was stopped by being pulled around in tight circles to the left. He becoming very crooked and even resented going around in a horse walker in one direction to the extent that he would turn around and even go backwards!

If your horse worked well with one pole, in your next training session set two poles at 2.5 m (8 ft) or two trot strides apart. Setting them at this distance prevents the horse trying to jump them as he can take a step in between. Once he is happy with this, add a third pole at the same distance away. This helps him to regulate his rhythm, and not race over them. When he is executing this exercise well, place the three poles closer together at 1.3 m (4 ft) apart so that he trots over the poles without a stride in between them. Because the horse is free to move in a straight line, he is encouraged to aim for the centre of each pole.

Pole work can be used for a few minutes at any time during a training session but three or four times in each direction should be enough. Your goal is to have a calm, relaxed horse that uses his joints and generally loosens up his muscles. If pole work suits your horse, you can build up to four or even six in a row over a time span of six to eight weeks.

LOOSE SCHOOLING OVER SMALL JUMPS TO DEVELOP CONFIDENCE

Most horses love jumping, especially without the hindrance of a rider, and it can be valuable loosening work, developing freedom through the shoulders and power from the haunches. The horse uses his neck as a balancing pole, stretches his neck muscles and develops flexibility through his back. It is interesting to observe how your horse tackles obstacles when working loose as this can say a lot about his training, natural ability and character. Any correctly trained horse should be able to jump well provided he has no physical problems. An experienced show jumper will place himself accurately for take-off each time, and visibly adjust his gait accordingly, often being conservative with the height that he jumps owing to a correct technique and the ability to tuck his legs up underneath himself. A dressage horse will have the balance to come at the jump in a controlled manner but if he has been incorrectly trained and not allowed to stretch through his back in his general training he may jump higher than necessary to clear the jump, have a tight neck and may leave his legs trailing. A confident horse will jump over much bigger obstacles with pleasure on his face, whereas a less-than-brave horse will be cautious with small obstacles. (Figures 16.2 and 16.3.)

A horse must be familiar with the ground-pole exercises before attempting small jumps. Again, he needs leg protection, and a lunge cavesson

285

or bridle without reins. He does not need a roller as neither side reins nor a lunge line will be used.

Place one pole on the ground between two wings or plastic blocks as a ground line making sure that the outside wing, or block, is right against the wall to prevent him nipping up the side and set a second pole at 0.5 m (1½ ft) high to make a small jump. To prevent him running out to the inside, make a barrier with two poles, as with the poles exercise. Send your horse around the school at a steady trot, and aim him towards the jump with your whip. Stay alongside him as he jumps, and pick up control of him after the jump by keeping your whip aimed at his hocks at all times. If he speeds up, use your voice to steady him. If your preparatory work has been thorough, you should not experience problems. Five or six jumps in each direction will suffice and the total session should take about ten to fifteen minutes, including loosening him up and cooling him down on the flat .

If you need to lunge him at any time to calm him, then do so but if you are going to lunge him over the jump, make sure you use plastic blocks; jumps with wings and lunge lines do not mix!

To introduce a second jump, set another pair of wings 7 m (23 ft) away

Figure 16.2 'I am a show jumper!' Trevor enjoys his weekly free-jumping session. The two poles raised on blocks act as wings to prevent him running out.

Figure 16.3 'I can do it too!' Amadeus, who competes in dressage, enjoys proving he really can do it over a small ascending spread.

from the first jump (6.5 m [21 ft] if your horse is short-striding) with a pole on the ground between the jumps as a ground line, with another at 0.5 m (1¹/₂ ft) high to form the second jump. Send your horse over both jumps a couple of times in each direction.

Keep the jumps small to check that you have them a suitable distance apart for your horse before you raise them any higher, and make sure your horse is confident. If all is well, then raise the jumps in two increments to 0.75 m (2¹/₂ ft) high, raising the ground poles on one side by 0.3 m (1 ft) so that they are on an angle and filling the gap between the top rail and the ground. This ensures your horse is not faced with a large gap under each obstacle and helps him to focus on each individual jump. It may take three or four sessions to get to this point and 0.75–1 m (2¹/₂–3 ft) high will be sufficient for most horses.

You may have a talented jumper who is happy jumping well over 1 m (3ft). If this is the case use just one jump built as an ascending spread jump to make it more inviting and encourage him to really stretch through his

Figure 16.4 'This is more like it!' Trevor happily taking on a larger spread.

back (Figure 16.4). On no account test a horse to his limit to see how high he can jump. At some point he will refuse when the jump is too much for him and this may destroy his confidence. If you plan the session well, he should be challenged, but not afraid. Always finish with a well-performed jump. If you have overfaced him and he stops, lower the jump to a height he is happy with and finish the session. Learn from your mistake and do not be so ambitious next time.

At one yard I used to visit there was some serious rivalry as to how high the horses could jump. Each morning these huge jumps appeared overnight and there was no way any horse in the yard could have managed them. It turned out that a couple of young lads were putting the jumps up as high as they would go, insinuating that their horses had jumped them. Having rumbled their prank, a couple of the girls built the most enormous spread using every pole and wing in the place. The boys never bothered again!

DEALING WITH A HORSE THAT DOES NOT UNDERSTAND LOOSE SCHOOLING

If your horse is not used to being loose schooled and his preliminary training was scrimped on or even missed out altogether, you will undoubtedly have problems. All horses have days when they have so much energy that they just want to run around or simply feel mischievous. If you have let your horse loose in the school and he just kicks up his heels and rushes all over the place, you have to ask yourself, is he getting enough turnout, is he being overfed, or is he not having sufficient work? It is a grave mistake to loose school because you are afraid to ride him as he will learn that if he is naughty, you let him do what he likes. A better solution would be to lunge him with plenty of transitions and work over poles to get him mentally focused again. Leave the loose schooling for another day.

When left to their own devices, horses that lack confidence will rush about as they are unsure of what to do. In this case, more work on establishing his trust is needed so that he does not think removal of the lunge line means you are abandoning him. If he is worried, 'mock' lunge him for a few moments, then reattach the lunge line before he becomes anxious. Each time you do this leave the lunge line off for a few moments longer, until he can happily work loose around you for about ten minutes. This should be enough time for most horses; any longer and they will lose concentration. In total a lunge/loose schooling session should last about half an hour.

If he refuses to move when you let him loose, he is either extremely lazy or does not understand what to do. If this happens, reattach the lunge line, and go back to the walk-with-me, stop-with-me exercises in the in-hand chapter. You will need a schooling whip to tap him quickly and clearly to help him move with you. With this type of horse, you can go a little overboard with the praise, as they need all the encouragement you can give them but, again, do not give it in an overloud or heavy-handed way. You can progress to running alongside him as he trots, gradually lengthening the lead rein/lunge line to increase the distance between you, when he is going forward more of his own accord. Try to detach the line without him noticing so that he is working loose beside you and keep going as though nothing has changed. Then walk, stop and praise him. Finish this particular session and resume the lesson tomorrow. It will take time for the unconfident horse to find enjoyment in his training but that is the essential ingredient: he must enjoy working with you.

It is highly unlikely that your horse might attack you when loose schooling if you have already built up a good relationship with him during his training so far but it is possible with a strange horse. If you have any doubts about a horse, do not loose school him but if a horse becomes unexpectedly confrontational, you have to act quickly. You might have volunteered to help with a horse that has probably been the dominant one in his partnership with his owner and he objects to your confidence and rises to the challenge.

The first thing that usually happens is the stand-off. The horse plants himself in front of you lifts his neck, and looks as though he is going to rear up at you. This is not too frightening if dealing with a small pony, but pretty intimidating when dealing with a broad-chested cob! You must deal with this in exactly the same way as you would when a horse runs at you on the lunge. Do not panic, stand your ground, and keep eye contact with a good authoritative stare. Calmly raise your whip to one side and take a couple of steps in that direction so that you are level with his belly. Raise your other arm out to the side to make yourself appear large and very wide. Send him forward with a sharp flick of the whip, making sure you get an accurate shot to his thigh. Smacking the ground with the whip or waving it around is pointless; it is much better to use it once properly to obtain the desired effect. It is, however, important to remember that the whip should *never* be used in anger. When a horse is intimidating you, think how another horse would react to such a threat: he would present his backside to this horse and give him both hind hooves in the chest; it is a shock tactic as much as a punishment. Your whip is a hooves substitute! If you time it well, you should only need to do this once to establish yourself as 'top horse' but if he challenges you again, repeat the process. Consistency is everything. If he runs at you baring his teeth, bare yours back at him, and deflect him with your whip as before. You have to appear more aggressive and powerful than he is.

I learnt this lesson trying to cope with a flock of geese at a farm where I kept my horses. The gander would approach anyone or anything with outstretched wings at a run, hissing loudly. By running at him as though aiming for a head-on collision with my arms outstretched and doing a reasonable impression of the hissing, he would side-step away honking in irritation and let me pass and so we reached an understanding; I became am honorary goose for the four years I was there. The moral of the tale is: if in doubt as to your next move, do to the horse what he is doing to you.

LOOSE SCHOOLING WITH TWO PEOPLE

If you have an assistant, loose schooling is far easier, especially when using poles and jumps. The assistant should, like you, be suitably dressed for the exercise and also carry a lunge whip. Each of you should stand at one end of the school on the centre line, as though you were in the centre of a 20 m circle.

Send your horse around the arena as you did when on your own. He may want to circle around you as before, but your assistant must take over as he comes passed you on to the long side. To do this she needs to leave her spot, and stand near to you, ready to move alongside your horse to guide him up the arena so that he does not make a circle. She may need to walk briskly or even jog slowly along beside him, but on no account should either of you chase the horse. You need to follow her, but stay behind her, as she has control. When she reaches the middle of her 20 m circle, she must stay put, with you close behind her. As your horse goes passed her towards the next long side, it is your turn to move with him along the straight and your assistant's turn to follow behind you. It is a matter of passing the horse from one of you to the other. Talk to each other as you work together so that you do not bump into each other or end up too far apart.

It is most important not to get in front of your horse when doing this, as this will make him stop and turn around. If you do this, you must switch roles and hand the control to your friend. She must then remain level with his belly to stay with him, and allow him to continue in the other direction. What you must not do is get too far apart with one of you too far in front

291

of the horse and the other too far behind him because he will ping pong between you like a table-tennis ball, especially if you are both brandishing your lunge whips. Regain control with the system of passing him from one of you to the other around the arena.

To ask him to change the rein, hold your whip at arm's length in the hand nearest to his head and point it in front of his nose. Stretch your other arm out so that you appear very wide; your assistant must lower her whip so that she is not giving any signals. He should turn easily and once he has turned, your assistant resumes control with her whip pointed at his haunches to encourage him forward in the new direction. You should both keep your whips aimed at his haunches in the hand nearest to his quarters unless you want to turn him.

To stop him, you should both tuck your whips behind you and stand still. Use your verbal cues to ask him to walk and halt. If you have trained him to come to you when he has finished, he can come for a titbit, if your preference is for him to stay where he is, go to him to reward him. Attach him to the lunge line, remove the side reins if you have been using them, and lead him around the arena to stretch and relax before returning to the stable.

With poles and jumps, one of you brings him into the exercise so that he comes in straight and in a steady rhythm. The other is positioned directly alongside the poles or jump/s with the whip aimed at his hocks, in order to keep him straight after the exercise. Work with one end of the school apiece, so each of you has control of a short side and half of each long side and either the approach or landing over the poles/jump.

INDEX